THE KING'S BOOK of NUMEROLOGY

Volume 12

ADVANCED PRINCIPLES

RICHARD ANDREW KING

© by Richard Andrew King
Published by Richard King Publications
PO Box 3621
Laguna Hills, CA 92654

No part of this publication may be reproduced or transmitted in any form or by any means, electronic or mechanical, including photocopy, recording, or any information storage and retrieval system now known or to be invented without permission in writing from the publisher, except by a reviewer who wishes to quote brief passages in connection with a review written for inclusion in a magazine, newspaper, online article, or broadcast. Contact Richard King Publications, PO Box 3621, Laguna Hills, CA 92654; RichardKing.net; Rich@RichardKing.net.

This book and its information contain copyrighted material, trademarks, and other proprietary information owned and copyrighted by Richard Andrew King and the King's Numerology^{tm}, including but not limited to numeric formulae, matrices, grids and diagrams. You may not modify, publish, transmit, participate in the transfer or sale of, create applications and/or derivative works of, or in any way exploit, in whole or in part, any Proprietary or other Material in any capacity in this work or in the King's Numerology^{tm} system.

This King's Numerology^{tm} system is neither intended to extol nor defame any featured individual, whether named or unnamed. Its purpose is to show the relationship between people's lives and their numbers in order to further the understanding of numerology as a science and the King's Numerology^{tm} system in particular.

Library of Congress Cataloging-in-Publication Data
King, Richard Andrew
The King's Book of Numerology, Volume 12: Advanced Principles
ISBN: 978-0-931872-27-3; Pricing: 90000
Date of Publication: 8 September 2018

ACKNOWLEDGMENTS

Many thanks to Liana Moisescu, Graphic Artist,
for her exquisite artistry in development of the book's cover

http://lianadesigns.crevado.com/
https://99designs.com/profiles/1544664

RICHARD ANDREW KING – BOOKS

Available through RichardKing.net and major online retailers.

KBN Series:

1. *The King's Book of Numerology: Volume I – Foundations & Fundamentals*
2. *The King's Book of Numerology 2 (II): Forecasting – Part 1*
3. *The King's Book of Numerology 3: Master Numbers*
4. *The King's Book of Numerology 4: Intermediate Principles*
5. *The King's Book of Numerology 5: IR Sets – Level 1*
6. *The King's Book of Numerology 6: Love Relationships*
7. *The King's Book of Numerology 7: Parenting Wisdom – Numerology & Life Truths*
8. *The King's Book of Numerology 8: Forecasting – Part 2*
9. *The King's Book of Numerology 9: Numeric Biography, Princess Diana*
10. *The King's Book of Numerology 10: Historic Icons – Part 1*
11. *The King's Book of Numerology 11: The Age of the Female – Volumes 1 & 2*
12: *The King's Book of Numerology 12: Advanced Principles*

Numerology books published separately . . .

The Age of the Female – A Thousand Years of Yin (KBN11)

Your Love Numbers – Discovering The Secrets of Your Life, Loves & Relationships (KBN6)

Destinies of the Rich & Famous – The Secret Numbers of Extraordinary Lives (KBN10)

Parenting Wisdom for the 21st Century – Raising Your Children By Their Numbers To Achieve Their Highest Potential (KBN7)

Blueprint of a Princess – Diana Frances Spencer, Queen of Hearts (KBN9)

Non-Numerology books . . .

Messages from the Masters – Timeless Truths for Spiritual Seekers

The Black Belt Book of Life – Secrets of a Martial Arts Master

The Karate Consciousness – From Worldly Warrior to Mystic Master

Parenting Wisdom – What to Teach the Children (Part 2 of KBN7)

The Age of the Female II – Heroines of the Shift (Part 2 of KBN11)

The Galactic Transcripts

99 Poems of the Spirit

THE KING'S BOOK OF NUMEROLOGY

Volume 12

ADVANCED PRINCIPLES

TABLE OF CONTENTS

Chapters	Title	Page
	Author's Introduction	9
Chapter 1	The Numerology of Dislike	11
Chapter 2	The Numerology of Betrayal	25
Chapter 3	Nemesis Numbers	57
Chapter 4	Common Name Dynamics	83
Chapter 5	Single Name Analysis Profile - SNAP	91
Chapter 6	Numerology and Past Lives	103
Chapter 7	Family Ties	115
Chapter 8	Life Journey Shifts and Changes	129
Chapter 9	Voids, Vacuums and Karmic Scales	183
Chapter 10	Life Matrix Diamond	197
Chapter 11	Professional Chart Analysis	217
Chapter 12	KBN Series Summation: Volumes 1 - 12	243
	INDEX	291

Richard Andrew King

AUTHOR'S INTRODUCTION

This twelfth volume of *The King's Book of Numerology*[tm] series concludes the first establishment of a foundational system for understanding the divine science of numeric coding. The first twelve volumes is an excellent and worthy beginning for those individuals who seek answers to life's most pressing and mystical mysteries.

Divine is an appropriate adjective because it is impossible for any serious minded student of numerology to not recognize the reality that there exists a Power operating this universe that transcends the comprehension of the human mind, an Intelligence so vast, enormous, immense and perfect that It creates specific destinies for every human being on this earth to the nth degree, destinies which are encoded in one's full birth name and birth date. Amazing? No doubt. Real? Absolutely. Verifiable? Indisputably.

A cursory study will reveal the Truth of numbers – labels for the formative energies of fate. A thorough comprehensive investigation will move one's initial forays into numerology from a beginning interest to a deep, unassailable understanding and profound awareness of the numeric superstructure of life and destiny. Such sentient perception will expand one's consciousness of creation and reality far beyond the superficial landscape of commonplace mindsets and mundane suppositions and assumptions.

Although the first twelve volumes of the KBN series offer a considerable amount of information regarding the science of numeric coding, it is by no means the final word on the subject. Quite the contrary. Numerology is vast and deep; expansive and limitless. Continued study and research will unveil great detail and knowledge of creation. Such study is not simply recommended, it is unquestionably encouraged.

Yours in the Infinite study of Life and Numbers,

Richard Andrew King

Richard Andrew King

CHAPTER 1

THE NUMEROLOGY OF DISLIKE

Have you ever wondered why some people dislike other people? They may have never met them, know nothing about them, but still they don't like them. Seems strange, right? Actually, it is quite natural.

As we know, numbers (and their corresponding letters) represent labels for energies and energy fields. As we also know, numbers clash and therefore their energies clash – invisibly. Fire and water clash. Likewise, their related numbers – 1 and 2 – clash. The 1 is a fire sign; the 2 is a water sign. The 1 represents logic; the 2, emotion. The 1 references direct action; the 2, indirect action. The 1 defines unification; the 2, division. The 1 shouts independence; the 2, dependence. The 1 is yang; the 2 is yin. The 1 is rational; the 2, irrational. Simply stated, the 1 and 2 are antithetical and therefore clash with one another by natural design.

And so it is with people. At our core each of us is energy. We are not our body. Our body is a human suit by and through which we operate in this worldly dimension. We may be able to cover our bodies with various types of clothing but we cannot hide our energy, which radiates invisibly and is as unaffected by clothing as X-rays are unaffected by skin. Therefore, when our energy is juxtaposed with another person's energy oppositional to ours, we intrinsically feel it and this uncomfortable feeling we label as *dislike* or worse. The greater the conflicting energies, the greater the discomfort and its varying degrees of *dislike*.

Of course the opposite is also true. When we are in proximity of another person whose energy harmonizes with ours, a natural feeling of comfort exists and we tend to *like* that person. The greater the connective tissue or MER – Mutual Energetic Resonance discussed fully in *The King's Book of Numerology, Volume 6 – Love Relationships* (KBN6), the greater the feeling of *like*. When

Richard Andrew King

the connective energies between two people are large, we feel love for that person. When the energies are mutual and large, people fall in love. In reality, love on a human level (not a spiritual level) is simply a mutuality of energetic resonance. The greater the resonance, the greater the love. Conversely, the greater the dissonance, the greater the *dislike*.

As humans, each of us has experienced people whom we've never met who don't like us and vice-versa. We may ask ourselves, "Why does this person dislike me when he/she does not even know me?" If we're introspectively astute we may even ask, "Why do I dislike that person when I've never met him/her?" The answer – a clashing of energies.

When assessing the degree of *like* or *dislike* between two people, a comparison of their Simple Basic Matrices will give us clues but not the whole story. For a greater understanding of why some people dislike other people, we need to access and analyze their Subcap Challenges, especially those in their full natal Expression as well as its parcel of individual names.

To validate this phenomenon of *dislike*, let's look at some real life examples. To protect people's identities, we won't use actual names. Rather, we'll use their numbers.

DISLIKE EXAMPLE #01

Person A was disliked by Person B for seemingly no reason. Person B even fabricated lies about Person A but Person A could not understand why. In consulting with The King's Numerology^{tm}, the answer became clear. It lies in the Subcap Challenges of Person B.

Person B's first name housed a 16 General root. Its Subcap Challenge is 5 (6 minus 1 = 5). Person B's second name housed a 27 General root. Its Subcap Challenge is also a 5. Together, the numbers of Person B's first and second names generate a 43. Its Subcap Challenge is a 1. Therefore, the Subcap Challenges of Person B's first name, second name and Common Name are 5-5-1. The Umbrella of Person A (Lifepath, Expression and PE) is, guess what? A 5-5-1! How much clearer could it be? Person A's entire persona and life reality, as identified by his Umbrella components, posed a complete challenge to Person B via the Challenges of his first, second and Common Name!

The degree of *dislike* has levels. In this example we see that Person B was challenged by not just one major energy field of Person A but three – his Lifepath, his Expression and his Reality. Thus, Person B was confronted with a triple dose of Person A and his life. Person B, with the 5-5-1 Subcap Challenges in his names, didn't like Person A's natural persona – his 5 Expression; his 5 Lifepath or his 1 PE.

However, if Person A's Lifepath had been a 4 his PE would have been a 9 (4 LP + 5 Exp = 9). This would have mitigated the intensity of Peron B's sense of *dislike*. In fact, since Person B's second name was a simple 9, he would have identified somewhat with Person A's 9 PE. Unfortunately, this was not the case. Person B's 5-5-1 Subcap Challenges clashed with Person A's 5-5-1 Umbrella energies, thus generating an understandably natural dislike of Person A.

To confirm the numeric science of Subcap Challenges being a major cause in the arena of *dislike*, let's take a look at another example.

DISLIKE EXAMPLE #02

Here we find Person A once again. As noted, his Umbrella is a 5-5-1. Person C's first name has a General root of 27. Her second name has a General root of 16. Does this combination look familiar? It should. Person B had the same set of roots but reversed – his first name held a 16 and his second name housed a 27. Thus, both Person B and C maintained a 5 Subcap Challenge in their first and second names, generating a 5-5-1 pattern matching Person A's 5-5-1 Umbrella.

What this simple process does not reveal is the full aggregate of numbers in the entire charts of the people featured here. There may be other numeric energies offsetting or mitigating a condition of *dislike*. This said, Subcap Challenge energies, although they may not translate to *dislike* specifically, they will always present a challenge to some degree.

Now let's see how a condition of *dislike* degrades into the sad situation of hate.

Richard Andrew King

DISLIKE EXAMPLE #03

By his own words, Person D hated his mother – a sad state of affairs. His day of birth was the 16th. The transition root of his 7 Expression is a 16. Here we see stacking. As we know, the 16 carries a 5 Subcap Challenge. What do you suppose his mother's Expression was? If you surmised a 5, you would be correct. Thus, with lifetime stacked 5 Challenges in his day of birth and his Expression he would certainly have been agitated by his mother's 5 Expression energy. But for him to hate his mother there had to be more. Dislike is one thing but hate is on a far more grievous level.

Person D's Grand and Crown Challenges in his Life Matrix were a 5, so here we see more compounding of the problem. With his 7 Expression, the IR Set for these Challenges is a 5/(7)/3. This reveals a condition in which the 5 LIST energy relates directly to his mother. When the 5 filters through his 7 Expression, the outcome 3 ROPE energy of communication, joy and happiness is negatively influenced in a Challenge position, thus exacerbating his dislike for his mother.

To compound the issue, the 3 is void in Person D's chart, creating a 5/(7)/3v energy field of unhappiness, negativity and lack of joy, morphing the dislike of his mother into the realm of hate for her. It should also be pointed out that the son (Person D) had no 3s in his Basic Matrix, thus generating a Grand Voided 3 Challenge PE – the most unhappy of all 3 components in a chart.

To make things even worse, his 7 Expression Filter houses a 16 transition root, which itself has a 5 Subcap Challenge creating even more disdain. The IR Set would look like this: 5/(16-7)/3v. The King's Numerology™ certainly does not condone hatred, but with this much negatively Challenged energy comprised of stacked 5 Subcap Challenges in dual 16-7 components (day of birth and Expression) generating a 3 void outcome revealing a lack of joy, happiness, communication and positive energy, it is understandable that the mother's son would hate her. This real life situation is glaringly unfortunate but true.

Sadly, this son also stated he hated his paternal grandmother! Once again, such negative feelings are present in his numbers.

The grandmother's Basic Matrix houses a 5 Nature. Bingo! Her personality rubbed the grandson in the same way as his mother. The 5/(16-7)/3v was activated with the grandmother, too.

Additionally, the grandmother's Expression is a 9. When combined with the grandson's simple 7 Expression the result is a 16-7 – the most difficult of all Mix vibrations. Its simple IR Set becomes 7/(9)/16-7. When his 16 Expression transition cipher is inserted into the pattern, the IR Set becomes a 16-7/(9)/16-7, generating an energetic paradigm where the LIST and ROPE energies are both 16-7s, which contain more 5 subcap energy! Thus, "chaos in/chaos out."

As if this were not enough corroboration of this man's hatred for his paternal grandmother, besides his 3 void, his Life Matrix housed Grand and Crown Voided 4 Challenges. Contrastingly, the grandmother's Soul and Material Nature are both 4s. This generated a 4v/(7)/11-2 IR Set for the grandson, more exactly ciphered as 4v/(16-7)/11-2. Notice the problem? The 11-2 and 16-7 numeric patterns in combination manifest the most conflictive (11-2) and turbulent (16-7) energy of all binary combinations.

To generate more darkness regarding this man's hatred, his grandmother's Material Soul is a 3. This negatively resonates with his 3v ROPE in his 5/(16-7)/3v Grand and Crown Challenges!

And there's still more. This son/grandson's wife stated that people working for him didn't even like him, and at parties people did not want to talk with him. No wonder! As we know, the 5 is the *Number of Man*. Therefore, in his 5/(16-7)/3v Grand and Crown Challenges, the 5 represents all people, i.e., his work mates. The 3 void manifests as a poor attitude, acerbic language, negative persona and unhappy disposition.

This most tragic account of Person D's hatred for his mother and grandmother is clearly revealed in his numbers and, once again, validates the Pythagorean maxim that *Numbers rule the universe. Everything is arranged according to number and mathematical shape.* "Everything" obviously includes personal feelings such as dislike and hatred. The numerological moral of the story is that *numbers tell the story* and all we have to do is access those numbers to discover the truth of life and destiny.

Richard Andrew King

DISLIKE EXAMPLE #04

Person E was the target of extreme hatred by Person F via his own statement. Person E was born on the 11th – a simple 2 day. His Expression and Nature were both 2s. Person F's Lifepath housed a 2 Subcap Challenge; his Expression housed a 2 Subcap Challenge and his PE contained a double 2 Subcap Challenge. This generated a quadstack of the 2 Subcap Challenge in Person F's Umbrella. In other words, his entire outer destiny via his Basic Matrix was saturated in 2 Subcap Challenge energy which directly targeted Person E's 11-2 day of birth, his 2 Expression and 2 Nature.

Furthermore, Person F's Life Matrix 1st Challenge, 3rd Challenge (Grand) and 4th Challenge (Crown) all revealed a 2 in the LIST position. His 2nd Challenge housed a 2 in the ROPE position. Combined with the four Subcap 2 Challenges in his Umbrella and the four Life Matrix 2 Challenges, Person F was plagued with an octostack (eight stack) of 2 Challenge energy – all directed toward Person E and his 2 energy. As we see, it is the intense stacking of the 2 Challenge energy that translated as Person F's hatred for Person E.

Another fact. Person F's Expression is a 7. When the 2 LIST energy of his 1st, 3rd and 4th Life Matrix Challenges filter through his 7 Expression with its 16 transition root, the outcome ROPE is a 9, generating an IR Set of 2/(7)/9; more specifically as 2/(16-7)/9. Interestingly, the object of his hatred, Person E, has a 9 Soul – the energy driving his most primal needs, wants and desires. The 9 Subcap Challenge ROPE of Person F was in direct conflict with the primal 9 desires of Person E, which only added to the intensity of Person F's hatred for Person E.

Furthermore, the 2/(16-7)/9 IR Set in Person F's 1st, 3rd and 4th Challenges contains both Person E's 2 energy in his day of birth, Expression and Nature as well as the 9 energy in his Soul. Translating these numbers into words creates the following IR Set word string:

Person E's 2 Birth day, Exp. and Nature + Person F's 16-7 Exp. = Person E's 9 Soul.

As is obvious, Person F's Subcap Challenges in his Umbrella and Life Matrix were so concentrated that Person F's feelings toward Person E manifested not as simple dislike but as extreme hatred.

The King's Book of Numerology, Volume 12 – Advanced Principles

CELEBRITY CASE STUDIES

One way to verify the veracity of numerology is to study the lives of known people, correlating their numbers with their destinies, which are "out there" for the whole world to see. The King's Numerology^{tm} has illustrated this method often, especially in *The King's Book of Numerology, Volume 6 – Love Relationships*; *The King's Book of Numerology, Volume 9 – Numeric Biography, Princess Diana*, and *The King's Book of Numerology, Volume 10 – Historic Icons, Part 1*.

The following cases involve celebrities whose lives are well known. Whether the parties involved actually disliked each other is personal to them, but their relationships have generated media stories involving their differences, challenges and problems. What is chronicled here are the numeric reasons for their relationship "issues."

PATRICK SWAYZE AND JENNIFER GREY

If you were to research actors, celebrities or co-stars who disliked each other, one pair that always seems to make every list is that of Patrick Swayze and Jennifer Grey – the couple who made the classic movie *Dirty Dancing* an iconic exposition of cinematic success.

Using the birth data of *Patrick Wayne Swayze*, born 18 August 1952, and *Jennifer Grey*, born 26 March 1960, it is easy to see why this couple has garnered such a contentious reputation. The following information highlights some of the challenges each of them faced in their relationship, challenges which are clearly delineated in their numbers.

One of the first critical issues that pops up involves their Lifepath numbers. Swayze had a 7 Lifepath; Grey, a 9 Lifepath. Their Relationship Mix therefore generates a 16-7 Mix Lifepath – the most problematic number to have in a Relationship Mix (for more on the science of relationships, read *The King's Book of Numerology, Volume 6 – Love Relationships*). This 16-7 Mix Lifepath guarantees some level of turmoil and chaos between them. As we recall, the 16-7 is the *Great Purifier* – an energy forcing us to purify our consciousness by inflicting karmic retribution for previous sins and misdeeds. With a 16-7 in any Mix Umbrella component (Lifepath, Expression or PE), red flags portend troubled waters ahead.

The Mix Material Soul between Swayze and Grey is an 11-2 – the energy of conflict and opposition. Coupled with their 16-7 Mix Lifepath, some degree of angst is guaranteed. As KBN6 states, the two most problematic numbers in a Relationship Match and Mix chart are the 11-2 and the 16-7 in combination. There may be other numbers which increase or mitigate the disturbance caused by these two red-flag energies but without a doubt the 11-2 and 16-7 are precarious and must be given their just dues.

A prominent issue between Swayze and Grey is that they're both dominant individuals, and dominant individuals usually clash. Swayze has four 9s in his Basic Matrix: 9 Day of Birth (18th), 9 PE, 9 Soul and a 99-9 Material Nature. Grey's Lifepath is a 9, and her first name of *Jennifer* is a 9, thus generating a Name Timeline IR Set of 9/(9)/9 for the first forty-five years of her life. Given that symbols for the 9 are a scepter, throne, crown and microphone, a conflict of power is natural and understandable between these two mega stars.

Jennifer Grey's Umbrella is composed of a 9 Lifepath, 1 Expression and 1 PE, creating a 9/(1)/1 IR Set. No two numbers are more dynamically individualistic and potentially egotistic than the 1 and 9 in combination. When the powerhouse *Grand Elemental, Grand Ruler* and *Grand Amplifier* 9 is in the LIST position (Lessons, Influences, Subjects and Themes), it empowers both the 1 Filter and the 1 ROPE (Reality, Outcome, Performance, Experience). Therefore, Grey's 9/(1)/1 Umbrella, in conjunction with the 9/(9)/9 Name Timeline (NTL) of *Jennifer*, generates a powerful and dominating ego, especially for the first forty-five years of Grey's life.

Furthermore, her surname of *Grey* is a 1 with roots of 55-28-10. The 55-1 is the only pure fire master number. It is powerfully rebellious, mercurial and hard to control. The 55-1 is all about freedom, independence and self.

Not only is the name *Grey* a 55-1, but when the 28 General Expression of *Grey* filters through her 27 General Lifepath root, a second 55-1 is generated, doubling and intensifying the 55-1's already rebellious and renegade energy. With this in mind, the NTL of *Grey* is a 55-1/(9)/55-1! Add this to her 9/(1)/1 Umbrella and 9/(9)/9 NTL of *Jennifer* and you have an energy of massive power, ego, rebellion and independence. And since we're discussing last names, *Swayze* generates a 99 specific Expression! Combined with his 99 Material Nature, 9 simple Day of Birth, 9 PE and 9 Soul, his power is also off the charts!

So what happens when two individuals, whose charts are overflowing with massive 9 power, collide? The result is a tumult of titans. Thus, how could there not be problems between Swayze and Grey? Answer: there could not be a problem-free environment. Each wants to dominate, to sit on the throne of power. Hence, a clashing.

But there's more, of course. Swayze's voids are a 4 and 6. Grey's voids are a 2-3-4-8. He has two social energies missing (4 and 6); she has three (2-4-8). In effect, between them all the social energies are missing (2-4-6-8). Actors, although individual by design, have to get along with their co-stars to some level, each of whom is vying for stardom and to be in the spotlight. With their combined lack of social energies, it would have been difficult for Swayze and Grey to have a friction-free relationship.

Another major problem is that Swayze's 1st, 3rd and 4th Challenges house a 1 LIST energy. This large amount of 1 Challenge energy would have caused him problems in relation to Grey's 1 Expression and 1 PE. Added to this, Swayze's 1st Pinnacle, 2nd Epoch, 3rd Epoch and 4th Pinnacle ROPE all manifest a 1 energy. With his 9s in tow, these 1s in both the LIST and ROPE positions give him an air of ego. Therefore, not only was there a clash of 9 energy between him and Grey, there was the 1 energetic conflict as well.

Remember what we've said about the 1 and 9 together? They're filled with egocentricity. Thus, the problems between Swayze and Grey could not have been avoided. On screen, they made for a powerful pair. The phenomenal success of *Dirty Dancing* is proof of their individual talent and universal power. But it is exactly the power of the ego via their 1 and 9 energy that played a major role in the dramatically contentious role of their personal relationship, giving birth to the media's observations and assessments.

Richard Andrew King

MARILYN MONROE AND TONY CURTIS

Another celebrity relationship often appearing in the "troubled category" is that Marilyn Monroe and Tony Curtis, both legendary thespians. Monroe was born Norma Jeane Mortenson on 1 June 1926. Curtis was born Bernard Schwartz on 3 June 1925. Monroe is one of twelve historic individuals featured in *The King's Book of Numerology, Volume 10 – Historic Icons, Part 1*, aka KBN10.

In assessing the numerology charts of Monroe and Curtis it is obvious this pair had issues, a few are outlined below. If you're interested in their relationship issues on and off screen, please feel free to do your own research. The goal of this chapter is simply to identify problematic concerns between the two of them, not to explain their personal history, although reports of them having issues are definitely real based on the analysis of their numbers.

Let's start with Tony Curtis's simple Challenges. His 1st Challenge is a 3/(9)/3; 2nd Challenge is a 2/(9)/2; 3rd Challenges are a 1/(9)/1 and 8/(9)/8; 4th Challenge is a 5/(9)/5. Every one of these Challenges involved some numeric aspect of Marilyn Monroe's chart, which is obviously problematic.

Of note: Monroe's voids are 3-7-8. Curtis's voids are 6 and 7.

Curtis's 1st Challenge is a 3/(9)3. Marilyn Monroe's Material Nature is a 3. The Subcap Challenge of her first natal name *Norma* is a 3 (General Expression is a 25). The 3 is also voided in her chart. The 3/(9)/3 IR Set addresses communication, art, pleasure, image and images, beauty, vanity, narcissism, acting, self-expression, health and well-being, entitlement. Curtis had issues with this energy and Marilyn Monroe's 3 Material Nature and 3 void were definitely part of those issues.

The 2nd Challenge of Tony Curtis is a 2/(9)/2; specifically an 11-2/(9)/11-2. Monroe's life PE was an 11-2. The name *Marilyn* is a 38-11-2. Curtis's Nature is an 11-2. The name *Tony* is a 2, and the Subcap Challenge of his natal name *Bernard* is a 2, stemming from a 35 General Expression. Thus, there was a great deal of innate tension in the relationship aspect of these two actors.

The King's Book of Numerology, Volume 12 – Advanced Principles

Curtis had two IR Sets in his Grand Challenge position: 1/(9)/1 and an 8/(9)/8. Monroe was born on the 1st of June 1926, so this would have resonated with his 1/(9)/1 Challenged energy. Monroe's Soul is an 8. His Lifepath and PE are both 8s, generating an 8/(9)/8 Umbrella. His natal name of *Bernard* is an 8. All of these 8s would have resonated with Curtis's 8/(9)/8 Grand Challenge energy, which is as much an internal issue with him as it is an external issue with Monroe.

The Crown Challenge for Curtis is a 5/(9)/5. Monroe's Nature is a 5, as is the Subcap Challenge of the name *Marilyn* with its 38 General Expression. Plus, Monroe's 1st Challenge is a 5/(4)/9.

As is obvious, the interconnection between Curtis and Monroe is heavily laced with problematic energy threads.

The Mix Nature energies between Curtis and Monroe reveal a 16-7 – his 11-2 Nature plus her 5 simple Nature. How many times have we seen the 16-7 popping up in problematic situations? Answer: a lot. Furthermore, it is the major red flag energy in cases of betrayal and adultery, which we'll discuss in the next chapter.

Another difficulty between Curtis and Monroe besides the Mix 16-7 is that their Relationship Mix houses three sets of 15-6 energy: Mix Lifepath (her 7, his 8); Mix Soul (her 8, his 7); 1st natal Names of *Norma* and *Bernard* (her 7, his 8). It is interesting, isn't it, that each one of their three Mix 15-6 energies are combined exclusively with the numbers 7 and 8 – exact opposites. The 7 is void in his chart and the 8 is void in hers. Therefore, their Mix 15-6s were negatively harnessed, as if the 15-6 needed more darkness in it.

From all of the foregoing data, it is understandable that the relationship between Marilyn Monroe and Tony Curtis would be a difficult one and that they would have issues with each other. Oh, how tangled are the numeric/energetic webs destiny has woven for some people.

Richard Andrew King

PRESIDENT DONALD TRUMP AND CONGRESSMAN JOHN LEWIS

Politics is, unfortunately, a nasty and ugly profession. With so much power, egocentricity, special interests and corruption saturating the political landscape it is not difficult to find people who openly dislike, even hate, other people.

One example is that of Congressman John Lewis (born John Robert Lewis on 21 February 1940) who openly does not like President Trump (born Donald John Trump on 14 June 1946), to say the least.

Lewis, a Democrat, refused to attend President Trump's Inauguration, as well as that of George W. Bush, both Republicans. Lewis didn't see Donald Trump as a legitimate president, even though President Trump was elected in an open, free and quite legitimate election. Lewis's dislike of Donald Trump is another prime example of how numbers "tell the story." Numbers and their energies are a-political. Take politics out of the equation and Lewis would still dislike Trump.

As we've been seeing, Challenges play a major role in one person's dislike of another. Voids also are major players. John Lewis's dislike of Donald Trump is extremely obvious. One quick glance at their numbers reveals the open truth.

Donald Trump's Soul and Nature are both 7s. His Lifepath is a 4. Therefore, both his Soul Layers and Nature Layers generate a 7/(4)/11-2 energy field. Trump has no voids in his chart.

John Lewis's voids are 7 and 4 – the precise LIST and FILTER energies of Donald Trump's Soul Layers and Nature Layers! Need more be said? Not really, but there is more.

Both John Lewis's Grand Challenge and Crown Challenge house a 7v/(4v)/11-2 IR Set, which are the *exact* Soul and Nature Layers of Donald Trump!

In unambiguous terms John Lewis's primary obstacles in his later life – the time when Donald Trump is serving as President of the United States – are the *exact* numbers relating to Trump's

The King's Book of Numerology, Volume 12 – Advanced Principles

deepest needs, wants, desires and motivations (Soul Layers) and personality (Nature Layers). Since Donald Trump has no voids, his Soul and Nature Layers reveal a 7/(4)/11-2 IR Set. Because John Lewis has a 4 and 7 void in his chart, the same IR Set that Trump's chart reveals manifests as a 7v/(4v)/11-2 in Lewis's Challenges. Remarkable and perfect.

It is no wonder John Lewis does not like Donald Trump. It makes no difference what profession they shared. If they were kids in a school yard, athletes on the same sports team or members of the same family, Lewis would still not like Donald Trump. Lewis's Challenge energies and voids clash, exactly, with Trump's Soul and Nature energies, thus creating a state of complete dissonance, which translates in John Lewis's chart as a complete dislike of President Donald Trump.

SUMMARY

The examples presented in this chapter reinforce the reality of numbers and their energies and how numbers reflect reality in its many forms, especially in relation to the aspects of dislike and hatred. As we have learned, Challenges and voids play a dynamic role in how people get along with each other. Two people can be wonderful individuals but their intrinsic energies may clash in degrees from mild to severe. Whether people are family members or not makes no difference. It is the numeric/energetic fabric of their destinies that "tells the story" of *dislike* or worse. This reality echoes the Biblical statement from St. Matthew 10:36 – *And a man's foes shall be they of his own household*.

Knowing this information should help people, particularly young people, to learn to be whole within themselves and not worry about what other people think of them because what other people think of them is based in numbers and energies. A person may be an absolutely wonderful human being but be disliked, even hated, by another person whose energies are diametrically opposed to his. These examples all reveal this truth. The moral of the story – don't worry about what other people think of you. Just be who you are and do the best you can to keep purifying and perfecting yourself while working to expand your own divinity.

Richard Andrew King

CHAPTER 2

THE NUMEROLOGY OF BETRAYAL

Betrayal is, arguably, one of the most egregious human behaviors. In contrast to an act of *dislike*, betrayal involves personal relationship, the foundation of which is trust. When trust is violated and betrayal occurs, the heart, mind, emotions, and soul are negatively enjoined, generating pain and sorrow in the process, often destroying the relationship itself.

The amount of suffering created by betrayal is in direct proportion to the intensity of the attachment between the individuals involved. People may dislike another person without ever having a relationship with that person, but betrayal is personal, very personal, and that's the issue.

Degrees of betrayal run the gamut from a drop of rain to a hurricane; from a mild shake to a super quake; from a campfire to a forest fire; from a question asked to a nuclear blast. Betrayals may be among friends, lovers, business partners, married couples. As far as the latter group is concerned, adultery generates the greatest rift and rupture because it involves the most intimate union and energetic fusion of souls, individuals who made an open commitment of devotion to the marriage.

Before we proceed let this be known. In discussing acts of betrayal, even adultery, The King's Numerology[tm] makes no judgments. Judgements rest with God. Besides, none of us knows what the karma is between people. As Saint Dadu says, *What you have not done will never befall you. Only what you have done will befall you.* In other words, we cannot experience what we have not created, but we will experience what we have created. What we do to others will be done to us at some point in time in this life or the next. This is the inescapable truth of karma – *the* ruling law of this dimension. So . . . no judgements rest with the following examples, only numeric analysis.

Richard Andrew King

BETRAYAL AND THE NUMBER 16

The *Great Purifier* – the number 16 – is quite prevalent during those times when betrayals occur, which is when the 16-7 is manifested negatively, not positively. The 16-7 is highly spiritual on its positive side, but its negative side can be quite dark. A brief glimpse at the 16-7 capset tells us why betrayals can occur within its environment.

As we see in the following image, the 1 of self, action and initiation is focused on the 6 of love and lust; the 5 Subcap Challenge represents the senses, sensuality, stimulation, excitement, experience, change, adventure; the 7 Addcap Pinnacle is the most secretive and private of all numbers. Remember, too, that no two numbers are more sexual than the 5 and 6 together, and when they combine in an energetic atmosphere of action (1) and secrecy (7), betrayals and adulteries can and do occur.

    7 ← secrecy/privacy

   16 ← action (1) /love/lust (6)

    5 ← sensuality/stimulation

The 16-7 Great Purifier is not the only number represented in betrayals. Yet, it is the most common, especially in the case of partnerships, friendships, love relationships and marriages. Let's take a look at some actual case studies of betrayals. Names and situations have been slightly modified for personal privacy.

BETRAYALS – CASE STUDIES

Case #01

When this couple originally married, there was some resonance in their numbers, enough to attract the wife to the husband. Her Soul was a 9. Her Material Soul was an 8, and obviously her Lifepath was an 8. Her husband, although he had no 8s in his Basic Matrix, did have the 8 in his 1st Epoch, 1st Pinnacle and 1st Challenge (1st E-P-C Triad). It was this triune eightplex that attracted her to him. With an 8 Lifepath and an 8 Soul, she was naturally attracted to his 8s. But remember, the 8s were in his Life Matrix, not his Basic Matrix. Furthermore, they were only in his chart for the 1st E-P-C Triad, which ended when he turned thirty-five years of age. After that, his chart was void of 8s. It was at this exact time that the wife lost interest in him and the marriage began to erode.

The timeframe involved is important to understand because this couple's marriage occurred during the transitional period of his eightplex – the 1st E-P-C Triad. Destiny aside, if they had known about the numerological aspects of relationship and how temporary theirs would be, they could have avoided it. Yet, destiny always rules and, therefore, their marriage was doomed to be impermanent.

During this early time of their marriage, there were no 16-7s active in either of their Life Matrices. However, when his 1st E-P-C Triad ran its course, the marriage began to degrade with the exiting of the 8 energy to which she had been strongly attracted. No 8s, no attraction. When she entered her 3rd Pinnacle at age 38, which generated a 14-5/(2)/16-7 IR Set, they separated. The wife began actively dating during their separation, which was not appreciated by the husband who felt betrayed, and the marriage ended in her filing for divorce. The husband had no 16-7s in his Life Matrix at this time, which indicates that if there were untoward behaviors going on they would have been a result of the wife's actions, not his.

Richard Andrew King

Case #02

This next situation involves the two numbers in combination which are capable of generating more darkness and chaos than any other two numbers – the 15 and 16. Interestingly, in the Tarot deck the 15 is the Devil card representing negativity and carnality; the 16 is the Tower card signifying a fall from grace, chaos and destruction.

Interestingly, the 15-6 is very often present in cases where illicit drugs are involved. The word *drugs* houses a Specific Expression of 69, thus generating a 15 transition root and a 6 crown.

As the story goes, Paul was a yoga instructor. Flo was one of his students. She had studied with him for several years. There was an attraction between them so he asked her out to dinner and a movie. She accepted. Their dinner was pleasant but things changed when they entered the theater.

Upon being seated, Flo got up and left for a few minutes. She said nothing to Paul. When she returned after ten minutes or so, she retook her seat for a few minutes and then left again, never offering a reason to Paul as to why or what she was doing. This time she was gone for around twenty minutes. This same pattern occurred a third time with her sitting for a couple minutes and then getting up and leaving for another twenty minutes or so without any explanation to Paul, who was obviously becoming suspicious at this point. Upon returning after the third episode, she told Paul she was going to go sit outside and for him to stay and watch the movie, obviously alone. Wondering what was going on, he followed her after a minute or so. After searching for her in the theater, he finally saw her sitting at a table holding her cell phone and looking down. As he approached her, she spotted him and quickly put the cell phone away. When he got closer to her, Paul stated she had a shocked look on her face, as if to say, "What are you doing here?" Paul simply asked, "What's going on?" Flo could offer no reasonable answer.

Paul's account was that Flo's mood had changed drastically, becoming short-tempered and snarky. This was not the woman Paul thought he knew. He had never seen her like this before. Why was she being so rude, insensitive, secretive and indifferent, he thought. At this point they left the theater. She guided them back to his car and he drove her home. Obviously, their date was over, but many questions arose for Paul, who felt quite disturbed and betrayed by Flo's actions.

In seeking answers to her bizarre behavior, Paul sought help from The King's Numerology™. On that particular day Flo had a quadstack (four stack) of 15-6/(1)/16-7 energy. Plus, their combined Mix PE was a 16-7, which is not a good sign for an harmonious relationship. A 16-7 in the Mix PE, or any Mix component for that matter, always creates some degree of turmoil (see KBN6) and should raise red flags. Plus, Flo's surname housed a 2/(14)/16-7 specific Subcap Challenge, adding more dark energy to her quadstack of 15-6/(1)/16-7, therefore creating a quintstack (five stack) of 16-7 energy. Two days later, Flo sent Paul an email saying she was no longer interested in studying yoga and terminated her attendance as well as their relationship, fueling more suspicion as to her weird behavior.

Paul had no idea if Flo was involved with drugs or not, but the quadstack of 15-6/(1)/16-7 energy is quite dark, and it is not inconceivable to think that drugs were involved with Flo's aberrant behavior, especially when Paul, who had known her for several years in a teacher-student business capacity, had never seen her in such a state before. Paul queried, "Why would anyone terminate a long-standing relationship when confronted with the simple query, 'What's going on'?" Obviously, it was easier for Flo to sever their relationship than explain her unsettling and bizarre conduct, behavior which most certainly was reflected by a 15-6/(1)/16-7 energy of darkness, betrayal and secrecy.

In such cases of betrayal, both parties often have a 15-6 or 16-7 because the drama affects both of them. Paul's simple Personal Year Timeline was a 2/(5)/7, more fully ciphered as 11-2/(14-5)/16-7. This pattern reveals turmoil and betrayal (16-7) originating from females, others or relationships (11-2). This pattern was also present in the second month of his Universal Timeline (UTL) when the event occurred.

Richard Andrew King

Case #03

A marriage that was doomed from the beginning is the subject of case #03. The Relationship Match and Mix between this husband and wife manifested a 16-7 Mix Expression, a 16-7 Mix PE and an 11-2 Mix 1st Names. Multiple red flags were flying high in this marriage that was sure to have problems.

We've seen the results of a 16-7 Mix PE between Paul and Flo. Now we see it in the partners of Case #03 where the 16-7 Mix Expression and 16-7 Mix PE generate stacking, which we know makes things worse. Plus, the 11-2 Mix 1st Names creates tension with one ego clashing with another. And which two binary numbers always generate red flags in a Relationship Match and Mix? If you surmised the 11-2 and 16-7 you would be right, which means you're probably familiar with *The King's Book of Numerology, Volume 6 – Love Relationships* (KBN6).

The Mix 16-7 stacking and 11-2 Mix 1st Names signal problems in the relationship and marriage but not necessarily betrayal, let alone adultery. Factually, however, the husband did commit adultery, which led to the wife filing for divorce.

The time period of the husband's betrayal was during his 4th (Crown) Pinnacle/Challenge Couplet in which his Pinnacle reflected a 1/(15)/16-7 IR Set; his Challenge was a 16-7/(6)/4. Therefore, his Crown PC Couplet contained the 16-7 energy in both the LIST and ROPE positions. These 16-7 energies bolstered the Mix 16-7 Expression and Mix 16-7 PE, thus creating a 16-7 quadset.

Of course the wife's chart would also have to show the betrayal, and it does. Her 3rd (Grand) Pinnacle, where the betrayal and divorce occurred, is a 6/(1)/7 IR Set, a more expansive version of which would be 15-6/(1)/16-7. Her Letter Timeline also housed a 15-6/(1)/16-7, and her Name Timeline contained a 16-7/(1)/17-8 IR Set. Once again, numbers tell the tale of life's dramas.

Case #04

At age 50 during a 5/(11-2)/16-7 energy field, a woman left her husband and children for her female companion. Because age 50 begins her 50s decade, the decade itself would also contain a 5/(11-2)/16-7. Plus, the Addcap and Subcap of the 50 gestation cipher house a 5/(11-2)/16-7 energy. All of these components generate a quadstack of the 5/(11-2)/16-7 vibration.

This woman's Lifepath was a 5; her Expression was an 11-2, and her PE was a 16-7. This, of course, generated a 5/(11-2)/16-7 LIR Umbrella. This increased her 5/(11-2)/16-7 quadstack to a quintstack. Her Soul Layers were an 11-2/(5)/16-7, adding yet another 16-7, thus generating a hexstack (six stack) of 16-7 energy in the ROPE position. Obviously, her life was filled with massive turmoil and heartache.

Sadly, and to make matters worse, the woman suffered a debilitating stroke a few years later. The stroke occurred in a Personal Year Timeline (PTL) of 5/(11-2)/16-7; an Age Timeline (ATL) Cycle Month of 5/(11-2)/16-7 and within a 5/(11-2)/16-7 Lifetime Monthly Timeline (LMT).

The female partner's 2nd Epoch in which this drama played itself out was a 5/(11-2)/16-7. She was also transiting her 5th 9 Cycle, which housed a 5/(11-2)/16-7 IR Set. Compounding the 16-7 energy was her Name Timeline – a 16-7/(1)/17-8. Her 2nd Challenge maintained a 16-7/(11-2)/18-9 energy revealing the ending of the relationship when her partner's stroke occurred.

Here again we see that when one person's life involves turmoil and suffering, other people close to them will also be engaged, which makes common sense when we think about it. When people whom we love hurt, so we hurt also. How could it be otherwise unless we had hearts of stone?

Richard Andrew King

Case #05

This next account involves a woman who stated, "I love being the other woman." By "other woman" she meant the mistress to a married man. Therefore, she was a major player in the drama of betrayal. When asked why she liked being the "other woman," she said it was because she always was treated extremely well.

So what does the numerology chart of a female who said, "I love being the other woman" look like? Let's take a look.

This woman's Soul Layers and Nature Layers both manifested a 1/(15-6)/16-7. Her 1 Soul indicates that her most primal desires are about her and the need to be the center of attention, as is verified by her own words. A 1 Soul in a woman also identifies her desire for males, who are naturally ruled by 1 energy. By being the "other woman" to a married man also corroborates her need to feel special. After all, it wasn't single men to whom she was attracted. It was married men and by being with a married man, she would, to some extent, exercise dominance over the man's wife, thus placing her in the number one "lover" position, literally and figuratively.

Her 1 Nature resonates perfectly with her 1 Soul's desire and signals that her life is, indeed, about her. Because the 1 is also the number of action and initiation, it speaks to her aggressiveness and willingness to lead and seek out males who would treat her well, as are her stated desires.

The 15-6 Filter in her Soul and Nature layers references her Lifepath, which is one of personal love and sex. Remember, the 15 is the Devil and Lovers card in the Tarot. Remember, too, that the numbers 5 and 6 in combination create the most sexual energetic pairing. When her 1 energy of self, men and action filters through her 15 energy of love, lust and sex, the outcome is the most potent number associated with secrecy and betrayal – the 16-7. Thus, it's easy to understand why this woman said, "I love being the other women," i.e., the mistress.

When analyzing her Life Matrix, another puzzle piece stands out. She has life linkage of the 7 energy, which is contained in the LIST position of her 1st Challenge, 2nd Pinnacle, 3rd (Grand)

Pinnacle, 3rd (Grand Challenge) and 4th (Crown) Challenge. In fact, of these five 7s, four reflect a 16-7! Her 2nd Challenge PE and Crown Pinnacle PE are also 16-7s. Therefore, from birth to death this woman's entire life is saturated with the energy of betrayal and adultery, as is clearly delineated in her Basic Matrix and Life Matrix.

Case #06

The woman in this scenario had an EIR Umbrella of 14-5/(11-2)/16-7 (14-5 Expression, 11-2 Lifepath, 16-7 PE). Since the individual's Umbrella is a blueprint of the outer life, this IR Set portends trouble for her.

Interestingly, her Material Soul was a 65-11-2. What does this 65 signify? We just discussed this in the previous example. Her Nature is a 68-14-5. The 68 references interaction and engagement (8) of love, lust and sex (6). Her Material Nature is a 16. The 11, 14 and 16 are the exact components of her Umbrella.

As one might surmise from the above data alone, this woman's life was destined to be difficult and troubling. As one example, when she was 29 years old her Age Timeline was a 2/(5)/7, the extended form of which is a 29-11-2/(14-5)/16-7. Notice, once again, that the IR Set components are the same as her Umbrella, Material Soul, Nature and Material Nature, compounding all of them and generating stacking.

The betrayal. In the 2nd Cycle Month of her 29th year, which housed a 2/(14-5)/16-7 IR Set, she was discovered cheating on her boyfriend. Her Lifetime Monthly Timeline (LMT) was also a 2/(14-5)/16-7. Notice the stacking of this pair with the other components mentioned above.

The boyfriend says that after he caught her cheating, within two months she moved away with what was apparently her "other" boyfriend, and married him! In effect, she was "seeing" two guys at the same time, and the other boyfriend, it turns out, didn't know she was betraying him either. Not long after her marriage to the "other" guy she divorced him! Such nefarious unfaithfulness. *Oh, what a tangled web we weave when first we practice to deceive* ~ Sir Walter Scott, *Marmion*.

Richard Andrew King

FAMOUS BETRAYALS

John Edwards – U.S. Senator

In the political arena one of the most publicized betrayals involving adultery was that of John Edwards (born Johnny Reid Edwards on 10 June 1953), a U.S. Senator from North Carolina who was a candidate for the Democratic presidential nomination in 2008. Edwards had an extramarital affair with a woman named Rielle Hunter (born Lisa Jo Druck on 20 March 1964), which was disclosed in the media in 2007, all going on while his wife was dying from cancer. His behavior and indiscretions damaged his image immensely and ended his political career (Wikipedia).

The number 16-7 saturated Edwards' chart. First, both his Lifepath and Expression house the 16-7 *Great Purifier*, thus reflecting dual Filters creating a 16-7/(16-7)/32-5 Umbrella. His affair was disclosed in 2007 when Edwards was 54 years old, generating a 9/(16-7)/16-7 Age Timeline (ATL). His Universal Timeline (UTL) in 2007 was also a 9/(16-7)/16-7. His Name Timeline (NTL) of *Reid* was a 9/(16-7)/16-7; his Letter Timeline (LTL) in the "I" of *Reid* was a 9/(16-7)/16-7. All these 16-7s generated a decastack (ten stack) of problematic energy. Whew! This is a massive amount of betrayal and trouble, which obviously destroyed John Edwards' personal and public life.

Rielle Hunter's chart reveals a split cipher 88-16-7 Lifepath where both the 7 and 8 are void. Her Expression is a 6 with roots of 15, 42 and 123. The Umbrella created from her Lifepath and Expression is, therefore, a Grand Voided 88v-16-7v/(15-6)/22-4. Her Lifepath 43 Specific root carries a Subcap Challenge of 1/(15)/16-7v. This generated internal stacking of the 16-7 energy in the Lessons, Influences, Subjects and Themes (LIST) of her life's journey. Her affair with Edwards occurred in her 3rd (Grand) Pinnacle, which houses a 1/(15)/16-7v. Her Grand and Crown Challenges house a 9/(15-6)/15-6. Obviously, she too had a life script filled with betrayal.

Mrs. Edwards (born Mary Elizabeth Anania on 3 July 1949; died on 7 December 2010, age 61) had a 2/(14)/16-7 IR Set in her Crown Challenge – the exact time of her husband's betrayal. It was also during this period in which she unfortunately died.

Newt Gingrich – U.S. Senator

Across the political isle, the Republican Newt Gingrich was also involved in marital betrayal and adultery. Born Newton Leroy McPherson on 17 June 1943, his first wife was Jackie Battley (born Jacqueline May Battley on 21 February 1936; died 7 August 2013). They married in 1962. In 1980 Gingrich started an affair with Marianne Ginther, subsequently divorced Jackie and married Marianne in 1981. They divorced in 1999 after Gingrich's extended affair with Callista Bisek, whom he married in 2000.

Gingrich's Expression houses a 16-7 which acted as the Filter for every one of the eleven components of the Life Matrix (Epochs, Pinnacles, Challenges). His Grand and Crown Challenges both contained a 9/(16-7)/16-7 energy. His Crown Pinnacle is a 16-7/(16-7)/14-5. With the highest and lowest parts of his Life Matrix having concentrated 16-7 energy, his relationship challenges become obvious.

Gingrich's initial affair with Ginther was in 1980 – a 9/(16-7)/16-7 Universal Timeline (UTL) year for him. His 2nd Challenge when the affair took place housed an 11-2/(16-7)/9 energy indicating the ending (9) of a relationship (11-2). The 16-7 Filter of course played its normal role.

Gingrich began his second affair with Callista Bisek in 1993 when he was in his 3rd (Grand) Challenge, a 9/(16-7)/16-7. His Personal Year Timeline (PTL) was also a 9/(16-7)/16-7. He did not marry Callista until the year 2000 after his divorce from Ginther in 1999.

Without even assessing the wives' charts, the amalgam of Gingrich's 16-7 energy tells the story of his relationship endeavors, affairs and marriages. Regardless who the players were, Gingrich's destiny was to experience multiple marriages and affairs.

It should be obvious by now how the numbers 11-2, 14-5, 15-6 and 16-7 play a major role in the drama of betrayal and adultery. The greater the saturation and stacking of these energies, the greater the problems of infidelity become.

Richard Andrew King

Tiger Woods – Professional Golfer

Following is a three piece article on Tiger Woods – the most famous professional golfer in the world during his reign, which crumbled as a result of his own adulterous behavior. It was originally published in 2010 via The King's Numerology^{tm} article series. It gives a more thorough account of Woods' life and relationship issues than those cases explored previously.

[Article preface]

The entire world has been shocked by the Tigress Saga of Tiger Woods. It is one of the strangest, most tragic and saddest falls, if not the most tragic and saddest, of any sports icon in modern history. For the mass populace it came out of nowhere. Woods' image was that of the perfect athlete who had everything – the perfect role model of husband and father, or so it seemed. As Henry Wadsworth Longfellow noted in his poem, "A Psalm of Life:" *things are not as they seem.* Still, the one question is, "Why?" Why would Tiger Woods – the man who ostensibly had it all – risk it all in one of the most ignoble falls of all time. This article address that question.

TIGER WOODS: WHY?
Part One: Desires of Love

[This article is neither intended to extol nor defame Tiger Woods. It is offered simply as a means of relating his personal numbers in his numerology chart with the events and circumstances of his life and destiny to further the understanding of numerology as a science.]

The saga of Tiger Woods – his extraordinary rise to fame and fortune and his equally extraordinary fall from grace to depths of disgrace unknown by any sports figure in the history of the modern world was, as all things are, by design. Tiger Woods, as each of us, was born with a destiny already marked out for him by forces beyond his control and understanding. Why he was given such a destiny is known only to God, and while we are not in a position to judge, we can, nonetheless, look at his numbers to explain his destiny and answer the question, "Why would a man who ostensibly had everything – wealth, power, fame, name, a beautiful wife and children, as well as public acclaim – throw it all away in such a way that Shakespeare himself would find fodder for a human tragedy of unspeakable proportions?"

The fall of Tiger Woods in many ways eclipses those falls of other prominent personalities such as Michael Jackson, Kobe Bryant, O.J. Simpson and Bernie Madoff. For most of the world, Tiger's Saga of Tigresses came out of nowhere. Tiger Woods appeared to be the most wholesome of athletes, a good husband and father with an ostensibly squeaky-clean public image, which made him hundreds of millions of dollars through high-powered sponsorships. Here was a sports figure who was, ostensibly again, truly a role model for all to admire, especially in the wake of other prominent individuals who experienced tragedy-laden lapses, some leading to their demise, especially Simpson and Madoff and countless others throughout history.

The fact of the matter is that life is destined for all of us, and Tiger Woods' life, as well as his wife, Elin Nordegren, and their children, as well as the many alleged mistresses in this sad tale of a Tiger, are no different. Says Saint Charan Singh, *All men come into this world with a destiny of their own which goes on pushing them relentlessly on the course already marked out for them. Man is completely helpless. Then why worry?*

Our destinies are known to us through our birth names and birth dates. This article will explore Tiger Woods' destiny as it relates to the numbers 5 & 6, correlating these personal numbers of his numerology chart with the events of his life and tragic decline.

Tiger's Primal Desires and the Number 5

Tiger Woods was born *Eldrick Tont Woods* on 30 December 1975. This natal (birth) data houses the blueprint of his destiny. The nickname "Tiger" was given to him by his father in honor of one of his father's war buddies.

Within our natal names each of us has a set of desires which defines our needs, wants and motivations. It is these energies, defined by numbers, which drive us to perform certain acts. They are extremely powerful and occupy the core root of the individual. Tiger's most primal desires are marked by the number Five (5) whose attributes are freedom, detachment, sensuality, adventure, exploration, versatility, variety, excitement, experience, the five senses, motion and movement. This 5 is accompanied by a root of 32 (3 + 2 = 5), a social and party vibration indicating pleasure (3) with others and females (2). This 32-5 combination shows up again in Tiger's chart in multiple places. It is also interesting that the word *mistress* is a 32-5 energy, and the Soul of the word *mistress* is also a 5 – a perfect numerical representation for what a mistress is – a paramour seeking sexual gratification without restraint, often accepting financial favors as a quid pro quo for her services. The negative aspect of the 5 is risk-taking, recklessness, wildness, intemperance and slavery – the opposite side of the 5 energy's freedom aspect. It is these qualities that help fuel Tiger Woods' primal needs. He desires excitement, adventure, variety, motion and sensual experience. Anyone with a 5 Soul (the "Soul" is the numerology label for these primal desires), will also share these same needs and motivations to some degree.

Tiger's Secondary Desires and the Number 6

Each of us also has a second desire within our natal data which augments our primal desire. It is labeled the Material Soul or MS. Tiger's Material Soul is a 6, the energy of romance, personal love, sex, nurturing. Furthermore, this 6 has a 33 master number root which is, arguably, the most sexual of all master numbers. Master numbers are binary numbers of the same digit such as 11, 22, 33, 44 and so forth. They are extremely powerful, much like nuclear energy in which their negative aspects are as equally destructive as their positive aspects are productive.

The 33 master energy, when unchecked and unrestrained, is notably present in the charts of those individuals who have fallen from grace or experienced difficulties in their lives due to sensual and sexual gratification and addiction. This 33 energy is a major player in the Woods' saga. His "Humpty-Dumpty-esque" fall occurred when he was 33 years old (matching his Material Soul energy), and his first alleged mistress, Rachel Uchitel, carries a 33 energy in her last name, "Uchitel." Besides this energy, the name "Rachel Uchitel" also manifests a 5 Soul which is identical to Tiger's 5 Soul energy. The name "Rachel" manifests a 6 Soul, again matching Tiger's 6 Material Soul. The presence of these numbers in both their charts creates a natural intrinsic resonance between them as people. This "numeric resonance" is one of the keys to love and attraction which is explained in *The King's Book of Numerology, Volume 6 – Love Relationships* (available on Amazon.com and RichardKing.net).

The 5 and 6 as a combination governing one's desires, needs and wants is the most powerful set of numbers manifesting potentially unrestrained sensual and sexual interests, a variety of lovers, risk-taking, "partying" behaviors and pleasurable indulgences. Anyone with this 5-6 numerical set in their Soul and Material Soul respectively will have highly similar desires as Tiger Woods. It is this 5-6 combination which also creates an attraction between Woods and Uchitel, as mentioned. The problem is that the 5 energy seeks variety and multiple experiences and therefore does not bode well for a faithful, devoted, long term and monogamous relationship. Exceptions do exist, but the lives and events of both Woods and Uchitel have exemplified the essence of what the 5 and 6 energy in tandem represents in general terms – a variety of lovers and love experiences.

Intensity and Stacking

When a person's chart simultaneously contains the same number (energy) in various components, *stacking* occurs. *Stacking* is the simultaneous occurrence of the same number within a chart. Stacking creates intensity. It's like standing in the middle of multiple fires, not just one, all at the same time. For Tiger, the number 5 is present in more than just his Soul, thus adding to the 5's intensity and exacerbating its energies and characteristics. He also carries a 5 in his Material Nature (MN) – one of the components of the Basic Matrix of The King's Numerology^{tm}. This 5 Material Nature defines his personality and manner of doing things. Coupled with his 5 desire energy, this is a potent example of *stacking*, thus creating further intensity of the Five's fire. With this much 5 energy fueling a person's primal desires *and* personality, it would be most challenging to not stray or seek gratification in a variety of ways.

There's still more. The name "Tiger" is also a 5 and a 32-5 at that! As we recall, the 32-5 occupied the Soul component of Tiger's birth name, *Eldrick Tont Woods*. Additionally, the Soul energy of the name "Tiger" is also a 5! Thus, Tiger Woods' numerology chart generates a *hepstack* (stack of seven; also referred to as a septuple stack) of 5 energy in multiple places:

Richard Andrew King

Stacking of the Number 5 in the Woods' Saga

1. His Natal Soul
2. His Material Nature
3. The name *Tiger*
4. The Soul of the name *Tiger*
5. The word *Mistress*
6. The Soul of *Mistress*
7. The Soul of *Rachel Uchitel*

This septuple *stacking* of 5 energy creates enormous intensity of all that the 5 represents. It also reveals how interrelated our destinies are. Anyone with this combination would have a most challenging time managing his or her sexual/sensual energy. This is not to excuse Tiger Woods for his behaviors, but it is to explain them and to help answer the question of his reckless amorous behavior with its deleterious results, "Why?"

Tiger & Elin's Marriage

Successful marriages exude a resonance of numerical energy as explained in *The King's Book of Numerology, Volume 6 – Love Relationships* (KBN6). When there is a large amount of like-kind energy between two people in their combined charts, the marriage union is strong and lasting. However, when there is a lack of like-kind energy, the marriage is at risk of dissolution.

Professionally speaking, and if destiny could be altered, which it can't, the marriage between Tiger Woods and Elin Nordegren was not a good mixing and matching of energies, and the result is as the world is now seeing – a familial and professional tragedy.

If two people are going to be happy and fulfilled in their marriage, both of their most internal drives, needs and wants must be satisfied. As we have seen, Tiger Woods' desires are motivated heavily by 5 energy. This is what he needs to be fulfilled and content. Yet, the numerology chart of Elin Nordegren (born: Elin Maria Pernilla Nordegren on 1 January 1980) has no 5 energy whatsoever in her Basic Matrix. Thus, Tiger's 5 energy has no reflection in her chart. Her chart is basically indifferent to the desires that motivate him. There is no corresponding reverberation or reciprocity of his basic needs, wants and desires.

Compounding this, their Mix energies – those which describe the relationship and marriage – are also devoid of 5 energy. This creates a painful scenario for both of them. Through no fault of either of them, Tiger was simply unfulfilled and deeply lacking in resonant energy in his marriage, which is why he has commented that his marriage was boring. To him it was because the total lack of 5 energy created a void lacking the kind of excitement and adventure he intrinsically needs. Had both Tiger and Elin married a partner whose energies were more compatible with their own, their marriages would most likely have endured and the whole sad saga of Tiger Woods would never have materialized. Yet, this is a hypothetical situation and unrealistic from a destiny standpoint.

Perhaps the silver lining in all this is that both Tiger and Elin will look more deeply into their intrinsic needs and seek professional counseling as to what, in fact, constitutes an enduring and fulfilling marriage numerologically. If their destinies do not allow this, then perhaps their story will motivate others to seek answers *before* any nuptial knots are tied, thus avoiding the heartache, heartbreak, sadness, suffering, tragedy and tumult of divorce and all of its attending agonies and miseries and instead create a loving, fulfilling and harmonious union.

Richard Andrew King

TIGER WOODS: WHY?
Part Two: Power, Fame and Ego

Fortune does not change men, it unmasks them.

Suzanne Necker

18th Century French Patroness

Power tends to corrupt, and absolute power corrupts absolutely. Great men are almost always bad men, even when they exercise influence and not authority.

Lord Acton

19th Century English Historian

Humility is the true sign of greatness. The branches of a tree laden with fruit bend low. So it is with the truly great.

Jagat Singh

20th Century Saint

Unnumbered suppliants crowd Preferment's Gate, athirst for wealth and burning to be great; delusive fortune hears the incessant call; they rise, they shine, evaporate and fall!

Dr. Samuel Johnson

18th Century English Writer, Lexicographer, Poet

Vanity of Human Wishes

As the Saga of Tiger Woods continues to unfold, its lessons emerge magnetic, microscopic, telescopic and educational. As sad as this human tragedy is, its lessons are replete with timeless and universal principles and lessons of life – its successes, failures, lures, traps, heartaches and heartbreaks. It is indeed a potpourri of both how to live and how not to live one's life. Yet, it is a common life story familiar to us all. No one in this world is perfect. We all make mistakes and have most likely several closets full of both fresh and decaying skeletons. The thing with this drama is that Tiger Woods was the most publically recognized sports icon in the world, notwithstanding the fact that the reality of who he is was so drastically different from the persona he portrayed. This article continues to delve into that one question the entire world is asking, "Why?"

Tiger and the Power of the Numbers 8 and 9

As Eighteenth Century French Patroness, Suzanne Necker, succinctly stated, *Fortune does not change men, it unmasks them.* What the world is seeing of a thirty-four year old Tiger Woods is really the unmasking of who he is intrinsically. All of our lives are destined . . . to the breath. It is no different for Tiger Woods. Plus, leopards never change their spots. Nor do we. All of us are born with a blueprint that is set for life. We go through different phases of our life, especially those marked in our Life Matrix, and we can, with effort, rise to a higher frequency of a particular intrinsic energy that defines us, but our basic patterns are set and determined by higher powers even before we are born. Why they are the way they are is known only to God. Our job is to do the best we can with them, learn from them, grow from them, and even discharge past karmas involving them.

Tiger: 9 Expression

In numerology, the Expression identifies the individual as a composite whole, replete with assets, liabilities, desires, and personality traits. Tiger Woods was born "Eldrick Tont Woods" on 30 December 1975. His birth name equates to a simple 9 number, referred to as the "Grand Elemental" in The King's Numerology^{tm} system. As a cipher, Nine (9) is unique because when it is added to any other single cipher, the result is always that number. For example, 9 + 8 = 17: 1 + 7 = 8. Notice that when 9 is added to 8, the result is 8. Were 9 added to 3, the result would be 3 in reduction: 9 + 3 = 12: 1 + 2 = 3. It is the same with every number. No other number has this quality. It is unique exclusively to the 9.

This Grand Elemental attribute makes the 9 very charismatic. Since people are really energy identified with a numerical label, when engaging with Tiger Woods [or any 9 person], they would feel a connection because their specific energy would be reflected to them by the 9 individual. This is one reason why 9 is powerful – it naturally mixes with everyone and everyone identifies with it because it reflects themselves to themselves.

Nine (9) is also dominate, and it would be an appropriate phrase to say, "9 rules." Why is this? If all the single ciphers in the alpha-numeric spectrum [the single digits 1 to 9] are added together and reduced to a single digit, the outcome is a 9. For example: 1 + 2 + 3 + 4 + 5 + 6 + 7 + 8 + 9 = 45: 4 + 5 = 9. Therefore, 9 contains all of the single numbers within itself, corroborating its charismatic and chameleon attributes. The caution is that 9 is potentially so powerful it can become domineering to a grievous fault.

Nine (9) dons other characteristics as well. In numerology it is the number of the public stage, fame, notoriety, travel, art, theater, expansion, the global spotlight, universality, philanthropy, broadcasting, finalizations, endings and the termination of cycles.

As all numbers, 9 has two sides, one good; one bad. 9 can be the magnanimous ruler or the nefarious and malevolent tyrant. Power is power, whether it's nuclear or personal. Used appropriately, it generates great and wonderful benefits for all; used inappropriately, it creates a living hell for everyone. And furthermore, whatever it creates it generates a karmic payback for itself. What we put onto the circle of life always circles back to encircle us, regardless of whether the energy is positive or negative. We sow; we reap. It is the immutable law of this creation and no one – no king, queen, pauper, prince, celebrity or even global golf icon escapes it.

The misuse of power is common, which is why Lord Acton stated in a letter to London's Bishop Mandell Creighton, *Power tends to corrupt, and absolute power corrupts absolutely. Great men are almost always bad men, even when they exercise influence and not authority.*

Money, and lots of it, always creates a sense of worldly power. Since people are attracted to money and power, it places the one in power in a dangerous position, especially men who lack self-restraint and are immersed with a sense of enjoying the spoils of their ephemeral potency with the female sex. With this power in tow, so in tow are the numbers of hangers-on, sycophants, predators, yes-sirs, mistresses, vultures and flies. And since the number 9 mixes with everyone, it can, if it's not careful, become mixed with those souls and beings who are of a dark, usurious, untoward and negative nature. If desirous of being in power, or being placed in power, but lacking in strength and wisdom, it is easy to see how one would fall into the clutches of such contaminated characters and thereby suffer the slings and arrows of outrageous fortune, and certainly the Woods' Saga fits the "outrageous fortune" bill (respects to you, Mr. Shakespeare). It is this power aspect of the 9 which helps to plague Tiger Woods, creating a scenario that was exposed, ostensibly and coincidentally, with a powerful, and reportedly, raging 9 iron.

Tiger's Name Timeline PE of 9

In numerology, each of our birth names carries with it a timeline or period in which the name is active. Tiger's first name is "Eldrick." This equates to an 8. When we add his Lifepath number, a 1 (we'll discuss this next), the result is a 9 outcome, the energy of power, fame and notoriety. This second 9 in Tiger's chart creates *stacking*, a condition creating greater intensity of the 9 energy. This 8/9 Influence/Reality Set (I/R Set for short) rules Tiger's life from birth through age thirty-five. It is also a combination indicating success (8) with a powerfully public outcome of domination (9), which Tiger has been privileged to have since birth. The sad part is that unless one with this combination has an understanding of spiritual matters accompanied with a sense of humility, worldly success often goes to people's heads, swelling and inflating them with the importance but false sense of their own egos, blinding them and subsequently causing them enormous grief. Had there been more humility than ego, the grief would never have existed. Power would be given to God, not to the self, so the self could not fall into the abyss of self-acclaim, self-centeredness, self-importance and self-made troubles.

Tiger's First Challenge: 9/9

Increasing the *stacking* of 9 energy is that the first Challenge period in Tiger's life [from birth to age thirty-five] is a 9/(9)/9 IR set. This increases his power, domination, public and global influence as well as mixing among many people. With the addition of this first Challenge 9/(9)/9 set, Tiger Woods' chart reveals a quadstack of four 9s:

1. 9 Expression
2. 9 First Name [Eldrick] Timeline PE
3. 9 First Challenge
4. 9 First Challenge PE

This is certainly a large amount of the energy of power, domination and public appeal. Yet, as all things cycle, so does power. None of us has it forever.

Tiger's Sense of Ego, Self, Uniqueness and the Number 1

Tiger Woods was born on 30 December 1975. This date creates a 1 Lifepath, the script of his life indicating the issues, events and lessons – both positive and negative – he will be experiencing. Combined with his 9 Expression, this 1 Lifepath also generates a 1 Performance/Experience cipher or PE, the component of one's Basic Matrix defining the role a person will play on the great life stage. Here again is an example of stacking, this time involving the 1 energy.

The number 1 is the cipher of the ego, self, yang/male issues, action, independence, strength of will, self-reliance. When the 9 and 1 are combined, as they are in Tiger's case, the 1 PE (or reality cipher) is saturated with the vibration of self and ego. "E Online" quotes Tiger Woods' high school girlfriend, Dina Parr, as saying that when he was in college he developed an "untouchable arrogance" that escalated with the number of women in his life. It is this 1 and 9 set of ciphers that certainly played and continues to play a dominate role in Woods' troubled life.

What is the solution to all this self-absorbed, power-dominating plague? The answer lies, as it always does, with adjusting one's life to encompass the only true One (1), God, and His power, while subordinating the little, ego-saturated and me-first driven self to a higher reality. If we have power, it is because God gave it to us. If we have money, it is because God gave it to us. If we are fortunate enough to have skills and abilities that outshine others, making us the best in the world, it is because God allowed it. Everything comes from God; nothing from self.

The trap is that we think our talents and success belong to us and were created by us. They don't and aren't. They belong to God and are gifted to us by Him, and when we put ourselves first and engage in the great sin of ingratitude by not putting God first and thanking Him for our good fortune, then we're headed for a fall, and the bigger the illusion, the bigger our ego, the bigger our sense of personal greatness, the bigger the fall. Humpty-Dumpty got a big head. He fell, and he fell from such a high place and in such an explosion when he hit the ground that "All the king's horses and all the king's men couldn't put Humpty Dumpty back together again."

Tiger Woods has experienced a Humpty-Dumpty fall. Can he put his life back together again? Perhaps to a degree, but only if he reverses his thoughts, principles, actions and behaviors by putting God first, not himself. That's how it is with all of us. When it comes down to it, no matter how big we think we are, we're nothing. Science has proven that there are more stars in the universe than all the grains of sand on all the beaches of the world. With that kind of immensity, how insubstantial is any of us, including our fame, fortune, power, status or celebrity?

To wrap himself in humility is the first thing Tiger Woods, or any of us for that matter, needs to do to fix his life.

As Saint Jagat Singh states: *Humility is the true sign of greatness. The branches of a tree laden with fruit bend low. So it is with the truly great.*

Richard Andrew King

If Tiger decides not to revolutionize his life, his thoughts and behavior, then he will, no doubt, continue to become one of the endless numbers of souls Dr. Samuel Johnson referenced in his *Vanity of Human Wishes*:

Unnumbered suppliants crowd Preferment's Gate,
athirst for wealth and burning to be great;
delusive fortune hears the incessant call;
they rise, they shine, evaporate and fall!

TIGER WOODS: WHY?
Part 3: Missing Wiring

In Part 1 of "Tiger Woods, Why?" we discussed the issues of love and sex as they relate to the numbers 5 and 6. In Part 2 we addressed the numbers 1, 8 and 9 as they relate to concepts of power, fame, success and ego. In this article we will explain how the numbers 7 and 8 play a major role in the concept of "missing wiring" in the Tiger Woods Saga.

In numerology there are nine basic numbers: 1-2-3-4-5-6-7-8-9. These nine single ciphers represent the composite "wiring" of the individual. Each number, as a wire, manifests specific characteristics and attributes (identified as keywords or key phrases). Across these "wires" flow the energy which allows the individual to operate as a conscious living being. When an individual's full natal name houses all of the single numbers, his wiring is complete and his ability to operate as a balanced, harmonious and functionally integrated human being is enhanced. When a number or numbers are missing in the chart, the wiring is incomplete and the individual's chances of living a full, whole and effective life are compromised.

Voids are missing wires in the birth name. They are major problematic players in the destiny of an individual. Simply said, voids create problems; the more voids, the more potential problems. Furthermore, if a void is located in a Challenge position in the numerology chart, its problems intensify in the area associated with its characteristics and attributes for the time the void is active in the chart. If the void not only occurs in a Challenge position but also does not occupy one of the seven components of the Basic Matrix, it becomes a Grand Voided Challenge and its problematic status creates havoc for the individual during the time frame in which the void occurs.

Think of an automobile and its structure. It is filled with all kinds of wires which send mechanical or electrical signals to its various parts, thus allowing the car to run smoothly and efficiently. For example, assume the ignition system has no wiring. The car couldn't start even if the remainder of the car's wiring were complete. Perhaps the ignition system is in tact but there are no break lines from the brake pedal to the wheels. The car will not be able to stop even if it gets moving. If there's no wiring from the steering column to the front end wheel assembly, the car may be able to start, it

Richard Andrew King

may be able to go, it may be able to stop but it won't be able to turn. Obviously, then, an automobile's wiring system is critical to its health, integration and functionability. Without all of the wiring in tact, an automobile may not only be inefficient but dangerous . . . to itself and others.

So it is with people. If their wiring is complete, their lives and happiness will be potentially enhanced. If their wiring is lacking, they will be lacking, their lives manifesting problems and causing potential disruption to themselves and others. Numerology "wires" are identified by numbers and their corresponding letters as depicted in the following chart.

BASIC LETTER VALUE CHART

A-J-S	=	1
B-K-T	=	2
C-L-U	=	3
D-M-V	=	4
E-N-W	=	5
F-O-X	=	6
G-P-Y	=	7
H-Q-Z	=	8
I & R	=	9

Tiger Woods, who was born "Eldrick Tont Woods" on 30 December 1975, has no Gs, Ps or Ys in his birth name. This gives him a 7 void. He also has no Hs, Qs or Zs which give him an 8 void. Plus, he has no 7s or 8s in the Basic Matrix of his numerology chart. This condition makes each number a Grand Void. Furthermore, Tiger's chart manifests a double 8 void in the Challenge aspect of his chart, thus creating a Grand Voided Challenge. In layman's terms, all this void structure creates very demanding times for Tiger Woods which will tax both the internal and external aspects of his life.

The 7 Void

In numerology, the number 7 rules all things internal – the mind and spirit. This includes the depth of thought or lack of it (the opposite side of its energetic coin); discretion and indiscretion; wisdom and foolishness; nobility and ignobility; calm and chaos; purity and impurity; sanctification and adulteration; saints and sinners; analysis, reflection, examination, evaluation, reclusion, recession, privacy and secrecy.

It is this 7 void which has negatively impacted Woods' ability to assess, examine and evaluate his actions wisely. Generally speaking, a 7 void manifests as a lack of depth of thought, an absence of wisdom and discretion. This is not always the case, however, as sometimes a person with a 7 void will work hard to fill up the void positively. Too, other factors in the chart may offset or mitigate negative 7 potentials. This said, with the combination of Tiger's 1, 5, 6 and 9 energy of self, ego, sensual stimulation, variety, love and power (see article Parts 1 and 2), it is understandable that the 7 void in his chart played itself out as a total lack of thought, wisdom and discretion which were overpowered by his ego, sexual and sensual energies. In effect, the "wiring" is missing between Tiger's depth of thought and his actions.

The 8 Void

In numerology, the number 8 rules all things external. 8 is the energy of connection and its opposite polarity, disconnection. It is the most powerful social number of the alpha-numeric spectrum (the single numbers One through Nine). 8 also rules management, administration, marketing, coordination, orchestration, continuity, commerce, execution, engagement, worldly comfort, flow and a sense of being 'in the loop.'

With an 8 Grand Voided Challenge in his numerology chart, there exists a deep disconnect in Woods between his private and public life, between the promotion of his wholesome family-man image and his libidinous menagerie of mistresses. This kind of hypocrisy has been perhaps the most disturbing aspect of the Woods Saga. In some ways, it's much like the Bernie Madoff scandal. He also had fooled and deceived many people, and his disconnect finally caught up with him and

Richard Andrew King

disconnected him not only from his fortune but his freedom. Madoff also had a 7 and 8 void in his chart but his voids were both Grand Voided Challenges and thus more severe. Too, Madoff, like Woods, had the 33-6 master number present as the identifier of his needs, wants and desires, and the numbers 1 and 9 dominate in his Challenge positions as well. The 1 and 9 rule ego and power – the same energies plaguing Woods. Madoff, like Woods, duped many people but his was certainly more criminal, bilking people out of approximately sixty-five billion dollars with absolutely no remorse for his actions or the immense catastrophic effect it had on the people he deceived and damaged.

Both Madoff and Woods express extreme egos and power bases and court an extreme disconnect to what is considered normal reality. As far as Woods is concerned, how could he engage in such a plethora of sexual relationships with total disregard not only for his own health and well-being but more grievously for that of his wife and children? The sexually transmitted disease issues are enormous, not to mention the psychological, emotional, familial, financial and social implications. What was he thinking? And this is the root of the problem. He wasn't thinking. Either that or he just didn't have the depth of thought to make a connection between his actions and how those actions could and would negatively affect his wife, children, their future, the rest of his family, the PGA, his fans, sponsors, the public in general and his own life and success. Certainly, he couldn't have been blind to his global iconic image, popularity and hero status. Or could he? Did his 1 and 9 power combination delude him into thinking because he was the great Tiger Woods that he would escape detection or accountability? This is a perfect example of a 7-8 void combination, a total disconnect between himself and others, but a strong connection to his own needs, as reflected by the dominating combination of 1 (ego/self) and 9 (power) energy in his chart.

If Tiger Woods ultimately shows some genuine penitence and humility, it will be a positive move in the right direction for him. The key in his rehabilitation will be to fill these voids of the 7 and 8 with wisdom, as well as loving, not lusting, management of his personal life. It won't be easy, and he will have to exercise extreme discipline, self-control and strength of will to negate the negative effects of these voids, not to mention managing the damage that has been done to so many lives, as well as the rebuilding of his personal life. *You play, you pay* is the age-old saying, and sometimes the payback is harsh, brutal and catastrophic. Such is karma.

The whole Tiger Woods Saga has certainly been shocking, sad and extremely painful, especially for his wife and family. In consideration of their collective well-being, we wish all of them a sense of balance and harmony so they may move past this heartbreaking ordeal and ultimately lead harmonious and positive lives.

ARTICLE ADDENDUM

Do the numbers 11-2, 14-5, 15-6 and 16-7 – the numbers often appearing in cases of betrayal – appear in Tiger Woods' chart during the betrayal/adultery phase of his life? Yes. Let's take a look.

As we've seen, the number 5 is dominant in Woods' chart. The transition root for the 5 is the 14, so this number was strongly anchored in his life. The name *Tiger* carries a Specific Expression of 59, which of course reduces to a 14-5. The Soul of *Tiger* is a 14, and both his 5 Natural Soul and 5 Material Nature house a 14 root. The saga of Tiger Woods' tragic fall from grace is replete with mistresses. The word *Mistress* houses a 14-5 Soul.

The bombshell of Woods' betrayals, adulteries and serial cheating exploded during the Thanksgiving holiday of 2009 in the famous scenario of his wife chasing him with a golf club and smashing out the windows of his Escalade upon discovering his wayward indiscretions. The year 2009 houses an 11-2 transition master number. 2009 is also an energy referencing the ending (9) of relationship (2). Too, November is the 11th month. When the number 11-2 is added to Tiger Woods' 9 natal Expression, an 11-2/(9)/11-2 IR Set is created. Plus, the name *Rachel*, the first name of the first alleged mistress, is a 29-11-2.

The 15-6 is contained in Woods' Material Soul (MS). His 1st Pinnacle (from birth through age 35) is a 6/(9)/15-6. This stacked with his MS, increasing its energies.

The 16-7 plays a major role in Woods' tragic saga, of course. His birth date is 30 December 1975. When the "explosion" erupted during the Thanksgiving weekend of 2009, Woods was still in his natal 2008 at the age of 33 in his natal month of October – his 11th cycle month, which obviously added to his 11-2 stacking mentioned above. His natal year of 2008 maintained a 16-7/(9)/16-7

Richard Andrew King

Personal Year Timeline (PTL), and his Age Timeline (ATL) Universal column also contained the same 16-7/(9)/16-7 IR Set.

To make matters worse, Woods' middle name of *Tont* is a 15-6 Expression with a pure 15-6 Soul via the letter "O." Combined with his 1 Lifepath, the *Tont* NTL is a 15-6/(1)/16-7. It began at age 36, which was the exact year he entered his 2nd Pinnacle – a 16-7/(9)/16-7 period of nine years. Unfortunately, Woods' Crown Pinnacle is a 7/(9)/16-7, its energies raining down over his entire life.

Woods' wife was Elin Nordegren (born Elin Maria Pernilla Nordegren on 1 January 1980). At the time of the "explosion" she was 29 years old – an Age Timeline of 29-11-2/(8)/1. Her Cycle and Universal months during November of 2009 were both an 11-2. She was also transiting the "R" of "Maria," generating a Letter Timeline of 9/(11-2)/11-2. Her Natural Soul also housed an 11-2 root. Thus, between her and Woods there was a massive amount of explosive energy, as history has proven.

Interestingly, Nordegren did not have any major 15-6s or 16-7s in her chart at the time. Her Nature does house a 15-6 but that's all. However, her 2nd, 3rd and 4th Challenges house an 8/(8)/16-7 energy. Her 2nd Challenge began at age 35.

SUMMARY

History is awash, even overflowing, with cases of betrayal and adultery. This chapter has provided a foundation for understanding the numbers associated with such behaviors and should serve as a guide in the analysis process of one's destiny.

Now, to be sure, just because the 11-2, 14-5, 15-6 and 16-7 appear in a chart does not automatically translate to betrayal or adultery. This concatenation of interconnected numbers does, however, generate an amalgam of tension and turmoil. Of this there is no doubt. How much is the question. The antidote for mitigating their negative effects is to maintain a spiritual life of acceptance, balance, centeredness, purity, humility and resolve. We all have karmas which must be reconciled at some time in some life. What we sow, we reap, and we cannot reap what we do not sow, so when we are reaping turmoil, trouble, tears and chaos we must realize it is by our own doing. Blaming others is spiritually immature. As Guru Nanak, the famous Indian Saint stated: *I blame not another. I blame my own karmas. Whatever I sowed, so did I reap. Why then put the blame on others?* This is the reality of life in this dimension.

If we are the "victims" of betrayal, we would be wise to accept the reality that somewhere in our past we did the betraying. Otherwise, according to karmic law we could never be betrayed. Hopefully, if we are enlightened, we will never engage in such untoward behavior. Not only does betrayal cause immense pain and suffering for others, it will also rebound upon us. We would be wise to remember that God does not prevent us from making choices, but He also does not prevent us from experiencing the consequences of our choices. Let those who hear, truly hear.

Richard Andrew King

CHAPTER 3

NEMESIS NUMBERS

The Nemesis Number (or numbers) is that number serving as the catalyst for the activation of the 16-7 Great Purifier and its manifestations. Composed of a crown and its root structure, the Nemesis Number will generally be placed in the LIST position of an IR Set with the ROPE being the Great Purifier 16-7.

The FILTER of the Nemesis IR Set will either be the Lifepath number or the Expression number. If the Lifepath and Expression numbers are identical, then the FILTER for the Nemesis Number will only be one number for the entire life, in effect intensifying the Nemesis Number's energy.

Nemesis is the Greek goddess of retribution, of inexorable justice, forcing one to give back what is due. In other words, she is the goddess of the "pay back," of karmic reconciliation, usually of one's arrogance or hubris. A general definition of *nemesis* is that of an adversary or opponent. In the King's Numerology™, the Nemesis Number references the numeric energy acting as a catalyst to generate retribution and purification via the 16-7 Great Purifier – the instrument through which our negative karmas are reconciled and our inner awareness deepened and expanded. Everyone has the 16-7 in their charts somewhere; some have it more than others. Massive amounts of 16-7 energy can result in tumult, disgrace, humiliation, dishonor, a tragic fall from on high – all of which create pain, suffering, sorrow, trouble, tears, chaos. If managed positively, 16-7 energy will lead us to make spiritual gains in our evolution through a process of penitence and humility.

Although the 16-7 is often seen as baneful, the blessing of the 16-7 is that through its retributive process we are given the chance to balance our karmic debts and redeem ourselves. None of us is perfect in this world. We've all committed untoward actions in our past and their debts simply have to be repaid at some point in time. By paying our debts, our burdens are discharged and we become

Richard Andrew King

more whole. Therefore, we must not fear our Nemesis Number but embrace it because it allows us the opportunity of redemption, of reconciling our karmas, and reconciliation there must be.

It is understandable that the 16-7 Great Purifier is often regarded with some degree of trepidation. Verily, it is not a comfortable energy to experience but it is a necessary and imperative energy if we are to develop and purify ourselves. As both the King's Numerology™ and the Karate Institute of America™ teach . . .

Diamonds are made under extreme heat and pressure over an extended period of time; not by a mere and casual blowing of an intermittent wind.

If we want to be an old chunk of coal; if we are satisfied with that which is ordinary and common; if mediocrity is the level to which we aspire, then fine. We can be that way. However, if we wish to be a diamond, to be extraordinary, uncommon and as Confucius would say, a Superior Man, then we must be ready and willing to embrace the heat, pressure and time necessary to create the quality and value we wish to exemplify.

Helen Keller is one of the greatest human beings in history. Having lost her sight and hearing early in life, she struggled mightily with being blind and deaf – her personal nemeses. Yet, she embraced the adversities of her life, and her imprint on humanity is both colossal and legend. Keller said:

Character cannot be developed in ease and quiet. Only through experience of trial and suffering can the soul be strengthened, ambition inspired, and success achieved.

She also exclaimed:

Although the world is full of suffering, it is full also of the overcoming of it.

And . . .

We could never learn to be brave and patient if there were only joy in the world.

Kahlil Gibran, the famous Lebanese-American writer and artist beautifully remarked:

Out of suffering have emerged the strongest souls.
The most massive characters are seared with scars.

The 16-7 does generate circumstances which are difficult, challenging, trying. Under its influence there is the distinct possibility of tears, fears, turmoil, suffering, tragedy, chaos, heartache and heartbreak. Of this there is no doubt. Yet, the greatest people in history, the most substantive of souls, almost always have the 16-7 dominantly placed in their charts. The Great Purifier is that energy that forces us inward, turning our attention away from the pleasures and pursuits of the outer world to the eternal internal reality of the Great Within. In history there are few souls who achieved greatness by having easy lives. It is the 16-7 Great Purifier that forces us to think, ponder, reflect, examine, introspect, meditate, analyze – all of which deepen us, make us sensitive to the world around us and mold us into diamonds of extraordinary value and luster.

As mentioned in the beginning of this chapter, *nemesis* references an adversary or opponent. Adversity and opposition are absolutely requisite for us to become better, stronger, to grow and expand beyond our current state. No one gets better by doing nothing, by accepting the status quo, by being lazy or self-indulgent. We simply must be challenged to excel and grow. What athlete ever improved his skills by not being challenged by other athletes? What fighter ever expanded his martial arts acumen without being tested by other fighters, without actually fighting? What person ever became stronger by lifting cotton balls? The fact is, like it or not, we must be placed in the fire of adversity to grow, to improve, to develop, to excel. Therefore, when seen in this light, our Nemesis Numbers are to be welcomed and embraced, neither feared nor despised. They are major threads in the warp and woof of our lives, the fabric of our destinies, as well as being a critical and necessary stimulus to our spiritual growth and achievement.

Richard Andrew King

THE TWO PRIMARY NEMESIS NUMBERS

There are two principal Nemesis Numbers – one in which the EXPRESSION is the FILTER in an IR Set and the other in which the LIFEPATH is the Filter. These are illustrated in the charts below. Therefore, most people will have two Nemesis Numbers. The plural for Nemesis is *Nemeses*. Since most people's Lifepath is different from their Expression, they will have numeric *nemeses*.

Too, when the EXPRESSION is the FILTER, the LIST energies creating the Nemesis Number will be derived from the Lifepath (LP) itself, all eleven components of the Life Matrix (LM: Epochs, Pinnacles, Challenges); the Decade Timeline (DTL); the Lifetime Monthly Timeline (LMT); the Cycle of 9s; all of the Annual Cycle Patterns (ACPs) and their Cycle and Universal components.

When the LIFEPATH is the FILTER, only the Name Timelines (NTLs) and Letter Timelines (LTLs) will serve as the LIST for the Nemesis Number.

As a note, the ROPE will almost always contain a 16-7 Great Purifier due to the combinations generated by the root structures of the LIST and the FILTER numbers.

| NEMESIS NUMBER USING THE *EXPRESSION* AS THE FILTER ||||
| The LIST is the LP, LM, DTL, LMT, ACPs, CYCLE OF 9s ||||
Nemesis Number LIST	EXPRESSION Number FILTER	Great Purifier 16-7 ROPE	IR SET Simple
6	1	16-7	6/(1)/16-7
5	2	16-7	5/(2)/16-7
4	3	16-7	4/(3)/16-7
3	4	16-7	3/(4)/16-7
2	5	16-7	2/(5)/16-7
1	6	16-7	1/(6)/16-7
9	7	16-7	9/(7)/16-7
8	8	16-7	8/(8)/16-7
7	9	16-7	7/(9)/16-7

For example, the Nemesis Number for a 2 Expression person is 5; the Nemesis Number for a person with a 7 Expression is 9; a 1 Expression's Nemesis Number is a 6 and so forth.

The King's Book of Numerology, Volume 12 – Advanced Principles

NEMESIS NUMBER USING THE *LIFEPATH* AS THE FILTER			
The LIST is restricted to Name Timelines (NTLs) and Letter Timelines (LTLs)			
Nemesis Number LIST	LIFEPATH Number FILTER	Great Purifier 16-7 ROPE	IR SET Simple
6	1	16-7	6/(1)/16-7
5	2	16-7	5/(2)/16-7
4	3	16-7	4/(3)/16-7
3	4	16-7	3/(4)/16-7
2	5	16-7	2/(5)/16-7
1	6	16-7	1/(6)/16-7
9	7	16-7	9/(7)/16-7
8	8	16-7	8/(8)/16-7
7	9	16-7	7/(9)/16-7

For example, a person with an 8 Lifepath will have a Nemesis Number of 8; a 3 Lifepath's Nemesis Number is a 4; a 2 Lifepath is coupled with a 5 Nemesis Number and so forth. If both the Lifepath and Expression are the same number, they will have only one Nemesis Number, thus intensifying the individual's life lessons via Dual Filter Umbrella stacking of the Lifepath and Expression.

NEMESIS NUMBER: *LIFEPATH & EXPRESSION* AS DUAL FILTERS			
Nemesis Number LIST	LP & EXP DUAL FILTERS	Great Purifier 16-7 ROPE	IR SET Simple
6	1 LP – 1 EXP	16-7	6/(1)/16-7
5	2 LP – 2 EXP	16-7	5/(2)/16-7
4	3 LP – 3 EXP	16-7	4/(3)/16-7
3	4 LP – 4 EXP	16-7	3/(4)/16-7
2	5 LP – 5 EXP	16-7	2/(5)/16-7
1	6 LP – 6 EXP	16-7	1/(6)/16-7
9	7 LP – 7 EXP	16-7	9/(7)/16-7
8	8 LP – 8 EXP	16-7	8/(8)/16-7
7	9 LP – 9 EXP	16-7	7/(9)/16-7

Richard Andrew King

The following chart addresses the LIST issues of the Nemesis Numbers and their IR Sets.

NEMESIS NUMBER: IR SET LIST ISSUES		
Nemesis Number	**IR SET**	**LIST Issues of the Nemesis Number Generating a 16-7 ROPE**
6	6/(1)/16-7	Personal love, romance, heart, home, family, domicile, duty, community, country, nurturing, support, responsibility, helping
5	5/(2)/16-7	Freedom, detachment, change, movement, motion, letting go, adventure, wildness, sensory stimulation, experiences, sensuality
4	4/(3)/16-7	Work, service, security, stability, constancy, convention, tradition, stubbornness, recalcitrance, discipline, control, rules, order
3	3/(4)/16-7	Communication, words, fulfillment, joy, happiness, image and images, health and well-being, vanity, entitlement, narcissism
2	2/(5)/16-7	Close personal relationships, others, females, opposition, duality, deceit, dependence, indirect behavior, passivity, emotion
1	1/(6)/16-7	Independence, ego, self, males, direct action, leadership, authority
9	9/(7)/16-7	The public at large, power, arrogance, dominance, endings, travel, rulership, universality, theater, art, education, medicine, mankind
8	8/(8)/16-7	Social interaction, engagement, management, status, connection
7	7/(9)/16-7	Secrecy, withdrawal, alienation, isolation, separation, privacy, solitude, perfection, criticism, betrayal, adultery, thinking

EXAMPLES

2 Expression; 8 Lifepath (Nemesis Numbers are 5 and 8 respectively)

The Nemesis Number for an individual with a 2 Expression is the 5. The 2 Expression will normally have a transition root of 11, which is a master root as well. The Nemesis Number serving as the LIST is the 5, the 2 Expression is the FILTER and the ROPE is a 16-7, thus generating a 5/(2)/7 simple IR Set, which can also be ciphered as 5/(11-2)/16-7.

If the 5 is derived from a 14 root, the IR Set can be ciphered as 14-5/(11-2)/16-7. If the 5, 2 or 7 are void, the IR Set can reflect the void. For example, if the 7 alone is void, the simple IR Set becomes 5/(2)/7v. A more expressive ciphering would be 14-5/(11-2)/16-7v. If the 5 and 7 are both void, the simple IR Set would be 5v/(2)/7v; more fully as 14-5v/(11-2)/16-7v. If all three IR Set components are void, the simple IR Set would be 5v/(2v)/7v; more fully as 14-5v/(11-2v)/16-7v.

With the 2 Expression as the Filter, the Nemesis Number of 5 (LIST) can occupy the Lifepath (LP), every component of the Life Matrix (LM: Epochs, Pinnacles, Challenges), the 50s Decade Timeline (DTL), the 5th 9 Cycle (from ages 37 through 45), the Age Timelines (ATLs): 5, 14, 23, 32, 41, 50, 59, 68, 77, 86, 95, 104, 113, etc.; every Universal/Calendar year (Universal Timeline or UTL) reducing to a 5, every Personal Year Timeline (PTL), every Lifetime Monthly Timeline (LMT) and the Cycle and Universal columns of the Annual Cycle Patterns (ACPs). All of these components must be taken into account when generating a King's Numerology^{tm} chart in order to accurately assess the puzzle of one's destiny at any point of one's journey through this incarnation.

The 8 Lifepath, serving as the Filter of the individual in this example, will generate a 16-7 ROPE when any Name or Letter manifests an 8 energy (8 + 8 = 16-7). This becomes a second Nemesis Number for the individual. Thus, if any of the letters H-Q-Z appears in one's name, its 8 numeric designation will become a Nemesis Number and the 16-7 ROPE will be active for eight years. If any name within the full birth name is an 8, a 16-7 NTL ROPE will result. Names such as *Allen, Armstrong, Brian, Cook,* and *Jefferson* all carry a simple 8 crown. Thus, any person with an 8 LP and one of these names (or others) will have a 16-7 NTL for the General term of the name.

Richard Andrew King

If any individual with an 8 Lifepath has an 8 name (full natal Expression or any name of the full Expression) and an H, Q or Z within any name, 8/(8)/16-7 stacked IR Sets will occur, which would indicate a challenging and difficult period of life for the individual.

In this current example of a person with a 2 Expression and 8 Lifepath, a stacked 16-7 ROPE can occur. For example, if any Epoch, Pinnacle, Challenge, Decade Timeline, 5th year of a 9 Cycle, or a Lifetime Monthly Timeline is a 5 then a 5/(11-2)/16-7 will be active (5 LIST, 11-2 Expression FILTER and 16-7 ROPE). If during one of these periods the letters H, Q or Z also appear, they will generate an 8/(8)/16-7 LTL IR Set and stacking of the 16-7 Great Purifier will be present. Likewise, if any single name within the full natal name maintains an 8 Expression (such as a first name, middle name, surname or other name), its 8/(8)/16-7 NTL IR Set will generate stacking.

For example, an 8 Lifepath individual with an 11-2 Expression born in May (the 5th Month and 2nd Epoch of twenty-seven years from age 28 through 54) will create a 5/(11-2)/16-7 IR Set. If during this 27 year period, he/she also has an 8 Name or 8 Letter or both, an 8/(8)/16-7 will be generated and stacking will occur in the outcome ROPE position – one for the 5/(11-2)/16-7 2nd Epoch IR Set and the other for the 8/(8)/16-7 Name or Letter timeline IR Set.

<u>Tiger Woods: 9 Expression; 1 Lifepath</u> (Nemesis Numbers are a 7 and 6 respectively)

As mentioned earlier, Tiger Woods' natal data is: Eldrick Tont Woods, born 30 December 1975, with voids of 7 and 8. His two Nemesis Numbers are 7 and 6.

Woods' 2nd Pinnacle and 4th (Crown) Pinnacle house a 16-7v serving as the LIST energy. With his 9 Expression FILTER, a 16-7v ROPE is generated. Plus, as we see, the LIST and ROPE energies are both a 16-7v. The IR Set of these Pinnacles is a problematic 16-7v/(9)/16-7v. Very difficult.

This previous example reveals a red flag for any 9 Expression individual because, as is clear in Woods' chart, when a 7 is in the LIST position the ROPE will also be a 16-7. Think of all the components of a chart which potentially carry a 7 energy – the Lifepath, Life Matrix and its eleven components (Epochs, Pinnacles, Challenges), Lifetime Monthly Timeline, Decade Timeline, Cycle of 9s, Annual Cycle Patterns, etc. And since 9 is the energy most associated with fame and universality, if a 7 shows up in the LIST components mentioned, a 16-7 will be the resulting ROPE. This is why celebrity status can be precarious, especially if a 7 rests in a LIST position with a 9 FILTER. Thus, individuals aspiring to fame, fortune and a celebrity status should be wary. As the saying goes, *Be careful what you wish for*. Fame and fortune via the 9 Grand Ruler has a dark side. Remember, too, that 9 is also the Grand Amplifier, so when it serves as a FILTER, the 16-7 ROPE is more empowered than the 16-7 LIST energy.

Certainly, this 16-7v/(9)/16-7v IR Set energy was, and continues to be, a major player in the tragic fall of Tiger Woods.

Woods' second Nemesis Number is a 6, which serves as the LIST for a 1 Lifepath FILTER. Woods' middle name *Tont* is a 6 with roots of 15 (General) and 69 (Specific). This 15-6 energy became activated when Woods' was 36 years old and will terminate at the end of his 50th year. Therefore, his Name Timeline for this period is a 15-6/(1)/16-7v.

Furthermore, the "O" of *Tont* is active from ages 38 through 43, thus creating a 15-6/(1)/16-7v of its own. These two 15-6/(1)/16-7v IR Sets generate stacking during this time. Adding to his dilemma, Woods' 16-7v/(9)/16-7v 2nd Pinnacle was active from age 36 through 44, creating even more stacking.

As is clear, Tiger Woods' Nemesis Numbers of 7 and 6 played a major role in his most tragic fall from grace and the public stage. And . . . it is obviously a condition of his numbers. Fame, fortune, power, popularity and celebrity for him came early in his life but it was not to last. Had he been made aware of his destiny early on in his life perhaps he could have then acted on the positive side of the 15-6 and 16-7 energies, mitigating their severity.

Richard Andrew King

Elvis Presley: 9 Expression; 9 Lifepath – Dual Filters (Nemesis Number is a 7)

Elvis Aaron Presley was born on 8 January 1935. Presley's life is well known, as is his demise. Once again, the 9 Grand Ruler, Grand Amplifier and Grand Elemental played its role in his celebrity and massive universal appeal. Presley's Lifepath, Expression and PE are all 9s, thus creating dual 9 Filters whose only Nemesis Number is the 7.

In his entire Life Matrix, the only 7 in the LIST position among the Epochs, Pinnacles and Challenges was his 1st Challenge – a pure 7 (8 day of birth minus 1 birth month of January = 7). The IR Set during this period of 27 years was a 7/(9)/16-7. This was the time his beloved mother, Gladys, died. During this period of his youth, Presley was shy and regarded as a loner. There were also issues with his father.

The difficulty of Presley's 1st Challenge period was made worse because the 16-7 ROPE was actually an 88-16-7. Presley had two voids in his chart – the 2 and 8. Therefore, his 1st Challenge IR Set can be ciphered as 7/(9)/88v-16-7. The grand voided 88 master reveals the strong and tragic loss of his mother.

The only 7 Presley had in either his Name Timeline or Letter Timeline was in the "P" and "Y" of *Presley*. However, the "P" LTL wouldn't have become active until Presley was 45 years of age. He died at age 42 on 16 August 1977.

Note the day Presley died – the 16th. This generated a 16-7/(9)/16-7 energy field. The 16-7 ROPE also contained the same 88v-16-7 energy of his 1st Challenge, creating a 16-7/(9)/88v-16-7 IR Set. The 88 is generated from combining his 81 General Expression with the 7 LIST energy.

Other times Presley's 7 Nemesis Number was active were during his ages 7, 16, 25 and 34. These years generated a simple 7/(9)/16-7 IR Set. His 16th year was a 16-7/(9)/16-7. With the 88v added to the equation, the all-too-familiar 16-7/(9)/88v-16-7 IR Set reared its tragic head. Every one of Presley's 7 based ages (7, 16, 25 and 34) created a 7/(81)/88v-16-7 IR Set.

The King's Book of Numerology, Volume 12 – Advanced Principles

Yet, there's still more regarding Presley's 7 Age Timeline years. Sadly, his Universal Timeline and Personal Year Timeline were also 7s. Therefore, every one of his Annual Cycle Patterns in a 7 year housed a 7/(9)/88v-16-7 IR Set! Because he was born in January, the Cycle and Universal columns of his ACPs during September – his 9th Cycle month and the 9th Universal month – contained only the 7/(9)/88v-16-7 energy! When this hexstack (six stack) is added to the 7 year's ACP tristack, a whopping nanostack (nine stack) of the 7/(9)/88v-16-7 is generated! These were the most challenging and trying times, in spades, for Presley, to be sure. Yes, Elvis Aaron Presley's destiny was filled with fame beyond belief, but his life, at certain times, was also filled with grief beyond belief.

[Note: read more about Elvis Presley in *The King's Book of Numerology, Volume 10: Historic Icons – Part 1* (KBN10) and *Destinies of the Rich & Famous – The Secret Numbers of Extraordinary Lives* available at RichardKing.net and online booksellers.]

Lance Armstrong: 9 Expression; 9 Lifepath Dual Filters (Nemesis Number is a 7)

Disgraced professional road racing cyclist Lance Edward Gunderson was born on 18 September 1971. He was convicted of the greatest doping scandal in professional sports, stripped of all his titles and banned from professional cycling for life.

Like Elvis Presley, Gunderson's Lifepath, Expression and PE are all 9s with voids of 2 and 8. Because Gunderson was born on a 9 day (18th) in the 9th month (September) in a 9 year (1971), every one of his eleven Life Matrix components houses a 9/(9)/9 IR Set! This is power to the max. However, it does not explain Gunderson's Humpty-Dumpty fall from grace, which would normally be reflected in the 16-7 energy. So what happened? The answer lies in his Common Name, *Lance Armstrong*.

As a result of his mother's second husband adopting him at two years of age, *Lance Edward Gunderson* became *Lance Edward Armstrong*, and his Common Name became *Lance Armstrong*.

Richard Andrew King

The adopted name *Lance Edward Armstrong* is an 8, which is void in his chart. Thus, every one of his Life Matrix components morphed from the 9/(9)/9 of his birth name to a 9/(8v)/8v of his adopted name. Still, this does not reveal the massive disgrace history has noted. However, his newly adopted Common Name – *Lance Armstrong* – is a 7 with roots of 16, 61 and 160, generating a Name Timeline of 16-7/(9)/16-7. Additionally, using the name *Lance Armstrong* in his Life Matrix generates a 9/(16-7)/16-7 IR Set in all three Epochs, all four Pinnacles and all four Challenges – eleven components in all! In effect, Lance Armstrong became his own nemesis, and his Nemesis Number was the 16-7, situated in both the LIST and ROPE positions of his chart.

This case is interesting because normally the destiny is set with the full natal name. However, Armstrong's professional demise was the result of his Common Name, which shows the power and danger not only of a legal adopted name change but also of one's Common Name usage. The 9/(9)/9 IR Set saturating the Life Matrix of Lance Edward Gunderson is overflowing with universality and public recognition – traits which Armstrong initially enjoyed as a world champion cyclist. Had he kept his natal name, his life would have been quite different and positive. It was the legal name change and Common Name usage of *Lance Armstrong* which were the primary players in his fall.

Princess Diana: 4 Expression; 7 Lifepath (Nemesis Numbers are 3 and 9)

Princess Diana was born Diana Frances Spencer on 1 July 1961; dying on 31 August 1997 at the age of 36. Her life in numbers is fully featured in *The King's Book of Numerology, Volume 9: Numeric Biography, Princess Diana* (KBN9). She is also featured in *Destines of the Rich & Famous – The Secret Numbers of Extraordinary Lives*.

Diana's Lifepath was a 7 with roots of 16 and 25. Her Expression was a 4; her PE an 11-2. Her Soul Layers were a 9/(16-7)/16-7: 9 Soul/(16-7 Lifepath)/16-7 Material Soul (MS). Her Nature Layers were a 4/(16-7)/11-2: 4 Nature/(16-7 Lifepath)/11-2 Material Nature (MN). Her voids, like Elvis Presley and Lance Edward Gunderson, were 2 and 8. Her Nemesis Numbers are 3 and 9.

Diana's Basic Matrix reveals a life of conflict, turmoil, heartache and heartbreak with the 16-7 solidly anchored in her Lifepath and Material Soul along with the 11-2 situated in her life's PE and Material Nature. And what two numbers are most commonly associated with conflict and turmoil? The answer should be quite clear by now in this twelfth volume of the KBN series. They are the 11-2 and 16-7. As we see, Princess Diana had them both stacked in her Basic Matrix. Furthermore, every Name Timeline and Letter Timeline numeric energy had to pass through her 16-7 Lifepath as the Filter. From the outset, being a princess was not to be a fairytale but a scarytale for Diana.

Diana's 3 Nemesis Number never occupied a Life Matrix component. However, it was activated during her 3rd 9 Cycle from ages 19 through 27 and in her 30s Decade from age 30 through 39. Her 3 Nemesis Number combined with the 13 transition root of her 4 Expression during these two periods to generate an IR Set of 3/(13-4)/16-7. Age 19 through her death at age 36 was the exact timeline of her horror-filled adulterous fairytale-marriage-gone-bad to Prince Charles and the nightmare plight of being a Princess captivated in the House of Windsor. Both of these 16-7 ROPE periods – her 3rd 9 Cycle and 30s Decade – generated stacking with her 16-7 Lifepath and Material Soul.

To increase the darkness and foreboding of her life, her Letter Timelines of the "I" in *Diana* (ages 5 through 13) and the "R" in *Frances* (ages 27 through 35) created a 9/(16-7)/16-7 IR Set. This "R" LTL was the worst of her relationship years with Charles and the Royal family. She died one year later in the "A" of *Frances* at age 36 – a 1/(16-7)/8v energy field.

Marilyn Monroe: 4 Expression; 7 Lifepath (Nemesis Numbers are 3 and 9)

At first you may be thinking there is a mistake in the heading of this section because the Expression, Lifepath and Nemesis Numbers associated with Marilyn Monroe are identical to those of Princess Diana. Well, there is no mistake. They are indeed the same, but so should they be. The lives of these two iconic women were strikingly similar in fame, fortune, celebrity, darkness, turmoil, heartache and tragedy.

Richard Andrew King

Marilyn Monroe was born Norma Jeane Mortenson on 1 June 1926. She died on 5 August 1962 at age 36. Like Diana, Marilyn's Lifepath was a 7 with roots of 16 and 25. Her Expression was, like Diana's, a 4. They shared the 8 void (Marilyn also had voids of 3 and 7). Both Diana and Marilyn were born on the 1st day of the month (Diana on 1 July; Marilyn on 1 June). Both died tragically at age 36 in the month of August (the 8th calendar month, voided) under suspicious circumstances cloaked in conspiracies of murder.

Because they each shared a 4 Expression with a 13 transition root, their 3rd 9 Cycles and 30s Decades generated a 3/(13)/16-7 IR Set. Again, this was the exact time of their incandescent personas and tragic deaths. One difference is that Monroe's 3 and 7 voids generated an IR Set which can be ciphered as 3v/(13)/16-7v.

Diana had no 3s in her Life Matrix, as previously noted. However, Marilyn had a 3v 2nd Challenge which was active from age 30 through 38 – the timeline of her death at age 36. This timeline, like those of her 3rd 9 Cycle and 30s Decade manifested a 3v/(13)/16-7v IR Set, creating stacking. To make matters darker, Monroe had an 8 void in her chart as well as an 88 associated with the 16-7 of her 2nd Challenge. This created a 3v/(13-4)/88v-16-7v IR Set. Not good. Not healthy. Fatal.

The 3 Nemesis Number was a major player in Monroe's life. Her 9 Nemesis Number was only active in the "R" of *Norma* from ages 12 through 20. Its IR Set is a 9/(16-7v)/16-7v. She did have complications here being married early and divorced for the first time. She had two more marriages and many alleged relationships with famous men such as John and Robert Kennedy and others.

SOUL NEMESIS NUMBER

As we know, the Soul defines our basic needs, wants, desires and motivations. It is, arguably, the most critical of the Basic Matrix components because we are all driven by our most primal needs. As we also know, Soul Release is the #1 Secret of all great relationships. This is covered, of course, in *The King's Book of Numerology, Volume 6 – Love Relationships* (KBN6). Therefore, when one's Soul desires are confronted with the 16-7 Great Purifier, the old saying, *Be careful what you wish for* takes on an intensity like no other.

For example, let's say you have a 6 Soul and a 1 Expression. The 6 Soul seeks love, romance, family, heart, hearth and home. Now let's say that one or more of your three Epochs, four Pinnacles or four Challenges, or other chart components, houses a 6. Life is giving you exactly what you want, right? Yes, but not so fast. Why? Because when the 6 energy, serving as the LIST, filters through the 10 transition root of your 1 Expression (the FILTER), the ROPE becomes a 16-7! In plain terms, you got the love you wanted but it became problematic, to say the least. The IR Set is 6/(10-1)/16-7. Furthermore, what if the 6, 1 or 7 were void? And then what happens if the 6 is not in a Pinnacle position but a Challenge position or both? Now the 6 energy becomes, perhaps, more of a burden than a blessing.

Another example. Your Soul Layers are 9/(8)/8 – 9 Soul/(8 Lifepath)/8 Material Soul. Your Expression is a 2. If any of your Life Matrix components, Decade Timeline, Cycle of 9s, Lifetime Monthly Timeline, etc. contains an 8, your 8 Material Soul's desires, needs and wants are met. The IR Set developed from this combination would be an 8/(2)/1. No 16-7 is present. You got what you wanted, right? Yes and no again. Why? Well, what if one of your birth names creating your natal Expression is an 8? Then that 8 Name Timeline, when added to your 8 Lifepath, becomes a 16-7! The IR Set is 8/(8)/16-7. Once again, you got what you wanted – the 8 in your name – but along with it came the problematic issues always concomitant with the 16-7 Great Purifier.

Furthermore, what if you have an H, Q or Z in your name. Because the value of these letters is 8, when it merges with your 8 Lifepath the outcome is a 16-7 again, its Letter Timeline IR Set being 8/(8)/16-7. And then what if an 8 LTL is enclosed within an 8 NTL? The result is stacking. This is definitely bittersweet. You got what you wanted but its reality dampened your fulfillment.

There's another issue with this 8/(8)/16-7 IR Set. The 8 and 7 are diametrically opposed. The number 8 is the most social of all energies; the 7 is the most private and withdrawing. How calmly can you say "tug-o-war?"

In these two examples, the Soul number actually became its own Nemesis Number. It activated the 16-7 Great Purifier.

Richard Andrew King

A third example. You have a 2 Soul, a 2 Lifepath and a 5 Expression. The 2 Lifepath satisfies your 2 Soul. However, a 2 LP filtering through a 5 Expression generates a 2/(5)/7 IR Set. If the 2 LP carries an 11 master root (which is highly probable), and the 5 has a 14 root (practically a given) the result is a 16-7, the IR Set being an 11-2/(14-5)/16-7. With such an Umbrella, the destiny is inundated with turmoil, tumult, trouble, betrayal, chaos.

An 11-2/(14-5)/16-7 Umbrella is just the beginning. If any component of the Life Matrix contains a 2, more 16-7 ROPEs will emerge. Certainly the 2nd 9 Cycle and 20s Decade will house an IR Set of 2/(14-5)/16-7, so some degree of turmoil is guaranteed from age 10 (the beginning of the 2nd 9 Cycle) through the 29th year of life except for age 19, which offers a one year respite in this twenty year scenario. If any more 2s exist in other parts of the chart, such as the Life Matrix components, more 16-7 Great Purifiers will be activated. Once again, we see how someone's deepest desires, as defined by the Soul energies, can turn into problematic situations.

A fourth example: You have a 7 Material Soul and a 5 Expression. If any Life Matrix components or other timelines, except the NTL or LTL, house a 2, a 16-7 will emerge in a 2/(14-5)/16-7 IR Set. Interestingly, in this example the 7 Material Soul resonates with the 16-7 ROPE, so the individual's desires would be met and, hence, would not have the same negative effect that any other Soul number would have. In fact, the individual in this situation may be fulfilled with this arrangement, which could still be problematic but not disruptive. After all, a 7 Material Soul loves 7 energy, especially if it's in an outcome position. Also, the 2 is in the LIST position serving as the Nemesis Number, not the Soul number as in previous examples.

THE 9 CYCLE NEMESIS NUMBERS

Let's now turn our focus to the nine 9 Cycles. Beginning on the next page are nine charts, each pertaining to the nine simple Expression numbers acting as Filters for each of the nine Cycles through age 81. Each of the nine charts has one 9 Cycle acting as the Nemesis Number for its Expression number. The charts are in chronological order beginning with the number 1.

Notice that each of the nine charts, representing the nine basic numbers 1-9, contains one nine year cycle, acting as a LIST energy, in which the 16-7 occupies the ROPE position. In other words, no one escapes the 16-7 Great Purifier. All of us are affected by it at a time designated by our Expression number. For example, in the first chart the Expression is a 1. The 6th 9 Cycle from age 46 through age 54 generates a 16-7 ROPE. Therefore, the number 6 and its corresponding 9 Cycle becomes the 1 Expression's Nemesis Number for its nine year period.

Of interest is that the 6 Expression's Nemesis Number occurs in the 1st 9 Cycle from birth through age 9 creating a 16-7 ROPE. Therefore, its early years will be fraught with some degree of turmoil, trouble, angst, stress, etc. The good news is that 6 Expression individuals get the 16-7 out of the way early, as far as the 9 Cycle's 16-7 energy is concerned.

In contrast to the 6 Expression, a 7 Expression individual doesn't encounter his/her Nemesis Number until the 9th 9 Cycle beginning at age 73 and concluding at the end of age 81. The person might not even live long enough to traverse his/her 9th Cycle 16-7 energy.

At age 82, the 9 Cycles recycle to the 1, thus beginning a second round of 9 Cycles.

One additional benefit of the following charts is that the IR Sets for each Expression number are listed for each of the nine years of each 9 Cycle. This knowledge, if utilized, should help people manage their lives more successfully than not having such knowledge at their disposal.

Richard Andrew King

9 CYCLE NEMESIS NUMBER CHARTS: AGES 1 THROUGH 81
The LIST is the Nemesis 9 Cycle
The FILTER is the Expression

9 Cycle LIST	Ages	Expression FILTER	IR SET Simple
1st	1 to 9	1	1/(1)/2
2nd	10 to 18	1	2/(1)/3
3rd	19 to 27	1	3/(1)/4
4th	28 to 36	1	4/(1)/5
5th	37 to 45	1	5/(1)/6
6th – Nemesis #	**46 to 54**	**1**	**6/(1)/16-7**
7th	55 to 63	1	7/(1)/8
8th	64 to 72	1	8/(1)/9
9th	73 to 81	1	9/(1/)1

9 Cycle LIST	Ages	Expression FILTER	IR SET Simple
1st	1 to 9	2	1/(2)/3
2nd	10 to 18	2	2/(2)/4
3rd	19 to 27	2	3/(2)/5
4th	28 to 36	2	4/(2)/6
5th – Nemesis #	**37 to 45**	**2**	**5/(2)/16-7**
6th	46 to 54	2	6/(2)/8
7th	55 to 63	2	7/(2)/9
8th	64 to 72	2	8/(2)/1
9th	73 to 81	2	9/(2/)2

9 Cycle LIST	Ages	Expression FILTER	IR SET Simple
1st	1 to 9	3	1/(3)/4
2nd	10 to 18	3	2/(3)/5
3rd	19 to 27	3	3/(3)/6
4th – Nemesis #	**28 to 36**	**3**	**4/(3)/16-7**
5th	37 to 45	3	5/(3)/8
6th	46 to 54	3	6/(3)/9
7th	55 to 63	3	7/(3)/1
8th	64 to 72	3	8/(3)/2
9th	73 to 81	3	9/(3)/3

9 Cycle LIST	Ages	Expression FILTER	IR SET Simple
1st	1 to 9	4	1/(4)/5
2nd	10 to 18	4	2/(4)/6
3rd – Nemesis #	**19 to 27**	**4**	**3/(4)/16-7**
4th	28 to 36	4	4/(4)/8
5th	37 to 45	4	5/(4)/9
6th	46 to 54	4	6/(4)/1
7th	55 to 63	4	7/(4)/2
8th	64 to 72	4	8/(4)/3
9th	73 to 81	4	9/(4)/4

9 Cycle LIST	Ages	Expression FILTER	IR SET Simple
1st	1 to 9	5	1/(5)/6
2nd – Nemesis #	**10 to 18**	**5**	**2/(5)/16-7**
3rd	19 to 27	5	3/(5)/8
4th	28 to 36	5	4/(5)/9
5th	37 to 45	5	5/(5)/1
6th	46 to 54	5	6/(5)/2
7th	55 to 63	5	7/(5)/3
8th	64 to 72	5	8/(5)/4
9th	73 to 81	5	9/(5)/5

9 Cycle LIST	Ages	Expression FILTER	IR SET Simple
1st – Nemesis #	**1 to 9**	6	1/(6)/16-7
2nd	10 to 18	6	2/(6)/8
3rd	19 to 27	6	3/(6)/9
4th	28 to 36	6	4/(6)/1
5th	37 to 45	6	5/(6)/2
6th	46 to 54	6	6/(6)/3
7th	55 to 63	6	7/(6)/4
8th	64 to 72	6	8/(6)/5
9th	73 to 81	6	9/(6)/6

9 Cycle LIST	Ages	Expression FILTER	IR SET Simple
1st	1 to 9	7	1/(7)/8
2nd	10 to 18	7	2/(7)/9
3rd	19 to 27	7	3/(7)/1
4th	28 to 36	7	4/(7)/2
5th	37 to 45	7	5/(7)/3
6th	46 to 54	7	6/(7)/4
7th	55 to 63	7	7/(7)/5
8th	64 to 72	7	8/(7)/6
9th – Nemesis #	**73 to 81**	7	9/(7)/16-7

9 Cycle LIST	Ages	Expression FILTER	IR SET Simple
1st	1 to 9	8	1/(8)/9
2nd	10 to 18	8	2/(8)/1
3rd	19 to 27	8	3/(8)/2
4th	28 to 36	8	4/(8)/3
5th	37 to 45	8	5/(8)/4
6th	46 to 54	8	6/(8)/5
7th	55 to 63	8	7/(8)/6
8th – Nemesis #	**64 to 72**	8	8/(8)/16-7
9th	73 to 81	8	9/(8)/8

9 Cycle LIST	Ages	Expression FILTER	IR SET Simple
1st	1 to 9	9	1/(9)/1
2nd	10 to 18	9	2/(9)/2
3rd	19 to 27	9	3/(9)/3
4th	28 to 36	9	4/(9)/4
5th	37 to 45	9	5/(9)/5
6th	46 to 54	9	6/(9)/6
7th – Nemesis #	**55 to 63**	**9**	**7/(9)/16-7**
8th	64 to 72	9	8/(9)/8
9th	73 to 81	9	9/(9)/9

THE DECADE NEMESIS NUMBERS

Decade Nemesis Numbers are similar to those of the 9 Cycles except their timelines are different. The 9 Cycles begin at birth while the Decade timelines begin at age 10 – the first year in which the number 1 becomes active, generating a full ten year period.

As with the 9 Cycle numbering system, the Decade number serves as the Nemesis Number in the LIST position of the IR Set involved. For example, an individual with a 1 Expression, while transiting the 1st Decade will generate a 1/(1)/2 IR Set for that Decade. The 1 Expression person will not experience the 16-7 ROPE until the 60s Decade. The IR Set, of course, will then be 6/(1)/16-7.

Contrastingly, an individual with an Expression of 6 will be associated with a 1/(6)/16-7 IR Set in the 1st Decade from age 10 through 18. And so it goes for the remaining Expression ciphers.

As before, the 16-7 ROPEs are generated from the root systems of the numbers involved.

The ten Decade Nemesis Number charts follow.

Richard Andrew King

DECADE NEMESIS NUMBER CHARTS: AGES 10 THROUGH 99

The LIST is the Nemesis Decade
The FILTER is the Expression

Decade LIST	Decade Timeline	Expression FILTER	IR SET Simple
Tens Decade	10 to 19	1	1/(1)/2
Twenties Decade	20 to 29	1	2/(1)/3
Thirties Decade	30 to 39	1	3/(1)/4
Forties Decade	40 to 49	1	4/(1)/5
Fifties Decade	50 to 59	1	5/(1)/6
Sixties Decade - Nemesis	**60 to 69**	**1**	**6/(1)/16-7**
Seventies Decade	70 to 79	1	7/(1)/8
Eighties Decade	80 to 89	1	8/(1)/9
Nineties Decade	90 to 99	1	9/(1/)1

Decade LIST	Decade Timeline	Expression FILTER	IR SET Simple
Tens Decade	10 to 19	2	1/(2)/3
Twenties Decade	20 to 29	2	2/(2)/4
Thirties Decade	30 to 39	2	3/(2)/5
Forties Decade	40 to 49	2	4/(2)/6
Fifties Decade - Nemesis	**50 to 59**	**2**	**5/(2)/16-7**
Sixties Decade	60 to 69	2	6/(2)/8
Seventies Decade	70 to 79	2	7/(2)/9
Eighties Decade	80 to 89	2	8/(2)/1
Nineties Decade	90 to 99	2	9/(2/)2

Decade LIST	Decade Timeline	Expression FILTER	IR SET Simple
Tens Decade	10 to 19	3	1/(3)/4
Twenties Decade	20 to 29	3	2/(3)/5
Thirties Decade	30 to 39	3	3/(3)/6
Forties Decade - Nemesis	**40 to 49**	**3**	**4/(3)/16-7**
Fifties Decade	50 to 59	3	5/(3)/8
Sixties Decade	60 to 69	3	6/(3)/9
Seventies Decade	70 to 79	3	7/(3)/1
Eighties Decade	80 to 89	3	8/(3)/2
Nineties Decade	90 to 99	3	9/(3)/3

Decade LIST	Decade Timeline	Expression FILTER	IR SET Simple
Tens Decade	10 to 19	4	1/(4)/5
Twenties Decade	20 to 29	4	2/(4)/6
Thirties Decade - Nemesis	**30 to 39**	**4**	**3/(4)/16-7**
Forties Decade	40 to 49	4	4/(4)/8
Fifties Decade	50 to 59	4	5/(4)/9
Sixties Decade	60 to 69	4	6/(4)/1
Seventies Decade	70 to 79	4	7/(4)/2
Eighties Decade	80 to 89	4	8/(4)/3
Nineties Decade	90 to 99	4	9/(4)/4

Decade LIST	Decade Timeline	Expression FILTER	IR SET Simple
Tens Decade	10 to 19	5	1/(5)/6
Twenties Decade - Nemesis	**20 to 29**	**5**	**2/(5)/16-7**
Thirties Decade	30 to 39	5	3/(5)/8
Forties Decade	40 to 49	5	4/(5)/9
Fifties Decade	50 to 59	5	5/(5)/1
Sixties Decade	60 to 69	5	6/(5)/2
Seventies Decade	70 to 79	5	7/(5)/3
Eighties Decade	80 to 89	5	8/(5)/4
Nineties Decade	90 to 99	5	9/(5)/5

Decade LIST	Decade Timeline	Expression FILTER	IR SET Simple
Tens Decade - Nemesis	**10 to 19**	**6**	**1/(6)/16-7**
Twenties Decade	20 to 29	6	2/(6)/8
Thirties Decade	30 to 39	6	3/(6)/9
Forties Decade	40 to 49	6	4/(6)/1
Fifties Decade	50 to 59	6	5/(6)/2
Sixties Decade	60 to 69	6	6/(6)/3
Seventies Decade	70 to 79	6	7/(6)/4
Eighties Decade	80 to 89	6	8/(6)/5
Nineties Decade	90 to 99	6	9/(6)/6

Decade LIST	Decade Timeline	Expression FILTER	IR SET Simple
Tens Decade	10 to 19	7	1/(7)/8
Twenties Decade	20 to 29	7	2/(7)/9
Thirties Decade	30 to 39	7	3/(7)/1
Forties Decade	40 to 49	7	4/(7)/2
Fifties Decade	50 to 59	7	5/(7)/3
Sixties Decade	60 to 69	7	6/(7)/4
Seventies Decade	70 to 79	7	7/(7)/5
Eighties Decade	80 to 89	7	8/(7)/6
Nineties Decade - Nemesis	**90 to 99**	**7**	**9/(7)/16-7**

Decade LIST	Decade Timeline	Expression FILTER	IR SET Simple
Tens Decade	10 to 19	8	1/(8)/9
Twenties Decade	20 to 29	8	2/(8)/1
Thirties Decade	30 to 39	8	3/(8)/2
Forties Decade	40 to 49	8	4/(8)/3
Fifties Decade	50 to 59	8	5/(8)/4
Sixties Decade	60 to 69	8	6/(8)/5
Seventies Decade	70 to 79	8	7/(8)/6
Eighties Decade - Nemesis	**80 to 89**	**8**	**8/(8)/16-7**
Nineties Decade	90 to 99	8	9/(8)/8

Decade LIST	Decade Timeline	Expression FILTER	IR SET Simple
Tens Decade	10 to 19	9	1/(9)/1
Twenties Decade	20 to 29	9	2/(9)/2
Thirties Decade	30 to 39	9	3/(9)/3
Forties Decade	40 to 49	9	4/(9)/4
Fifties Decade	50 to 59	9	5/(9)/5
Sixties Decade	60 to 69	9	6/(9)/6
Seventies Decade - Nemesis	**70 to 79**	**9**	**7/(9)/16-7**
Eighties Decade	80 to 89	9	8/(9)/8
Nineties Decade	90 to 99	9	9/(9)/9

NEMESIS STACKING AND LINKAGE

As we certainly know by now, *stacking* and *linkage* are critical components of destiny. Stacking creates intensity; linkage generates continuity. These two dynamos should be at or near the top of any numerological assessment of a person's destiny, especially when the goal is to locate problems.

What is arguably the number one deciding factor in assessing the successes or travails in a person's life? It is *stacking*, purely and simply. A little stacking generates concerns and temporary challenges or short term success and fulfillment, but massive stacking generates large scale fortune or misfortune, the latter creating chaos, leaving a wasteland of wreckage in its wake and quake.

Along the same lines, what is the number one factor in determining the longevity of successes or travails? It is *linkage* of a numeric pattern through multiple timelines. The greatest form of linkage is life linkage – the same numeric pattern existing from birth to death.

We see examples of stacking and linkage everywhere in the charts of individuals who are famous or infamous. Amelia Earhart, Elvis Presley, General George Patton, Howard Hughes Jr., President John F. Kennedy, Marilyn Monroe, Michael Jackson, Oprah Winfrey, Hillary Clinton and Lance Armstrong comprise a miniscule list of individuals lifted by, or succumbing to, stacking, linkage or both.

When people go through difficult times, therefore, look for stacking and linkage in their chart. It will be there. It has to be there. In the case of turmoil, chaos, tragedy and tears look for stacking of their Nemesis Numbers. In cases of extended and long term fortunes and misfortunes look for linkage. In cases where great power is active over periods of time, look for both stacking and linkage. Where great and tragic falls are concerned, look for Nemesis Numbers and their Great Purifier 16-7 ROPE.

Richard Andrew King

SUMMARY

This chapter has attempted to create an awareness of the numerical combinations and arrangements generating their Nemesis Number(s) and its 16-7 Great Purifier. No one is exempt from troubles in life. It's simply a reality of existing in a world of karmic polarity. We all have the Nemesis Number in our charts somewhere to some degree. When one is aware of this condition, one is able to manage his/her life with greater efficiency, hopefully creating and/or maintaining some psychological, emotional and spiritual balance.

For those with heavy Nemesis Number energy in their chart, the advice is for them to focus on the spiritual aspects of the 7. They are advised to keep thoughts and actions as pure as possible; accept responsibility for their actions while not blaming others. Remember, we reap what we sow and we cannot reap what we do not sow. Contrary to popular thought, there are no innocent victims in this world.

Nemesis Numbers should not be feared. They should be managed and embraced. Their action initiates the Great Purifier 16-7 and its energies of reconciliation and redemption. Nemesis Numbers bless us with a wonderful opportunity to pay off old karmic debts, obligations which must be discharged at some time in some life. It might as well be now as then. The sooner the better. There is no virtue in waiting to pay up what we owe. Not taking care of spiritual business in the present only intensifies pay back in the future. Taking care of business in the present is itself a present, liberating us from debt and paving our way forward with aplomb.

CHAPTER 4

COMMON NAME DYNAMICS

A very simple and quick way to assess how any person will generally interact and relate with another person is to add the *Common Name* (CN) of one person to the full natal Expression name number of the other person. The *Common Name* is that name by which a person is generally known, such as Anthony, Ariel, Butch, Linda, Marcus and so forth. It can also be two names such as Tom Jones, Eva Smith, etc. The natal Expression, as we know, is the full birth name and its first name may be different from the Common Name the individual uses in the normal course of his/her life.

For example, John Fitzgerald Kennedy (35th President of the United States) was known as "Jack" or "Jack Kennedy" to the world, not John. Many males whose natal first name is Charles go by the Common Name of Charlie or Chuck; females born as Susan are often known as Sue, Suzie, Susie or Suzy; Robert becomes Bob, Bobby or Robby; Elizabeth, Liz and so forth.

The issue of import is that the simple Expression of *John* is a 2 but *Jack* is a 7. *John Fitzgerald Kennedy* is an 8 but *Jack Kennedy* is a 2. *Charles* is a 3; *Charlie* is a 2; *Susan* is a 2 but *Suzie* is an 8, *Susie* is a 1 and *Suzy* is also a 1. *Robert* is a 6 but *Bob* is a 1. *Elizabeth* is a 7, *Elisabeth* is a 9 but *Liz* is a 2.

Obviously, the natal first name and Common Name can be quite different. The full natal name establishes the blueprint of one's destiny in the greater number of cases. Lance Armstrong's case is an outlier but nonetheless real. Generally speaking, the Common Name acts as a covering, garb or piece of wardrobe over the natal name. We all have a body but adorn it with different clothes which don't intrinsically change who we are but do change how we look and are perceived. For example, individuals wearing a law enforcement or military uniform reveal clothing which defines their

Richard Andrew King

occupation but not who they are as human beings. The same can be said for doctors and nurses donning medical apparel, actors wearing costumes, cowboys wearing boots, jeans, hats and chaps.

Numerologically speaking, different names manifest different energies and, hence, different characteristics. Life is energy. Names are energy. They have purpose and meaning in the grand scheme of things. As the example of *John* and *Jack* (the two first names associated with John F. Kennedy) illustrate, the traits of the number 2 are different from those of the number 7. The 6's characteristics are very different from those of the number 1 (*Robert/Bob* example) and so forth.

When each name is spoken, its energy manifests a vibration, and vibrations can be as different as the sound waves emitted from the strings and notes plucked on a guitar. Sound waves are real. They have impact. Likewise, so does the utterance of names. Different names have different impacts. Hence, the reason for distinguishing between a natal first name and a Common Name. Thus, different names manifest different dynamics and the blending of names (energies) results in a wide range of dynamics which pertain directly to the way people interact and relate with each other.

On its surface this methodology of mixing one person's Common Name with the natal Expression of another person to assess conditions between them may seem too simple to be accurate, but give it a try. You'll be amazed. Besides, all we have to do is calculate one name in our heads – the CN of the other person and add that to our own Expression number. Do not expect, however, this technique to be as effective or as thorough as setting up a Relationship Match and Mix chart (KBN6) but it does have merit.

The formula for Common Name Dynamics is:

Person A: Common Name + Person B: Full Natal Expression = Mix Dynamic Energy (MDE)

To prove this formula for yourself, simply add the Common Name number of anyone you know to your natal Expression and check out the Mix Dynamic Energy of the resulting number. For example, let's say you have a friend whose Common Name is a 2. Your Expression is a 6. The Mix

Dynamic Energy (MDE) is an 8 (2 + 6 = 8). Assuming there are no voids in either name, the 8 should generate a warm and harmonious connection between the two of you. The numbers 2-6-8 are all social numbers and their elemental structure of water-water-earth blends well together.

Contrastingly, let's say you have a friend whose Common Name is a 1. This 1 CN plus your natal Expression of 6 creates a 7 (1 + 6 = 7). Most likely there will be a 16 root to the 7. This 16-7 MDE tells us that at some point to some degree there will be problems or issues between the two of you.

As another contrasting example, say you have a friend whose CN is also a 6. The MDE will be a 3 (6 + 6 = 12: = 3). This blending generates an outcome of happiness, joy, communication, fun, friendship and an overall feeling of goodness. The two of you should get along quite well, sans voids, voided Challenges or Grand Voided Challenges.

As you can tell, this is a simple process and do try it out. Create a Common Name list of people whom you get along with quite well; create another CN list of people you don't get along with. Utilize friends, family, acquaintances, work mates, etc. Follow the CN formula and assess the results. This information can be used for managing your relationship. In the least it will give you insight into the other person and the dynamics between the two of you.

As a note, the two MDE numbers creating the most problems will be the 11-2 and 16-7. We've seen this duo many times in the various examples of *dislike* and *betrayal* in Chapters 1 and 2 with the tension (11-2) and turmoil (16-7) they generate. However, in relation to the number 2, if both individuals have a 2 Soul or 2 Material Soul they may like the MDE. Same for the 16-7. This is why, for a more exact assessment, we need to know the full Basic Matrices of each individual and create a Relationship Match and Mix chart (see KBN6). Remember, this Common Name Dynamic methodology offers only a cursory, but still legitimate, assessment of how two people will relate and interact.

Richard Andrew King

Mix Dynamic Energy Characteristics

The following chart offers general characteristics of a Mix Dynamic Energy number. For a fuller expansion of its energies, cross-reference the MDE with each of the components of your Basic Matrix – the Lifepath, PE, Soul, Material Soul, Nature and Material Nature. You may be surprised by what you find.

Mix Dynamic Energy Characteristics Chart

MDE #	General Characteristics
1	Independent, individual, identity-laden, active, creative, leadership-oriented
2	Partnership, supportive, competitive, oppositional, conflicted, clashing, tense
3	Ease of communication, lots of talk, friendship, joy, happiness, fulfillment
4	Strong, secure, stable, rooted, conventional, potentially stagnant, boring
5	Adventurous, unconventional, stimulating, mercurial, detached, diverse, free
6	Loving, nurturing, domestic, family-oriented, supportive, dutiful, responsible
7	Internalized, introverted, private, separate, strained, troubled, tumultuous, chaotic
8	Externalized, extroverted, social, engaging, interactive, managerial, status seeking
9	Universal, public, expansive, artistic, dominant, charitable, travel-oriented, big

Internal Dynamics versus External Dynamics

To this point we have been discussing the *External Dynamics* of the Mixed Dynamic Energy, i.e., one person's Common Name added to our (or another person's) full natal Expression. *Internal Dynamics* are different. They involve a person's Common Name with *his/her own* full natal Expression. Seem strange? Not so much. Let's see.

Adding our own CN to our Expression doesn't make any sense, at least on the surface. Yet, it does. Our Common Names are not exclusive to us alone. Someone else may have the same CN as we do. A person named John will know other males named John; an Elizabeth will know other women named Elizabeth or Liz; a Robert will know other guys named Robert or Bob and so on. Therefore, a person with the same Common Name will be, obviously, a different person and utilization of the Common Name Dynamic formula becomes suitable.

But here's the thing: if we think of our own Common Name as another person the Mixed Dynamic Energy will be valid, so why would it not be valid to use our own CN with our Expression? The CN energy is still the same. If the CN theory works for others, it should work for us, and indeed it does. This is where the *Internal Dynamics* of the Common Name Dynamic formula come into being.

For example, let's assume the Common Name of Person A maintains a 15-6 energy. The simple Expression of Person B is a 1. Thus, the Mixed Dynamic Energy between Person A and Person B will be a 16-7 (15 + 1 = 16-7). This couple will most likely have problems at some point because of the darkness of the 15-6 and 16-7 duo.

Now, in another example, let's say the Common Name of Person C is also a 15-6 and their simple Expression is a 1, a scenario which is not unlikely. Therefore, Person C's *Internal Dynamic Energy* will be a 16-7! Having both the 15-6 and 16-7 within Person C will be quite problematic for that person. This example is an actual case from The King's Numerology^{tm} archives. The individual involved was plagued with darkness, chaos and a history of betrayal – characteristics common to the 15-6/16-7 combination.

Given this information, what is the MDE of your Common Name with your full natal Expression? How does the MDE number interact with the other components of your Basic Matrix? Does it resonate positively? Negatively?

Next, apply the same formula to your family members, friends and associates if you know their full natal Expression. This simple Common Name Dynamic process will expand the scope of one's understanding and is just another thread into the wonderful world of numerology.

A COMMON NAME PROJECT FOR YOU

In light of avoiding the Lance Armstrong catastrophe of Common Name usage, you might consider creating a chart of your Common Name (first CN only or first and second CNs together) to see how its energies contrast with your natal chart. The comparison may surprise you. Some forms are below to help you.

COMMON NAME (CN) BASIC MATRIX

Roots	Lifepath	CN	PE	Soul	M/S	Nature	M/N	Voids
Simple								
General								
Specific								
Transition								

YOUR COMMON NAME LIFE MATRIX

IR Set: Component #/(CN #)/PE #

Crown Pinnacle
/( )/

Grand Pinnacle
/( )/

1st Pinnacle	2nd Pinnacle
/( )/	/( )/

1st Epoch – Day:	2nd Epoch – Month:	3rd Epoch – Year:
/( )/	/( )/	/( )/

1st Challenge	2nd Challenge
/( )/	/( )/

Grand Challenge
/( )/

Crown Challenge
/( )/

Notes:

YOUR COMMON NAME MATRIX

	1st Name	2nd Name
Names		
Simple Crown		
General Root		
Specific Root		
CN (+ _ LP) = PE	_____/( )/_____	_____/( )/_____

Notes:

COMMON NAME WARNING

There is a warning when using a Common Name: make sure it resonates with your highest and best good, not your lowest and nastiest bad. Remember what happened to Lance Armstrong. It was his Common Name that reflected his unparalleled fall from grace. He was, after all, *the* #1 road racing cyclist in the world for years. He had a global following. He was a legend, but he sank into the depths of the disgraced with his professional doping scandal, never to recover with his tragic Humpty-Dumpty fall off the wall of fame and fortune.

Therefore, be wise in choosing and using a Common Name. Do the numbers. Make sure everything works well together for your good. It's your life, reputation and character. Protect them.

Richard Andrew King

CHAPTER 5

SINGLE NAME ANALYSIS PROFILE (SNAP)

As we continue to study Common Names, let's now focus more deeply on each single name of the full natal Expression as well as the Common Name. As we detail this knowledge, when it comes time to put pencil to paper it is recommended that you analyze each of your names first before proceeding to the names of others. No one really knows us better than we know ourselves and this Single Name Analysis Profile or SNAP allows us to gain greater insights into ourselves and others.

Just as we would analyze the full Expression by assessing its single cipher Crown, General root, Specific root, Transition root (if any) and a Master root (if any), we do the same for each single name. We also analyze the Soul, Material Soul, Nature and Material Nature of each name. We can also assess the House of Letters and the voids of each name.

Using the random name *Sally* with an 8 Lifepath, we can set up a grid like the one below.

SINGLE NAME ANALYSIS PROFILE - SNAP

Roots	Sally
Simple Crown	6
General Root	15
Specific Root	69
Master Root	none
IR Set = Name # (+ LP #) = PE #	6/(8)/5

Richard Andrew King

The Expression for *Sally* is a 6, so we know her vibration focuses on love, duty, responsibility, nurturing, home, community, beauty, harmony, art. The 15 serves as the General Root as well as the Transition Root for her 69 Specific Expression. When her 6 is added to her 8 Lifepath, the outcome is a 5 and Sally's IR Set is a 6/(8)/5; a full ciphering is a 69-15-6/(8)/77-14-5.

The 15 Transition Root is normal. Its energies focus on action and independence (1) and freedom, detachment, adventure, exploration, the senses, stimulation (5). The subcap 4 Challenge addresses order, security, discipline, control, boundaries, rules, regulations. Since the 4 and 5 are diametrically opposed, the 15 houses an intrinsic tug-o-war between freedom and practicality.

The 69 Specific Root conjoins the most *personally loving* of all numbers, the 6, with the most universal and *impersonally loving* of all numbers, the 9. This is an excellent energy for working with the masses (9) on a personal level (6).

The simple cipher structure of the name *Sally* is: 1-1-3-3-7; its specific structure is: 19-1-12-12-25. The simple version reveals strong independence, self and action (the two 1s); communication, words, health and well-being, image and images, joy, happiness, pleasure and children (dual 3s), and the 7 references analysis, examination, reflection, privacy, solitude, study. These three energies – the 1, 3 and 7 – comprise the foundational fabric of Sally's 6 energy. This tells us that Sally's loving and humanitarian energy (her 69-15-6 Expression) is strongly independent, friendly but still reserved. Of course, there are always the negative manifestations, but we'll stay positive.

Drilling deeper, the 19 of the "S" indicates a strongly independent energy (1) with a potential of being dominant and rulership-minded (9). The 8 subcap Challenge of the 19 focuses on social interaction, connection and engagement. The 1 of the "A" is pure self, action and independence. The two Ls and their 12s address action (1) in relationship (2), and the 25 of the "Y" indicates movement and motion (5) in the realm of others, relationships, competition, opposition (2).

The elemental analysis of *Sally* is quite interesting. The 1-1-3-3-7 cipher set is all fire and air. The two 1s are fire signs; the two 3s and the one 7 are air signs. Fire and air make a very hot duo. Lots of ego, action, imagination, isolation but no water (2 & 6) or earth (4 & 8) to neutralize the fire and bring it down to earth in this grouping. In some respects, therefore, Sally is fortunate to have an 8 Lifepath. Its earth element will act as a grounding energy to keep the 1s, 3s and solo 7 from becoming uncontrollable.

The Specific Inclusion/House of Letters table places the two 1s in the 1st House of self, ego, action, independence. The "S" and "A" combine to form 28.98 % of her name – 29% rounded up. This is calculated by adding the Specific value of the "S" (19) to the Specific value of the "A" (1) to get 20 and dividing it by the Specific Expression of *Sally*, which is 69.

The two "Ls" create a value of 24. Divided by 69, they equal 34.78% of her name – 35% rounded up. The solo "Y" and its 25 value generates 36.23% of *Sally* – 36 rounded down.

These three percentages of 29% for the 1s, 35% for the 3s and 36% for the 7 is fairly balanced. No one genera drastically outweighs the others. This tells us that the 1-1-3-3-7 cipher set of *Sally*, although imbalanced elementally, is fairly balanced proportionally.

There are two subcap Challenges in the name *Sally*: the 4, being derived from the 15 General root, and the 3 from the 69 Specific root. The 4 subcap Challenge focuses on roots, order, discipline, security, strength, service, control, organization, plodding along. This can be quite positive because the rootedness of the 4 can balance out the 5 PE generated from the 6/(8)/5 IR Set of *Sally* and her Lifepath of 8.

The 3 subcap Challenge addresses communication, words, health and well-being, children, joy, a positive cheery disposition, self-fulfillment and happiness. Sally will have to work on her attitude and communicative skills. People with a 3 Challenge, wherever it is in the chart, can reflect a pessimistic, dreary, sour, acerbic, discomforting, non-approachable, even negative disposition. It's not easy for a 3 Challenge person to be happy, joyful, positive and fun to be around. Health and children can also be an issue. Fortunately, the two Ls in *Sally* will help mitigate the severity of the her subcap 3 Challenge.

Richard Andrew King

Sally's SNO – Soul/Nature Overview

The Soul of *Sally* is an 8 with a Specific Root of 26 (1 of the "A" plus 25 of the "Y"). Knowing this, Sally has a natural need, want, desire and motivation to connect, interact and engage with others socially. The 26 Specific Soul Root reflects the most personally loving of all two digit combinations – the 2 and 6. This tells us Sally is driven to support and nurture others.

The simple Nature of *Sally* is a 7 (the 1 of the "S" plus the 6 of the two "Ls"). This is really interesting because, like the 4 and 5, the 7 and 8 are diametrically opposed. Sally's 26-8 Soul wants to connect and interact socially but her 7 Nature is reserved, withdrawing, reflective, private and solitary. She may feel this tug-o-war dilemma but not understand it.

The Specific Nature of *Sally* is a 43 (the 19 of the "S" plus the 24 of the two 12s of the "L"). Since the 7 is analytical, we know it is focused on order and structure (4) in communication, health/well-being, happiness, words, self-expression (3).

The Simple Soul/Nature Overview (SNO) of Sally is an 8-7-6. The SNO is a nice feature because it immediately gives us a cursory understanding of *Sally*. She's a loving, caring person (6 Expression) with a desire to interact, engage, connect, nurture and support (8 Soul) while manifesting a personality that is quiet, reserved, reflective, analytical, private.

Sally's Realities

We already know that the Reality, Outcome, Performance, Experience (ROPE) of *Sally* with her 8 Lifepath is a 5. Its IR Set is a 6/(8)/5. Therefore, she (6) will be engaged (8) in a variety of endeavors and potentially in multiple relationships (5). The 6 is all about love and family; the 5 is all about change, variety, detachment, freedom, letting go and adventure. A simple word phrase for this combination would be *changes in love*. Another would be *variety of relationships*. Another would be *dissolution of family or love*. Another would be *love in motion*. As we know, no two numbers are more sexual than the 5 and 6 together. Remember Tiger Woods' Soul Layers of 5 and 6? The 5 and 6 combined do not generally make for a stable, secure, long-term relationship.

Sally's Soul Layers

When the 8 Soul of *Sally* filters through her 8 Lifepath, her Material Soul is a 16-7. Uh-oh! Problem. This 8/(8)/16-7 IR Set will manifest in one of two ways – spiritually or materially. In its positive manifestation this 8/(8)/16-7 is *engagement of the spirit*. In a more mundane manner it is *interactive analysis*, which can be quite positive. However, on its dark side, this 8/(8)/16-7 can manifest as *secret connections*, i.e., lovers assignations, betrayals, adulteries. It all comes down to the consciousness level of the individual. With her 6/(8)/5 IR Set from her name *Sally*, and with this 8/(8)/16-7 IR Set in her Soul Layers, yellow flags, even red flags, should be raised. These two combinations can merge into a sexual dark side; not assuredly, but possibly.

Sally's Nature Layers

When the 7 Nature of *Sally* merges with her 8 Lifepath, the Material Nature is a 15-6. The "uh-oh" just got more intensified. The 7/(8)/15-6 IR Set of her Nature Layers, combined with the 8/(8)/16-7 IR Set in her Soul Layers definitely raises red flags now. We've seen multiple examples of the 15-6 and 16-7 in combination and the problems they generate. Sally is no different. Energies are energies. They don't lie. They have positive and negative sides but they don't lie. With Sally's comprised SNO of 8/(8)/16-7 Soul Layers and 7/(8)/15-6 Nature Layers creating a 6/(8)/14-5 Name Timeline, it would appear on its surface that she will quite possibly have a troubled love life, potentially dark and problematic. To have the 14-5, 15-6 and 16-7 energies mixed in a ROPE position does not bode well for a happy and harmonious life. Once again, though, it all boils down to the level and purity of her consciousness.

Sally's Voids

Sally is comprised of only three single numbers – the 1, 3 and 7. This means the voids in her name are 2, 4, 5, 6, 8 and 9. When her voids are juxtaposed with her SNO Layers, more concerning flags arise. One cannot expect to not have voids in a single name, but *Sally* has all four of the social numbers voided in her name – the 2-4-6-8. This is problematic, to be sure, given her SNO layers.

Richard Andrew King

Sally's Name and Letter Timeline

Now let's analyze Sally's Name and Letter Timelines. The name *Sally* has a Name Timeline of 15 years. Therefore, if Sally is the actual natal first name its timeline will be from birth through age 15. Combined with her 8 Lifepath, the IR Set is 6/(8)/14-5, which we've already discussed.

Regarding her Letter Timelines, the "S" and "A" will last for one year each and each letter will generate a 1/(8)/9 IR Set. The "S" LTL specifically houses a 19-1/(8)/27-9 IR Set. The difference between the Letter Timelines of the "S" and "A" is one of purity. The "A" is a pure 1 energy. The "S" is a more complex energy because of its 19 Specific value, which also contains an 8 subcap Challenge. The number 19 can be considered more powerful because the 1 of ego and self is combined with the Grand Elemental/Amplifier/Ruler 9 energy. As the King's Numerology^{tm} teaches, no two numbers in combination are more personally powerful and egocentric than the 1 and 9. Remember, too, that the "S" sound is the initial vibration generated every time the name *Sally* is spoken. Compare this "S" sound with names beginning with the letter "A." Say these combinations out loud:

Sally, Ava
Sally, Ann
Sally, April
Sally, Angie
Sally, Abigail
etc., etc.

The "A" sound is markedly softer and easier to pronounce than the "S" sound. You can almost breath the "A" words but not so with *Sally,* which takes more energy to pronounce. How do these two sounds make you feel? Different, right? Yet, they're both 1s but, obviously and specifically, very different 1s, not just in numeric ciphering but actual auditory perception and its concomitant emotional response.

Each of the two "Ls" in *Sally* generate a LTL of three years with an IR Set of 3/(8)/11-2. Together, they constitute a timeline of six years beginning at age 3, lasting through age 8. This 3/(8)/11-2 IR Set addresses communication, pleasure, words, fun, image, health and well-being (3) filtering through the 8 of interaction and engagement to generate a reality of others, relationships, female energy and support (2). Because of the 11 master number, the ROPE may involve some level of opposition, friction, contention and tension, as is natural to the 11-2 energy. It can also be highly charismatic, supportive, dynamic, diplomatic.

The "Y" of *Sally* begins at age 9 and continues through age 15. Its IR Set is 7/(8)/15-6. The 25 Specific root intimates potential conflict of some degree, especially with its ROPE of 15-6. It should not be overlooked that the name *Sally* is a 15-6 and the ROPE of her "Y" is a 15-6. Furthermore, the Name Timeline of *Sally* will be active for 15 years with an IR Set of 15-6/(8)/14-5. With such an amount of 14-5 and 15-6 energy there could be pejorative family issues for the first fifteen years of Sally's life if her first natal name is, indeed, *Sally*.

Sally's Basic Matrix

Although we have established a Lifepath of 8 for *Sally*, we have not as yet given her a complete birth date, so let's do that. Let's say she was born on 9 August 2007. This equates to her 8 Lifepath with a 26 General and Specific root structure (Note: this is a PFA date, i.e., plucked from air, totally random, just like the name *Sally* was a PFA name. Let's see where it takes us).

Given the name *Sally*, born on 9 August 2007, her Basic Matrix is as follows.

SALLY'S BASIC MATRIX

Roots	Umbrella – Outer Energies			Inner Energies				Voids
	Lifepath	Sally	PE	Soul	M/S	Nature	M/N	
Simple	8	6	5	8	7	7	6	2-4-5-6-8-9
General	26	15	41	8	34	7	33	
Specific	26	69	95	26	52	43	69	
Transition	n/a	15	14	n/a	16	n/a	15	

Richard Andrew King

We've already discussed the 8/(6)/5 IR Set associated with Sally's Umbrella – the Outer or External aspect of her Basic Matrix. What is interesting is that her Soul is an 8, matching her Lifepath. The 26 Specific Soul root also matches the 26 in both her General and Specific Lifepath components. This is excellent for her. It means her deepest needs, wants, desires and motivations of the 8 will be met through her Lifepath. In other words, there is Internal Soul Release for her – the #1 Key to great relationships, and even though she is not in a relationship with another person, her life will be satisfying for her, at least to some degree.

A major problem for Sally is that her Material Soul (MS) is a 7, as is her basic Nature. These two 7s are diametrically opposed to her 8 Lifepath and 8 Soul. Hence, she will be beset her entire life with a tug-o-war between her external, social, material, comfort-oriented, status-driven life and her internal, reclusive, private, solitary and reflective life. This is totally normal for the 7-8 pairing.

Sally's 6 Material Nature (MN) resonates perfectly with her 6 Expression of *Sally*. This is another positive for her. Both 6s of her Expression and Material Nature are 69s, so this adds to the harmony of the pair. Also of note is that her Material Nature houses a master 33 energy, which is not part of her Expression. No matter. The 33 simply adds to her communicative and artistic ability, empowering the 6 crown in both her Expression and Material Nature.

The 2-4-5-6-8-9 voids are not as critical as the full natal Expression, which may, in fact, nullify some or all of them. Since we don't know her full natal name we can't assess their actual manifestation. She may have no voids at all in her natal Expression.

What is certain is that the numbers of the Basic Matrix associated with the name *Sally* will be active for her whole life. If, indeed, Sally is her Common Name then every time her name is vocally expressed these Basic Matrix energies will be activated much more so than any other name she may have. This shows the importance and critical aspect of the Common Name.

Because the Name Timeline of *Sally* is fifteen years, the Basic Matrix numbers of *Sally* will be highly active from birth through age fifteen. As a young person, the conflicts between her 7s and 8s may be quite challenging because of her youth. This is where an understanding of numerology could be of great, if not critical, help to her. It's hard enough growing up, and having a 7-8 opposition in one's chart only adds to the challenge. If Sally, as well as her parents, even teachers and other interested adults, were aware of this conflict the situation could be more manageable.

Sally's Life Matrix

SALLY'S LIFE MATRIX
Born: 9 August 2007: Lifepath is 8

Crown Pinnacle
9/(6)/6

Grand Pinnacle
7/(6)/4

1st Pinnacle	2nd Pinnacle
8/(6)/5	8/(6)/5

1st Epoch – Day: 9	2nd Epoch – Month: 8	3rd Epoch – Year: 2007
9/(6)/6	8/(6)/5	9/(6)/6

1st Challenge	2nd Challenge
1/(6)/7	1/(6)/7

Grand Challenge
9/(6)/6

Crown Challenge
9/(6)/6

One of the first things about Sally's Life Matrix that jumps off the page is the number of duplicate IR Sets, the most dominate of which is her 9/(6)/6. It occupies her 1st Epoch, 3rd Epoch, Grand Challenge, Crown Challenge and Crown Pinnacle. Therefore, most of her life will focus on impersonal and personal love – the impersonal love of the 9 and the personal love of the 6. Because Sally's Expression is a 6, and five components of her Life Matrix house a 6 ROPE, her life's experiences will resonate with her. She will definitely be involved with the public in some capacity. As we know, 9 is the Grand Elemental, Grand Ruler, Grand Amplifier. Whether her career is in the medical, educational, theatrical, political, literary or athletic field, she will definitely be involved universally and engage a large number of people during her life.

Another major observation is her dual set of the 1/(6)/7 IR Set in her 1st and 2nd Challenges. This portends problems with males, her own identity, leadership and action. The 7 ROPE does house a 16 root, so the first thirty-seven years of her life (through her 2nd Challenge) will be strained. Early on, there could well be problems with her father or other males – familial or otherwise. There will be some type of discord during this time. The father, or mother with strong 1 energy, could abandon her. Alcohol, drug and sex issues could be a problem, as well as divorce. She may shun males and choose to live alone. Some form and degree of turmoil, heartache, heartbreak and isolation will occur. There is no doubt about this. Therefore, Sally would be well served to focus on her spiritual life, remain focused, balanced and centered. Studying, researching, analyzing, meditating – all will help her cope. These early years will be highly internal and developmental. A positive attitude on life will be beneficial.

The 8/(6)/5 IR Set is housed in three Life Matrix components: 1st Pinnacle, 2nd Pinnacle and 2nd Epoch. It resonates perfectly with her 8/(6)/5 Umbrella. It will be active from birth through age 54. Therefore, the 8's energy of interaction, connection and engagement will result in freedom, change, detachment, movement, experience and exploration.

The 8/(6)/5 and 1/(6)/7 IR Sets during the 1st and 2nd PC Couplets create a dual ROPE combination of 14-5 and 16-7 when their fuller ciphering is noted. We've seen this sequence many times. It creates an outcome of detachment, loss and freedom (14-5) married to conditions of internalization, isolation, withdrawal, concern, worry, turmoil, trouble, betrayal, potential adultery. Therefore, the most challenging time period of Sally's life will be from birth through age 37. It can be quite positive if she embraces her freedom and internalization, accepting them as an opportunity to be detached and introspective, as well as reconciling her past karmas. When any of us endure these energies, it's always advisable to focus on the positive aspect of the energies so as not to become suffocated and stagnated by their negative energies.

The remaining IR Set is the 7/(6)/4 of her Grand Pinnacle, which begins at age 38. She has now transcended the most challenging part of her life's journey. The nine years of her Grand Pinnacle will focus on structural analysis, in other words applying her mind and analytical abilities to her work. The 4 ROPE does possess a 22 master energy, so this could be a time for her to build some wealth and financial security. It all depends on what her full natal chart reveals.

SNAP SUMMARY

This chapter's purpose was to outline a SNAP process of delving more deeply into one's destiny by studying each separate name of the full natal Expression. Using a few simple techniques such as knowing the simple number associated with the single name in question, its SNO and letter composition gives a quick and easy way to understand people, even while conversing with them. More involved analysis can be done later. Try this process. Work with it every time you interact with someone. As long as you know their name, you can make fairly accurate assessments in almost no time at all.

Combining their energies with ours can also be accomplished easily and quickly. For example, how do your energies interact with the person with whom you're speaking? What is your Mix Expression of Common Names, for instance? How does their Soul energy harmonize with yours? Same for their Nature energies and yours. What about the elemental structure? What is the blend of fire, water, air and earth between the two of you? Are there any 11-2s or 16-7s between you? If so, be balanced, calm and centered. You may well feel some discord or tension between you if the 11-2 and/or 16-7 are in the Mix Common Name Expression. If there is Mix 3 energy, you should be able to speak easily with each other, enjoying the connection. An 8 Mix will generally create a feeling of connection. These are just a few ideas, but if you work with these SNAP ideas you will realize a level of understanding you never had before. Each engagement with any person will also add to your continuing storehouse of the knowledge of numbers and their manifestation, further cementing your conviction that, indeed, numerology is a science. Have fun!

Richard Andrew King

CHAPTER 6

NUMEROLOGY AND PAST LIVES

To access the blueprint of our destiny in this life via the science of numbers is a fact. Of this there is no doubt. The King's Numerology™ has offered a plethora of irrefutable proof in these twelve volumes as to the veracity of determining the general course of one's destiny in this incarnation. It has achieved this via a multitude of examples of people's lives and destinies, as well as establishing a process to follow through its educational books and articles.

However, the ability to process the numerology of past lives is questionable for many reasons. Can it be done? Only God knows, but there are clues in our current numbers that give hint to what part of our past existence beyond this current life was like. Do understand that the information in this chapter is pure speculation. The King's Numerology™ makes no claims of being able to generally or specifically determine past lives via numbers. The purpose of this chapter is to stimulate thought and expand consciousness beyond worldly limitations. With this said, let's proceed.

When we move beyond the scope of mundane worldly thought and study the writings of Saints, we learn that reincarnation is a fact of existence in this dimension. Following are a few quotes substantiating this truth.

The principle of reincarnation is a fact. It is part of the Creator's scheme.

The law of karma (results of past actions) and the doctrine of predestination
and preordination are true and inexorable. We reap what we sow! Our actions
in past lives bring about our "fate" in this life on which our bodies are fashioned.

Richard Andrew King

Like farmers, we are now living on the crop we gathered last, while we are preparing the soil and putting in the seed of the new crop. We, ourselves, are the architect of our fate.

The Karmic Law is inexorable.
~ Saint Sawan Singh, 19th/20th Centuries
(Spiritual Gems)

The Law of Karma is a self-operating law of cause and effect. A seed sown must sprout. Whatever you sow now, you will have to reap either in this birth or the next. Every action produces reaction, which in turn produces further reactions and this vicious circle goes on forever. Every karma originates from desire.

Not even a single grain that inadvertently enters your granary from a neighbor's field can go unaccounted. You simply must pay for what you get. The law is inviolable and it cannot be set aside. The payment may be either in kind, in coin or by transfer of an equivalent good karma, but payment there must be.
~ Saint Jagat Singh, 20th Century
(The Science of the Soul)

What thou hast not done will never befall thee; only what thou hast done will befall thee.

Modern Translation:
What you have not done will never happen to you; only what you have done will happen to you.
~ Saint Dadu Dayal, 16th Century
(Dadu: The Compassionate Mystic)

The above quotations are merely a drop in the bucket of statements regarding reincarnation and destiny. Yet, even if they were not available to be read, common sense says that reincarnation is a reality. Why? Because we live in an ordered universe. It may be chaotic but that does not negate its reality. The King's Numerology[tm] has preached this concept since the publication of KBN1.

Sir Isaac Newton, arguably the greatest scientist who ever lived, said:

God created everything by number, weight and measure,

and

It is the perfection of God's works that they are all done with the greatest simplicity. He is the God of order and not of confusion.

For example, how long and hard does one have to practice to become a professional musician, singer, athlete? Years, even decades, right? If that's the case, how do some souls come into this world with a level of excellence in their craft and art that seems as though they've been studying for a lifetime or perhaps lifetimes?

This book was published in 2018. During this early 2nd Millennium time period, talent shows for singers, artists and musicians often reveal children, as young as ten years of age or younger, exuding talent equaling the most professional artistry of the modern era. Is this happenstance? Quirks of nature? Hardly. Have you ever seen a tree, a redwood tree for example, grow to hundreds of feet in height in a year? No. It takes time to develop great talent, just as it takes time for redwood trees to become the beautiful giants they are. Such is the natural order of life in this creation.

So what's the answer? The answer is that these souls coming in with great talent are just continuing their lifetime's old journey of developing their art which, in this life, in this incarnation, comes to fruition. Thus, their talent is not based on a quirk of nature or luck. It is founded in order and in developing a skill lifetime after lifetime, incarnation after incarnation, until it matures and is recognized for its excellence. Therefore, the concept of reincarnation is one of practicality, of the natural order of this universe. Saints know this. Hence, their matter-of-fact quotes above.

Richard Andrew King

Let's return to Saint Dadu's quote (modern translation):

> *What you have not done will never happen to you;*
> *only what you have done will happen to you.*

Now think of the numbers in your Life Matrix – all eleven of its components. Why are those numbers there? What is the primal cause of their existence? Why were you born on the numerical day you were born? Do you have any voids? What's their provenance, their origin? Why do you have the name you do? What is the significance of the subnames of your full natal Expression?

We could continue this inquisition forever. The point is, there is a karmic reason why each of us was born with the name given to us at birth on the specific day of our birth. Nothing is happenstance in this world. As stated in *The King's Book of Numerology, Volume 1 – Foundations & Fundamentals*, "God did not drop us here without a plan or a way of knowing that plan." There are absolutely no coincidences in the universe. There is, without question, a divine design to all things, especially a divine design to our personal destiny.

Here's the point. Our day of birth – our 1st Epoch – is no accident. The same goes for our 1st Pinnacle/Challenge Couplet, our 2nd Epoch, our 3rd Epoch or any Life Matrix component. The numbers occupying each of these components reveal that we are reaping the harvests of the seeds we have sewn in previous lives – like them or not; love them or hate them; cherish or disparage them; it doesn't matter. They are what they are for a reason, a manifestation of natural order.

As Saint Dadu says: *What you have not done will never happen to you; only what you have done will happen to you.* Quite clearly, then, our numbers in our entire chart are a karmic payback, a reconciliation of seeds planted some time in our past lives. What these numbers are actually doing is returning to us in this life what we did in previous lives – positive or negative. Thus, we cannot play the victim. If we feel we are a victim, it's because we are a victim of our own making. We sow, we reap and we cannot reap what we do not sow. Karma, a 44-8 master energy, is the supreme law in this universe. It rules us. It rules everything and everyone. No one escapes it. No one can change it. Karma is *the* immutable, inviolable, self-operating law of this creation.

Therefore, when we look at our own numbers we would be wise in asking ourselves, *What did I do to deserve this fate, this destiny*? If we're sincere, we will get an answer. We may or may not like the answer but the absolute truth is that whatever we're getting we deserve. By then taking responsibility for our actions and their reactions – our destiny – we take a major step up the ladder of life and consciousness and move ever closer to becoming a self-realized soul. If we remain blind and refuse to acknowledge this great truth, well, we will remain stuck in the mud and mire of mundane thought and continue living in the darkness of ignorance, trapped in this labyrinthine nightmare of worldly madness.

SUPPOSITIONS

Suppose, for example, a group of people have stacked 16-7s in their individual charts. We've highlighted such cases already in this work. Stacked 16-7s portend turmoil of some sort in some degree. The greater the stacking, the greater the turmoil. If such people are wise, they will accept the reality that they created such turmoil somewhere, maybe not in this life but definitely in a past life or lives and that the current turmoil is the harvesting of previous plantings and actions. What we put onto the circle life, by karmic law, inevitably circles back to encircle us. This is axiomatic.

If such individuals accept responsibility for the turmoil they are experiencing, they will not make the major mistake commonly made by the majority of people with stacked 16-7s, which is to blame someone else, blame God, blame their parents, blame their spouse, blame the dog, blame the weather, blame, blame, blame anyone and anything except themselves.

Blaming others for the negative things that happen in our lives only intensifies our blindness and continued imprisonment. Remember Dadu's statement,

> *What you have not done will never happen to you;*
> *only what you have done will happen to you.*

In accordance with karma law it is incorrect to blame others for anything that happens to us. Indeed, we and we alone are the architects of our fate, as Saint Sawan Singh has declared.

Richard Andrew King

Who, in this day in age, ever blames themselves for what happens to them? Answer, practically no one, which speaks to qualities of ignorance and immaturity. And blaming God? God's not to blame for our troubles and miseries. We are. God doesn't prevent us from making choices and, likewise, He doesn't prevent us from experiencing the consequences of those choices. We choose to do things which are positive or negative and we will, by karma law, live the consequences of our choices. If we have turmoil, tragedies, chaos and disruptions in our lives, it is we who are to blame and no one else.

Another example. Suppose we have a 15-6 in our chart and the 6 is void. Suppose further that this energy occupies a component in our 1st Epoch-Pinnacle-Challenge timeline. What this tells us is that we will most probably have negative family love experiences, nurturing and support issues in the early stage of our life. We may even be hated, discounted and disowned. As a child, we may incorrectly blame our parents and family for the negativity we're experiencing. This would be natural considering our age and immaturity.

However, when we live by karma law we come to realize that our family issues involving a lack of love, nurturing, support, etc., are not happenstance and that we must have done certain things in a previous life to deserve what we're experiencing in this life. Were we a bad parent in another life? Did we not nurture our children? Were we abusive to them? Did we deny them love and care? Obviously, the answer is "yes" to some degree. Karmically, we could not be experiencing a negative home environment in this life unless we created it in a previous life. What we put onto the circle of life circles back to encircle us, eventually. Therefore, our family is not to blame, we are.

Perhaps we have the 15-6 located in multiple components of our Life Matrix. Maybe we even have life linkage of its energy. If so, this would create a lifetime of problems and issues involving love, home, heart, nurturing, duty, responsibility, caring, etc. Again, if we are wise we will look to ourselves and our own actions for reasons. We will not blame anyone else except ourselves. This is a hard truth to accept but it is the truth, and the sooner we reconcile ourselves with it the better for us, our health and well-being and those close to us in our own personal world.

How liberating is this concept? By blaming ourselves and not our parents or other family members for a lack of love, nurturing and support, we release all the negativity associated with our experiences because we realize we are to blame for any negative actions we experience and therefore hold no grudges or pejorative feelings for our parents, family or friends. In matter of fact, we cut the cord binding us to such conditions, are released from their incarcerating shackles and move on. Remember, we reap the deed as we sow the seed. If we are experiencing something – positive or negative – we created it. *We* created it. Other people are simply actors helping us play out the drama. This is not a philosophy. It is *the Law* of this creation. As Saint Sawan Singh reminds us: *Our actions in past lives bring about our "fate" in this life on which our bodies are fashioned*, and we could add, "On which our destinies are fashioned." And as Saint Dadu declares (using first person plural): *What we have not done will never befall us; only what we have done will befall us.*

Another supposition. A person has an 8 void. It also occupies a Challenge position in his chart. When the 8 is void, issues with connectivity arise; the flow of life is raggedy, not smooth; one thinks he knows when actually he doesn't know; things fall apart; relationships disconnect; efficiency becomes problematic; connecting the dots becomes challenging. Why?

One plausible answer to the disconnected nature of the 8 void is that perhaps in a previous life the individual made a concerted effort to disrupt other people's lives and well-being and, hence, in this incarnation his life is disrupted and conflicted. It makes perfectly logical sense that if we disrupt the lives of others, by karmic law, we generate a paradigm in which our lives reap the disruption we generated for others. The key question for the individual to ask is not, "Why is my life so disconnected?" but rather, "What have I done in the past to create such disconnection?"

The 11-2 energy poses some interesting suppositions. As we know, the 2 is the only single cipher whose transition number, the 11, is also a master number. The 2 is the energy of the female, socialization, and serves as the foundation of all the social numbers/energies: 2-4-6-8. Verily, the 2 is *the* energy of relationship. It is also the number associated with the bipolar, yin/yang, duality aspect of this creation. It rules both balance and imbalance, support and obstruction, help and interference, accord and discord, war and peace.

Richard Andrew King

When the 2 is positively aspected in a chart, the destiny will be focused on relationship of some kind to some degree. Working and being involved with "others" is a given.

Because relationships are common to life in general, having it in a chart is pretty normal for everyone. But why would a person have a large amount of 2 energy in the chart? Is it because they have many karmas, both good and bad, that need reconciling between people? Is it that they lacked any meaningful relationships in a previous life and now are given the opportunity to experience them? Is their calling in this life to continue building on previous relationship skills to help and support others? Think of all the main players featured in *The King's Book of Numerology, Volume 11 – The Age of the Female*. They had the number 2 strongly embedded in their charts to act, presumably, as vanguards ushering in a new millennium.

And what about a 2 void? It can raise strong conflicts in relationships because a lack of 2 energy most often manifests as the individual having little to no concern for others. The 2 void is common in people who exhibit qualities which are rude, inconsiderate, disrespectful, dismissive, indifferent, intolerant, careless, cold.

Many boxers, for example, have a 2 void in their charts, which makes sense because if they cared about their opponents they wouldn't want to beat them up or hurt them in any way. Of course the intriguing question is, "Why were they denied the 2 energy in this incarnation?" Was it to get even with others for hurting them in a past life but doing so in a socially-acceptable way? Or vice-versa?

Perhaps the most intriguing aspect of our numbers involves the Soul and Material Soul. Clearly, the primal Soul is the engine driving everything in life – its needs, wants, desires and motivations. Does a person have a particular Soul number because he/she craved its energy in another life but never had it? Simply having a number in a Soul doesn't mean the individual will even experience it in this life if that number isn't located in any of the timelines, especially those of the Life Matrix, NTL and LTL. So why is it there? Unfulfilled Soul or Material Soul desires create great frustration because their energy is never realized in life. This is one reason people lead lives of quiet desperation, as Thoreau would say. It is absolutely agonizing to have strong desires which are never experienced, therefore disallowing the person to have what he/she wants most of all.

Perhaps unrealized Soul Layer desires are a punishment or disciplinary action for an individual having denied those very energies to others in a prior life? Contrarily, it may be to motivate the individual to seek, more strongly, what he/she desires to learn.

And what about those fortunate individuals whose Soul or Material Soul energies are fulfilled in this life via their placement in their Umbrella, Life Matrix, NTL, LTL or other timelines? Is such fulfillment a reward for past good deeds? The culminating action of unrelenting effort in previous lives? Individuals who have one or both of their Soul Layer numbers fulfilled in their charts are generally very content people because their life is giving them what they want, what they most desire, even crave. Is this because of great sacrifices they made in previous lives, perhaps of doing for others but never doing for themselves? It would be reasonable, would it not?

Of equal interest are people whose charts house dual Filters – the same numeric energy in both their Lifepath and Expression. Regardless of the number, saturation of only one number generates a life that is very specialized and focused. As we know, most people's charts house different numbers in their Lifepath and Expression, thus diluting the effects of their Filters. But only one number serving as the Lifepath and Expression places such individuals in a very unique and concentrated situation. Why were such souls given such a destiny? That's the intriguing question?

For example, were 1 dual Filter individuals denied their independence in a previous life? Did they concentrate so much on other people they either didn't care about themselves or were told not to think of themselves? Did they not want to lead, go first, be independent and self-aware but now they're given the chance?

And 2 dual Filter souls. Perhaps they never cared about others or wanted to be involved in relationships but never had the opportunity. Maybe they had been loners for so long they were being given a break or made to take one in order to experience other people.

The 3 dual Filters in people's charts identify the energy of self-expression, ease of living, entitlement, joy, happiness, children, communication, vanity and narcissism. Why? Were their previous lives anchored in drudgery, suppression of self, happiness, communication, ease and fun?

Richard Andrew King

The 4s. Just think about how anchored and rooted dual 4 Filters are. Did people with 4 dual Filters never experience what is was like to be grounded, stable, secure, disciplined? There's a great deal of convention and tradition in dual 4 Filters, but certainly not much, if any, non-conventional or non-traditional energy. Why? There's very little freedom, adventure and versatility in such a large amount of 4 energy. Is it given to people in this life as a discipline from being too wild and uncontrolled in the past? Or rather a reprieve from lives which were constantly in motion and never stable?

Double nickel 5 Filters represent total freedom, detachment, variety, diversity, adventure, motion, movement, exploration. Were these souls so strongly enslaved in their past that finally they were given the opportunity of living life free of chains and shackles? Or perhaps their prior existences were so ho-hum they were given lives of excitement to bring them back into balance?

It would seem that people with dual 6 Filters have much to learn and/or gain from experiences based in love and family. Duty, responsibility, nurturing, community, country, service and the domicile saturate the heart-felt 6. Maybe they never had a family life in recent incarnations. Maybe they did and clung to them so much that they were given more. Maybe they, too, made great sacrifices for others in previous lives and returned to receive love and nurturing in this life. Without question, people with voided 6 Filters have much to learn about familial structure and love. Perhaps they abused family members in their past and now have to experience what it's like to be unloved.

For 7 dual Filters isolation, seclusion, privacy, internalization, inquisition, thought, study, analysis, knowledge, philosophy, religion and spirituality are the primary focus of these souls. Is it time for them to go Within and seek the deeper truths of life? Obviously, they're meant to be alone and solitary for the most part and, more importantly, to not be greatly social. Why?

It's just the opposite for 8 dual Filter individuals. Unlike the 7 they are meant to be social and external, to live in an environment of connectivity, engagement, orchestration, coordination, management. Were they so detached and cave-like in previous lives that now they must come out of their caves to experience what the outer life is like? Or perhaps in another life they craved to be social but were never given the chance and with dual 8 Filters they are given that chance now.

And 9 dual Filters, well, they are meant to be universal, public, humanitarian, expansive. This is the most broad and humanity-oriented of all dual Filters. There is no way these souls will live their lives in a cave unless it is a cave filled with masses of souls. Their lives will be public and large; definitely not small. Why? Was it a strong desire in the past which was finally made manifest? Or was it simply the result of having developed a skill or talent so big that it required a big audience to appreciate it?

SUMMARY

Regarding numerology and past lives, we could continue asking questions forever about dual Filters or any number now residing in our charts. For the most part, such activity may seem to be a waste of time because until we ascend to higher planes of existence we won't know, we can't know for sure, why we have the numbers we do.

Yet, asking such questions expands our consciousness beyond the mundane, the finite, beyond the entrance of birth and the exit of death. If we are to grow, and we must grow to move up the ladder of consciousness, asking questions is important because it forces us to think in broader terms and paradigms; to move outside the box of normal thought.

Ultimately, being inquisitive and seeking answers is critical to our growth, level of knowledge, understanding, degree of wisdom and consciousness. Isn't that why we read books like these anyway, to expand our mind and consciousness and learn deeper secrets of life and destiny? Of course it is, and such continued inquisition will expand our understanding, enabling us to move higher on the ladder of Life and Reality.

Richard Andrew King

CHAPTER 7

FAMILY TIES

Family. We all have one. What are their dynamics? Do family members get along, or not? Is there harmony among family members? Harmony among a few but not all? How about inharmony? Fighting among each other? What are the numeric ties, if any, that bind family members together or create an unbinding, fissure or total rupture in the family?

Saints tell us that our karmas bring us together. Were it not for karma we wouldn't have a particular family. Think of the billions of people in the world with whom we do not even have a relationship, yet somehow we belong to a small group of people whom we label as "family." The karmic ties that bind us, therefore, are obviously strong.

The beautiful fact about numerology is that we can develop an extremely accurate profile of the dynamics of any family – who gets along, who doesn't, who clashes with each other, who harmonizes well and why. All we have to do is compare everyone's charts with the others. When we have this information at our fingertips we can manage family relationships better than not having such knowledge, and the beauty is that acquiring this knowledge is easy.

The King's Book of Numerology, Volume 6 – Love Relationships (KBN6) contains all the information needed to create a personal family profile of every member and every familial relationship. The Relationship Match & Mix format, also called the Loveline Mix, is the tool we use to analyze any relationship. Updated versions are on the next page for your reference. Because KBN6 already fully explains this process, we won't repeat it here. Needless to say, to truly understand family dynamics, KBN6 is required reading, and it's worth it. Utilizing the Match & Mix format will be a great boon to understanding any family member and any family relationship – its positives and negatives, concords and discords, assets and liabilities, strengths and weaknesses.

Richard Andrew King

Note: this page is reproduced at the back of the book. Tear it out; copy it; save it; use it.

MATCH & MIX CHARTS

Full Natal Name and Date of Birth Person #1: _____ / Day/Month/Year

Full Natal Name and Date of Birth Person #2: _____ / Day/Month/Year

Basic Matrix	LP	Exp	PE	Soul	MS	Nature	MN	Voids
Name #1								
Name #2								
Mix								

LOVELINE MATCH – BASIC MATRICES

	Name #1	#1	#2	Name #2	
External	Life Path (Life Script)			Life Path (Life script)	External
External	Expression (Actor)			Expression (Actor)	External
External	P/E (Role in life)			P/E (Role in life)	External
Internal	Soul (Needs & Wants)			Soul (Needs & Wants)	Internal
Internal	Material Soul			Material Soul	Internal
Internal	Nature (Personality)			Nature (Personality)	Internal
Internal	Material Nature			Material Nature	Internal
Internal	First Name #1			First Name #2	Internal
	Numeric Day of Birth			Numeric Day of Birth	
	Voids			Voids	

LOVELINE MATCH & MIX

	Name #1	#1	MIX	#2	Name #2	
External	Life Path				Life Path	External
External	Expression				Expression	External
External	P/E				P/E	External
Internal	Soul				Soul	Internal
Internal	Material Soul				Material Soul	Internal
Internal	Nature				Nature	Internal
Internal	Material Nature				Material Nature	Internal
Internal	Name #1				Name #2	Internal
	Numeric Day of Birth				Numeric Day of Birth	
	Voids				Voids	
	Total Connections				**Total Connections**	

FAMILY ANALYSIS PROCESS

It is recommended that the family analysis process start with the parents, parent or guardian. Do their Basic Matrix. Use it as the hub of the numeric family wheel. If both parents or guardians are involved, a Match & Mix chart between them should be done first to assess their compatibility, strengths, weaknesses, challenges and degree of Mutual Energetic Resonance, aka MER (KBN6).

Next, construct a Basic Matrix chart for every person in the family. Then create a Match & Mix chart for each parent with each child. Finally, do a Match & Mix chart for any siblings. After the immediate family is concluded, follow suit with grandparents, aunts, uncles, cousins, etc.

FAMILY ANALYSIS NOTES

Soul Layer Release

The King's Numerology^{tm} believes the Soul is the most important number in a chart. Why? Because it represents the energies that drive the individual to meet one's most primal needs, wants, desires and motivations. The Soul is the core, the hub of the person's being. Everything revolves around it. Plus, the Soul is an internal energy which cannot be perceived externally, such as the Lifepath, Expression or PE and, in fact, its energies may be diametrically opposed to the outward persona the world sees via the Lifepath, Expression and PE.

Therefore, check the Soul number of every person first to determine what their most fundamental desires and needs are. Compare all of the Soul numbers of every family member with everyone else's. Does anyone share the same Soul number with another family member? If so, they will be driven by the same needs, desires and motivations. Axiomatically, there will exist a kinship between family members having the same Soul number.

If family members do have the same Soul number, cross reference it with their Lifepath number. If the Soul and Lifepath are the same in any family member, Soul Release will exist. Therefore, the person will feel extremely comfortable with his/her life because the Lifepath, matching the Soul,

Richard Andrew King

will guarantee the individual will get what they most want, need and desire. Unless a Nemesis Number is involved, the entire life of the individual will, for the most part, be fulfilling. If two members of the family have the same Soul and Lifepath numbers (a rare possibility), they will have a strong bond between them. Usually, however, a person's Soul and Lifepath numbers are different, at least the odds are more in favor of a difference than a likeness.

If one family member's Soul number matches the Expression of another person in the family, a magnetic attraction will exist between them with the Soul energy moving toward the Expression. In other words, the person with the Soul energy will be strongly attracted to the family member whose Expression matches his/her Soul energy, not vice-versa. Remember, the Soul identifies one's primal needs, and it will move toward the source that fulfills those needs. This is why Soul Release is the #1 Key to all successful relationships. When anyone's basic needs, wants and desires – the core of the individual – are met, the individual is fulfilled and that fulfillment is expressed as happiness.

Soul Release is the main connection to look for in the family assessment process, just as it is in any relationship. Of course, it is especially important in love relationships and marriages, even long term business partnerships. When everyone's primal needs are met, people are happy. It's that simple. When the Soul energy is not met, one's fulfillment will be comprised to some extent.

The Material Soul energies are important, too. They're not as pure as the primal Soul because they're a mixture of the Soul plus the Lifepath, but because they have a Lifepath aspect to them, they tend to describe one's worldly desires more than those of the simple/primal Soul. This is why the Material Soul is so named – the Lifepath represents the carnal/material aspect of the primal Soul when it enters the worldly environment and becomes "material."

Soul Layer Release (SLR) exists when either the Primal Soul and/or Material Soul matches one of the three Umbrella components consisting of the Lifepath, Expression or PE. We've covered this many times before, especially in KBN6. The strongest Soul Layer Release will be to the Expression, i.e., the person, because it's a mixture of pure energies – one person's Soul or Material Soul to the other person's specific energies. The Lifepath, being the script of a person's life, is not a person. It's a road map of destiny. The PE is not pure energy because it's a blend of the Expression and Lifepath. Thus, if there is Soul Layer Release between any members of the family, there will be a strong connection between them. This would be natural.

Soul Layer Release to one or more family members but not to all can cause issues, even problems, because any person who does not share in the Soul Layer Release connection may feel unloved, unappreciated, left out. Therefore, caution must be exercised. Just because SLR exists between some family members but not all, does not equate to a lack of love, although it may seem like it to the affected family member or members. Understanding the dynamics of SLR will assist all family members in managing their relationships. It is especially important for parents to grasp this principle in order to prevent other family members from feeling unloved, uncared for, ignored.

If there is no Basic Matrix Soul Layer Release, either within an individual family member's Soul or Material Soul to his/her own Umbrella or to another family member's Soul or Material Soul to the Umbrella of another family member, then check the Life Matrices to see if they house a Release window through one of its components – Epochs, Pinnacles or Challenges. For example, although a person may have no Soul Layer Release through the Basic Matrix for his/her 6 Soul, perhaps there is a connection between a 6 day of birth (1st Epoch), 6 month of birth (2nd Epoch) or a 6 year of birth (3rd Epoch). If all Epochs housed a 6, then the individual would have life linkage through the Life Matrix of the person involved – either him/her self or another family member. The same principle applies to the Pinnacles and/or Challenges.

If the Life Matrix offers no Soul Layer Release, check the Name Timelines or Letter Timelines. Other timelines can also be analyzed, such as the 9 Cycle Timelines or Decade Timelines. All of these components are possible windows for Soul Layer Release.

If there is absolutely no Soul Layer Release for any family member through any chart component, then the individual's destiny will not be as fulfilling as it would otherwise be, and he/she would be well-served to understand the spiritual aspects of the destiny. Some people traverse this life being quite fulfilled, while others are equally unfulfilled. Such is the reality of life. However, it may be a great blessing if there is no SLR because the individual will have to expand his awareness of this life and its meanings. Worldly fulfillment can lead to spiritual stagnation, and often does, but

Richard Andrew King

spiritual understanding trumps worldly satisfaction. In this sense, it may an extremely positive boon if there is no Soul Layer Release. For example, Saint Charan Singh's directive is:

Just live in the world and get out of it.

How can we get out of the world if we are attached to it? We can't. Therefore, we mustn't be disheartened if we have no SLR. In fact, considering the spiritual aspects we should be quite heartened. After all, our true self is spiritually based, not materially or worldly based. As the saying goes,

We are spiritual beings having a worldly experience,
not worldly beings having a spiritual experience.

If we're happy in the prison, why would we want to escape from it? Yet, imprisonment is not what our spiritual soul wants. It wants to be free, so understanding the full scope of both sides of Soul Layer Release is important for our well-being.

The blessing of having no SLR is that since the world offers no fulfillment for the individual, he/she is forced inward to find that happiness that the world cannot fulfill. Making the individual uncomfortable with the outer world of materialism is a clever trick God uses to force the individual to reverse and redirect his/her attention inwardly into the Inner World of divine reality and spiritual ascendance. Therefore, if we're not happy or fulfilled with our worldly lives, we should take heart and be comforted. It is most probably by divine design, and we would be well-served to turn Inward to discover the spiritual Truth of our existence and achieve the ultimate goal of God Realization. To this point, the tagline for The King's Numerology^{tm} is *Discovering the Divine Design of Your Life*, not "Discovering the Joys of The Material World." Through numerology we can see the design of this life, but our true purpose is to move up and beyond this material/carnal dimension, escaping its darkness and limitation.

Clashing Souls

It would not be unusual for family members to have Soul Layer numbers that are not only dissimilar but that clash. Therefore, when analyzing family charts, look for the three sets of numeric opposites: 1 vs. 2; 4 vs. 5; 7 vs. 8. Such opposites may not create a clashing of family members but they would create opposite needs, wants, desires and motivations.

If family members do house different Soul Layer numbers, expect the differences between individuals but respect their desires. The Soul energy cannot be changed. It governs the very core of a person's being. That's why it's called the Soul number, so there's no use arguing over differing points of view. Just realize that everyone has their own perception and agree to disagree. Opposite numbers provide an excellent way to understand basic energies and how they manifest. Such an understanding can create peace in a family rather than intolerance and chaos.

A parent's Soul energy may be directly opposite from their spouse, child or children. If this is the case, the parent needs to set the loving tone of the relationship and not be hostile to a child whose Soul's needs are different. The parent is older, more experienced and hopefully wiser than the child. After all, parents are the leaders; children the followers, at least in the formative pre-adult years. The relationship will change with age, no doubt, but from the natural point of view the parent will always be the parent and the child will always be the child, at least in this life. Who knows, maybe the relationship was reversed in a former life or will be reversed in a future life. In present tense, however, the relationship is set in stone, karmic stone.

Basic Matrix Harmonies and Inharmonies

Beyond analyses of the Soul Layer energies, the next step would be to focus on the other components of everyone's Basic Matrix. Following the same procedure, look for harmonies and inharmonies, not just from one family member to another but to the Mix of each family pairing.

If family members' Expressions fall into the opposition category of the 1 vs. 2, 4 vs. 5 and 7 vs. 8, the likelihood of opposing points of view should be expected. This would be totally natural.

Richard Andrew King

However, having opposing points of view should not translate to a lack of love or harmony. Relationships are best built on tolerance, respect, nurturing, understanding, caring, and love, even if the other person or persons hold a different point of view. After all, each of us is our own person with our own destiny to fulfill. The beautiful thing about applying numerology to the family paradigm is that we can know what the harmonies and inharmonies are and manage the relationship accordingly.

For example, two family members may share an 8 Expression. On the surface, this is good, right? The problem is that their Mix Expression will be a 16-7, not only a troubling number, as we know, but a single number – the 7 – that is exactly opposite from their single 8s. This combination would fall into the category of two people who are like two peas in a pod but who can't get along. Yet, knowing this connection is prone to problems, the two people can harmonize it through love and understanding. A lack of knowledge can obviously create problems. This is one reason why knowledge is power. Knowledge gives us insight; insight allows for understanding and love.

Contrastingly, if two people both had a 3 Expression, their Mix Expression would be a 6. If neither the 3 nor 6 is void, their relationship would be very loving and nurturing, assuming there were no other major numeric clashes in their combined charts.

If the Expressions of two people were a 4, their Mix Expression would be an 8. This is excellent. The 8 is the product of two 4s. Plus, the 4 and 8 are the only two earth elements of the Alpha Numeric Spectrum. These family members would be extremely comfortable in each other's presence. They would think the same and like to do the same things. They would be very earthy, ordered, rooted, conventional and traditional.

Two people sharing a 5 Expression create a 1 Mix Expression. Both the 1 and 5 are fire signs, so this is a good blend. Furthermore, the 1 represents independence and the 5 exudes freedom. Both individuals are free and independent spirits who would understand each other and have a relationship that is itself independent, even a little wild and never still. Unlike the 4s, this pairing would be unconventional, untraditional, free-spirited, fun and always on the go.

For those who share a 1 Expression, their Mix Expression will be a 2. This is interesting because the 1 is a fire sign and the 2, a water sign. Not only are the 1 and 2 opposites, their elemental structure is intrinsically oppositional. Fire and water don't blend. Furthermore, the 1 Expression likes to be the boss, the leader, the one in charge; never subservient, always dictative, so both may be in a constant battle for supremacy in the relationship. The interesting fact is that their 2 Mix Expression will challenge them both because it calls for balance, equilibrium, sharing, getting along, dependence and subordination in deference to the partnership itself. The 1 isn't about dependence but independence. Hence, family members with 1 Expressions may have challenges of ego and leadership which, if wisdom prevails, can lead to humility, forbearance and peace.

If family members share a 2 Expression, the Mix Expression will be a 4. The 2 is a water sign; the 4 is an earth sign. Plus, 4 is 2 doubled. This blending will result in a stable relationship which is quite compatible. Water and earth get along quite well. The 2 and 4 are also social numbers. Look for excellent harmony in this paring.

Six Expression individuals will create a 3 Mix Expression. This is also an harmonic blend. Not only is 6 a higher octave of the 3, both numbers exude beauty, communication, self-expression, words, fun, pleasure, enjoyment and artistry more than any two numbers. As we know, the master root of the 3 is 66 and the master root of the 6 is the 33. This creates mirrored siblings, so there is accentuated harmonious connectivity in the 6-6 pairing. The 3 is an air sign and the 6 is a water sign – a creative blending of artistry, beauty, communication, image. One of the challenges could involve vanity, narcissism and entitlement – all qualities of an exaggerated 3 energy.

A family relationship composed of two 7 Expression individuals will generate a 5 Mix Expression. This is an exciting blend – the most internal, analytical, solitary pairing of the same Expression. As we know, 7 is highly internal, mental and an air sign. The 5 is mercurial and a fire sign. Fire and air work extremely well together *if* the 5 fire storm created by the two 7s can be kept under control. Because of the mental nature of the 7 and the speed of the 5, this pairing will be full of ideas, quick thinking, freedom of thought and introspective action. There will also be change and diversity because of the 5's mercurial nature.

Richard Andrew King

If two family members share a 9 Expression the Mix Expression will also be a 9. Both people will be very dominant and seek to rule. They will be expansive, artistic, charismatic, even magnetic. The main issue here is one of power and who will rule the roost. The 9 is not a leadership energy, but rather a rulership energy. 9s like their scepters, crowns, thrones and microphones. They are quite comfortable in the public eye. This pairing could become a great team or great adversaries, with both family members seeking center stage. At some point, they will have to come to an agreement as to how to manage their separate but mutual power.

There are many other Expression combinations to consider. A couple guidelines when assessing the numbers of family members are:

1. Is the Mix one of opposing sets of numbers – the 1 vs. 2, 4 vs. 5 or 7 vs. 8?
2. Are the Expression numbers in the same elemental field?
3. Are the elements of the Expression numbers compatible while being different?
4. Is the Mix an 11-2 or 16-7? These can potentially create tension, trouble and turmoil.
5. Is there an harmonious blending of the numbers?
6. What are the potential inharmonies and conflicts of the numbers?
7. Does the Mix Expression number show up in any of the timelines of each person's life?
8. Is there a disparity of numeric energies in the family?
9. Is one individual very different from the others?

These are just a sampling of questions to consider when assessing the numbers of family members. The same formulae can be associated with the Lifepaths, PEs and Nature Layers of everyone in the family, and when they are considered, an energetic puzzle of the entire familial structure will emerge, offering extreme insight and understanding of family dynamics.

Voids

Voids can certainly cause problems and challenges in any family relationship. They should never be ignored. Cross reference any voids with the Basic Matrix and Life Matrix. Is the void in a Challenge position? If so, it will aggravate and intensify the voided energy. Is there a Grand Voided Challenge? This would create the most problematic manifestation of the void. It is also of note that other family members' numbers may fill up the voided energy if the number related to the voided number of their sibling is not voided. This can be a great benefit in mitigating the negative effect of a sibling's void or voids. Family members with identical voids will have similar issues, all other chart aspects being inconsequential. Focus should be on manifesting the positive characteristics of the voided number, i.e., filling it up and making it a strong link in the chain of one's life. Knowledge of voids can lead to understanding; ignorance of voids can lead to chaos.

As a review, the chart below recounts the basic issues of Alpha-Numeric voids.

#	Issues Related to Voids
1	Self-identity/self-worth, independence, leadership, action, strength, will, courage, yang
2	Others, relationships, dependence, balance, support, caring, indifference, emotion, yin
3	Self expression, image, words, communication, health, children, joy, sex, vanity
4	Work, service, organization, discipline, self-control, stubbornness, stability, strength
5	Freedom of movement, change, detachment, versatility, lack of self-control, sensuality
6	Personal, familial, social love, nurturing, support, duty, responsibility, pleasure, sex
7	Lack of discretion, knowledge, study, wisdom/foolishness, analysis, solitude, thought
8	Lack of engagement and connectivity, managerial skills, orchestration, coordination
9	Lack of universal and public compassion, respect, duty, power, rulership, big picture

Life Matrix Components

In understanding the life stream of a family member's life, pay close attention to the following:

1. Life Matrix components – Epochs, Pinnacles, Challenges. Know their timelines and cross reference them with the Basic Matrix energies and voids. How do they relate to other timelines such as Name Timelines, Letter Timelines, Decade Timelines, Cycle of 9s, Annual Cycle Patterns.

2. Look for stacking and linkage. As we know, stacking creates intensity and linkage determines continuity and longevity of the energies involved. Do any of the IR Sets match the Umbrella of the individual? Do they stack or link with other chart components.

3. Analyze changes from one energy field to another, such as a 1 Epoch moving to a 2 Epoch or vice-versa; a 4 Pinnacle changing to a 5 Pinnacle or vice-versa; a 7 Challenge moving into its opposite 8 Challenge period or vice-versa. Such shifts are important because of the oppositional nature of the energies and how they're manifested in a person's life.

4. Periods of 11-2 energy and 16-7 energy can be problematic, so pay attention to them. Prepare for them and teach other family members how to manage them if they are interested in knowing such things. Some people won't want to know, which is sad and unfortunate. If a person were about to traverse a mine field, wouldn't he/she be better off knowing where the mines are?

5. For newly born children and individuals under twenty-seven years of age, they will be transiting the first Epoch-Pinnacle-Challenge Timeline, which is the most crucial time of a person's life because it is *the* most formative period of one's life. Be sensitive to voids at this time, especially voided Challenges because their energies are hidden from external view. Pinnacle energy is visible to the outside world but not Challenge energy. Of the three E-P-C components, the Challenge is the most important because it houses hidden sufferings and personal problems. A 16-7 in any E-P-C component can reference turmoil in the home, alcoholism, betrayal, divorce and all the suffering and angst associated with such circumstances.

6. Be forward looking. The Life Matrix reveals the energy fields ahead. Whatever those may be, foreknowledge allows for proper management. No blind side punches can knock someone out. How can anyone protect themselves from a hurricane if they don't know it's coming? They can't. If storms are coming in the form of the 15-6, 16-7 or 11-2, then adequate preparation can be made and the storm planned for. Contrarily, if pleasant times are ahead the individual can be emboldened to keep on keeping on because there is light at the end of the tunnel.

7. Every family member's Life Matrix can be cross-referenced with every other family member. Remember, numbers represent people, not just situations or circumstances. A person with a 3 void, for example, may be troubled by a sibling with a 3 Expression, Lifepath, PE, etc. A family member with a 1 Challenge anywhere in the chart may have negative feelings about another family member with a 1 Soul, 1 Nature or 1 PE. A child with strong 9 energy in the first E-P-C Triad will have a relatively popular and/or expanded life, as opposed to a child with no 9s at all. Such a scenario may have a negative impact on children with no 9s because the spotlight won't be on them, and since popularity is such a valued characteristic for young people, feelings of unworthiness or inferiority may arise in those children with no 9 energy. In such a case it should be pointed out that character is more important than popularity, which is superficial at best. Children should be taught to appreciate who they are, not what they are, and certainly not worry about how they measure up to other people. Each child, each person, is unique in his/her own way. Each individual is an original creation, which should be honored and appreciated.

8. Looking forward, the final E-P-C Triad consisting of the Third Epoch, Crown Pinnacle and Crown Challenge will give clues as to where the child or family member is headed, unless they're already there. One can plan for such a time when the numbers are properly assessed.

Just considering the above combination of chart components reveals how full and extensive the numeric puzzle of one's family life can be. However, even considering a few connections between family members can generate powerful understanding of family dynamics and the ties that bind us together as a familial unit.

Richard Andrew King

CHAPTER 8

LIFE JOURNEY SHIFTS & CHANGES

Change. It is a constant in life. Yet, unlike the waves of the ocean, the changes in our lives are predictable in general terms. Being predictable, they are knowable and, hence, manageable. When we take the time to learn the changes in our life from birth to death, we will never get blindsided or caught off guard. Therefore, we can remain balanced, centered, stable and confident as we traverse the highways and byways of life.

This chapter is dedicated to sharing information regarding the changes relative to our destinies. To make the most of this knowledge, start with your own chart. You'll be able to see where you've been (if looking in hindsight) or where you will be (if looking forward). Obviously, the charts of anyone can be analyzed. Parents in particular would be well-served to understand the changes destined for their kids in order to help them negotiate their lives wisely and successfully.

The degree and number of changes in a person's life vary from person to person, destiny to destiny, number pattern to number pattern. Some people's lives are in constant flux. Individuals with a 5 in their Basic Matrix, for example, especially in the Lifepath and PE, will experience more change, movement and variety than anyone else. The 5 governs freedom, detachment, motion, movement, variety, uncertainty, curiosity, speed, adventure, excitement, stimulation. Its persona is nontraditional, unconventional and unpredictable. The number 5 is the epitome of change and movement, visually depicted by the Roman God Mercury with winged feet, thus symbolizing the 5's mercurial nature. The more saturated a chart is with 5 energy, the greater the degree of change. A person with Double Nickel Filters (Dual 5s in the Lifepath and Expression) will encounter more change in life than any other number or dual set of Filters. For 5 Expression people, life changes and shifts are part of their numeric DNA. Not only are changes and shifts in their lives common, they're expected.

Richard Andrew King

In contrast, the 4 generates little change. As we know, roots and anchors are symbols for the number 4, which doesn't like change. It loves roots, stability, security, order, the status quo, house and home, tradition and convention. Four Expression individuals generally do not like change. They embrace the boundaries, borders and anchors of their lives. For them, changes and shifts are not welcome and are totally antithetical to their numeric DNA.

The 4-5 juxtaposition is the poster child for anchors and wings. It is an exceptional pairing illustrating why people's lives and destinies are very different, not only in actuality but managerially. Changes and shifts in life affect everyone, but how everyone deals with them varies.

When considering changes and shifts, noting the polar and elemental structures of numbers is important. The odd numbers: 1-3-5-7 carry a positive charge; the even numbers 2-4-6-8, a negative charge. The 9 contains both positive and negative charges. The 1-3-5-7 quadset is independent, visionary, free and solitary, not greatly social. The 2-4-6-8 quadset is highly social, reflecting qualities of relationship, structure, family and interaction, not independence, freedom, solitude.

Like the 4-5 pairing, these quadsets are oppositional. Saturation of one quadset over another in a chart identifies how people will manage the vicissitudes of life. As a general rule, the 1-3-5-7 set will manage changes and shifts more easily than the 2-4-6-8 set. This is because the 1-3-5-7 quadset is focused on independence (1), self-expression (3), freedom (5) and solitude (7). Another word string for the 1-3-5-7 quadset is solo, artistic, detached and private. Relationships, anchors, domiciles and social engagements of the 2-4-6-8 are diametrically opposite from the 1-3-5-7. The energetic and vibrational architectures of these two quadsets are as different as night and day, male and female. Therefore, changes and shifts in a chart between these two sets will generally not be comfortable, and could be quite drastic.

In addition to their polar charges, elemental factors play a dominant role. The 1-3-5-7 quadset is all fire (1 and 5) and air (3 and 7). The 2-4-6-8 quadset is all water (2 and 6) and earth (4 and 8). Thus, it's easy to see how these two quadsets differ, and do so dramatically. Be very aware of these differences in both polar and elemental designs when analyzing a chart. They reveal much about people's lives and how people will perceive and manage those lives.

Voids are another data point to consider when analyzing changes and shifts. As we know, they can be highly problematic. Voids occupying a Challenge position are more problematic than in a Pinnacle location. Grand Voided Challenges are the most concerning.

LIFE MATRIX SHIFTS & CHANGES

There are two major fields of changes and shifts: 1. those pertaining to the Lifepath; 2. those relating to the Name and Letter Timelines. The former involves the script of our life; the latter focuses on us personally. We'll start our analysis with the Lifepath.

The first thing in assessing changes and shifts is to begin with single numbers. This will put us in the ballpark of each numeric field. Next, we can migrate to the root structures of each crown to gain more depth of understanding.

In our first example, we'll use the birthdate of 11 November 1885, which generates an 8 Lifepath. Reduced to single numbers, the Epoch pattern is 2-2-4. Immediately, this tells us there will be little change in the life. The result of little change is constancy of the vibrations from birth to death. Therefore, there will not be a great deal of drama in this life because there are no dramatic changes and shifts. There will be, however, great power in this destiny, as we'll soon see.

Of note is the polarity structure of the Lifepath (8) and the Epochs (2 and 4). These numbers carry a negative charge. The elemental structure is comprised of only water (2) and earth (4), elements that blend extremely well. Since there is little change in this life, the energies keep growing along one basic path – that of relationship and others (2); structure, order, work and service (4).

In chronological order, the Pinnacle structure of 11 November 1885 is 4-6-1-6: earth-water-fire-water; three negative charges and one positive charge. The Challenge structure is 0-2-2-2: all water with a negative charge. Except for the lone 1 Grand Pinnacle, the P/C structure is wonderfully compatible with the Epochs. Right away, we see that this life will be devoid of major changes or shifts. This is depicted in the following chart.

Richard Andrew King

CHANGES & SHIFTS: SIMPLE FORMAT
DOB: 11 November 1885 – 8 Lifepath

Crown Pinnacle
6

Grand Pinnacle
1

1st Pinnacle	2nd Pinnacle
4	6

1st Epoch – Day: 11	2nd Epoch – Month: 11	3rd Epoch – Year: 1885
2	2	4

1st Challenge	2nd Challenge
0	2

Grand Challenge
2

Crown Challenge
2

This Life Matrix shows little change from birth to death. The polar and elemental energies are extremely compatible. The consistency of the energy, sans changes and shifts, indicates a life that is stable and secure with an emphasis on relationships, others, teamwork (2); work, service, structure, order, organization (4); duty, loyalty, responsibility, home, community, country (6). The only change and shift exists in the Grand Pinnacle. Its 1 energy indicates ego, action, leadership.

From this Simple Life Matrix format we move to the Specific format where the power of this destiny is revealed.

The King's Book of Numerology, Volume 12 – Advanced Principles

CHANGES & SHIFTS: SPECIFIC FORMAT - A
DOB: 11 November 1885 – 8 Lifepath (44)

Crown Pinnacle
33

Grand Pinnacle
55

1st Pinnacle	2nd Pinnacle
22	33

1st Epoch – Day: 11	2nd Epoch – Month: 11	3rd Epoch – Year: 1885
11	11	22

1st Challenge	2nd Challenge
0	11

Grand Challenge
11

Crown Challenge
11

Just take a look at all those master numbers encased in this 44-8 Lifepath! The only Life Matrix component not housing a master number is the 1st Challenge, which is empty as a result of the day and month being the same (11). Obviously, this is not a common chart, and it clearly and incontrovertibly is testimony as to why simple numbers do not, cannot, reveal the depth of a person's destiny. We must always look deeper into the numeric patterns of our lives to generate the most comprehensive analysis possible.

Richard Andrew King

The next chart reveals a fuller representation of this Life Matrix.

CHANGES & SHIFTS: SPECIFIC FORMAT - B
DOB: 11 November 1885 – 8 Lifepath (44)

Crown Pinnacle
33-6

Grand Pinnacle
55-1

1st Pinnacle	2nd Pinnacle
22-4	33-6

1st Epoch – Day: 11	2nd Epoch – Month: 11	3rd Epoch – Year: 1885
11-2	11-2	22-4

1st Challenge	2nd Challenge
0	11-2

Grand Challenge
11-2

Crown Challenge
11-2

Pretty stunning, isn't it, this chart with a birthdate of 11 November 1885? It belongs to an actual historic figure. Any guesses? If you surmised General George Smith Patton, Jr. you'd be correct. Adding Patton's 6 Expression to the chart, his Life Matrix IR Sets are revealed.

CHANGES & SHIFTS: IR SET FORMAT – 6 EXPRESSION
DOB: 11 November 1885 – 8 Lifepath (44), 3 Void noted

Crown Pinnacle
33v-6/(6)/3v

Grand Pinnacle
55-1/(6)/7

1st Pinnacle	2nd Pinnacle
22-4/(6)/1	33v-6/(6)/3v

1st Epoch – Day: 11	2nd Epoch – Month: 11	3rd Epoch – Year: 1885
11-2/(6)/8	11-2/(6)/8	22-4/(6)/1

1st Challenge	2nd Challenge
0	11-2/(6)/8

Grand Challenge
11-2/(6)/8

Crown Challenge
11-2/(6)/8

The 8 ROPE stemming from a 2 LIST reveals Patton's executive, leadership and command abilities in the arena of others and the "team" (2). The 1 ROPE (1st Pinnacle and 3rd Epoch) and 1 LIST Grand Pinnacle indicate leadership, especially the 55-1. The 3 ROPE (2nd and 4th Pinnacles) is void. This created Patton's issues with communication. The 7 ROPE in his Grand Pinnacle references turmoil. General George Patton is also featured in *The King's Book of Numerology, Volume 10 – Historic Icons* and separately in *Destinies of the Rich & Famous – The Secret Numbers of Extraordinary Lives*.

Richard Andrew King

The second example involves a birthdate of 1 June 1926, which generates a 7 Lifepath. This birthdate also features an historic individual. Any guesses? If you have been a student of The King's Numerology™, you should know who this person is by now. The answer will be revealed at the end of this section.

CHANGES & SHIFTS: SIMPLE FORMAT
DOB: 1 June 1926 – 7 Lifepath

Crown Pinnacle
1

Grand Pinnacle
4

1st Pinnacle	2nd Pinnacle
7	6

1st Epoch – Day: 1	2nd Epoch – Month: 6	3rd Epoch – Year: 1926
1	6	9

1st Challenge	2nd Challenge
5	3

Grand Challenge
2

Crown Challenge
8

What is particularly interesting in this second example is the first E-P-C Triad with its 1st Epoch being a 1, first Pinnacle a 7 and first Challenge a 5. This tells us there will be issues involving male energy via the 1 Epoch. There will also be isolation and some degree of turmoil and suffering because of the 7 Pinnacle. The 5 Challenge references changes, loss, detachments, movement. The 5 and 7 do not appear in any other LIST position for the entire life, and the 1 1st Epoch will be reprised in the Crown Pinnacle. Therefore, the beginning part of life for this individual will be difficult. This is problematic because the 1st E-P-C Triad establishes the foundation for the remainder of the life. Thus, this life is not getting off to a good start.

The 1-5-7 triad is not a social energy pattern. It is solo, solitary and mercurial. For a newborn child, therefore, the first part of this life lacks meaningful relationship and support (2), love and nurturing (6), stability, security and foundation (4) and continuity (8) – characteristics required for a child to have a stable life and all the benefits accruing to such a life.

Another consideration is that this 1-7-5 E-P-C Triad is encased in a 7 Lifepath which contains roots of 16 and 25, making the Lifepath problematic. When the split-cipher theory is applied, a 52 root also appears (1 + 6 + 19 + 26 = 52). Both the 25 and 52 harbor a 3 Subcap Challenge, which speaks to issues lacking fulfillment, self-worth, happiness and a positive image. The 16 houses a 5 Subcap Challenge which reinforces the 5 Challenge itself.

The 7 in the 1st Pinnacle resonates perfectly with the 7 Lifepath, intensifying this person's experiences. This adds to the troublesome environment of the early life. Problems will be generated here that affect the life to come beyond the 1st E-P-C Triad.

The 2nd E-P-C Triad is much different, revealing a 6 2nd Epoch, 6 2nd Pinnacle and a 3 Challenge. Therefore, there will be a major shift after the 1st E-P-C Triad runs its course. The 6 references love, nurturing, sexuality, artistry. The 3 indicates issues with one's image, happiness, joy and fulfillment. Unfortunately, the individual never lived beyond the 2nd E-P-C Triad, offering a clue as to who this person is.

Richard Andrew King

CHANGES & SHIFTS: SPECIFIC FORMAT - A
DOB: 1 June 1926 – 7 Lifepath

Crown Pinnacle
19

Grand Pinnacle
31

1st Pinnacle	2nd Pinnacle
7	24

1st Epoch – Day: 1	2nd Epoch – Month: 6	3rd Epoch – Year: 1926
1	6	18

1st Challenge	2nd Challenge
5	12

Grand Challenge
7

Crown Challenge
8

The King's Book of Numerology, Volume 12 – Advanced Principles

CHANGES & SHIFTS: SPECIFIC FORMAT - B
DOB: 1 June 1926 – 7 Lifepath

Crown Pinnacle
19-1

Grand Pinnacle
31-4

1st Pinnacle	2nd Pinnacle
7	24-6

1st Epoch – Day: 1	2nd Epoch – Month: 6	3rd Epoch – Year: 1926
1	6	18-9

1st Challenge	2nd Challenge
5	12-3

Grand Challenge
2 & 7
5 - 3 = 2; 12 - 5 = 7

Crown Challenge
8

Richard Andrew King

CHANGES & SHIFTS: IR SET FORMAT – 4 EXPRESSION
DOB: 1 June 1926 – 7 Lifepath

Crown Pinnacle
19-1/(4)/5

Grand Pinnacle
31-4/(4)/8

1st Pinnacle	2nd Pinnacle
7/(4)/11-2	24-6/(4)/1

1st Epoch – Day: 1	2nd Epoch – Month: 6	3rd Epoch – Year: 1926
1/(4)/5	6/(4)/1	18-9/(4)/22-4

1st Challenge	2nd Challenge
5/(4)/9	12-3/(4)/16-7

Grand Challenge
2/(4)/6 & 7/(4)/11-2
5-3=2; 12-5=7

Crown Challenge
8/(4)/3

CHANGES & SHIFTS: IR SET FORMAT – 4 EXPRESSION
DOB: 1 June 1926 – 7 Lifepath, 3-7-8 Voids Noted

Crown Pinnacle
19-1/(4)/5

Grand Pinnacle
31-4/(4)/8v

1st Pinnacle	2nd Pinnacle
7v/(4)/11-2	24-6/(4)/1

1st Epoch – Day: 1	2nd Epoch – Month: 6	3rd Epoch – Year: 1926
1/(4)/5	6/(4)/1	18-9/(4)/22-4

1st Challenge	2nd Challenge
5/(4)/9	12-3v/(4)/88v-16-7v

Grand Challenge
2/(4)/6 & 7v/(4)/11-2
5-3=2; 12-5=7

Crown Challenge
8v/(4)/3v

Although the 1st E-P-C Triad was difficult, we see that the 2nd PC Couplet houses the most troublesome energy of the entire life with its 12-3v/(4)/16-7v Challenge. Life (3v) will turn dark (16-7v) at this time, quite dark, and so it was. This chart is that of Marilyn Monroe who died under suspicious circumstances on 5 August 1962 at age 36. In fact, the 16-7v incorporates an 88v, creating an IR Set of 12-3v/(4)/88v-16-7v where all three of Monroe's voids collided, tragically, in this 2nd Challenge, ending her life.

Richard Andrew King

As is obvious, the changes and shifts in the life of Marilyn Monroe were clearly marked from birth. Her destiny's drama mandated a troublesome early life via her 1st E-P-C Triad followed by a fatal 2nd PC Couplet with its 12-3v/(4)/88v-16-7v Challenge being the smoking gun.

Also obvious is that the 12-3v/(4)/88v-16-7v IR Set in her 2nd Challenge was the only time of her life in which this pattern was active. Therefore, it was destined to be the most difficult part of her life.

Furthermore, the 16-7v ROPE portends difficulty, but in combination with her 3v and 88v it escalated into disaster. Even if the IR Set had been 12-3/(4)/88-16-7, having no voids, it would have been a huge red flag, but with all three of her voids simultaneously active in an IR Set housing the Great Purifier to create the 12-3v/(4)/88v-16-7v energy field the result proved lethal.

As tragic as Monroe's life was, her chart simply and clearly reveals the power of foreknowledge, confirming the veracity of numerology as a science, once more. Her 2nd Challenge is the key to her tragic demise. It reveals the troublesome 12-3v/(4)/88v-16-7v energy field with its voided 3-7-8 triumvirate in conjunction with the 16-7v Great Purifier, which also occupied her Lifepath. Her 2nd Challenge also underscores the importance of being able to assess changes and shifts in one's life.

Regarding forecasting changes and shifts, the good news is that discovering this information is easy and quick. A simple Life Matrix chart, erected in minutes, can reveal massive changes in one's life. Marilyn Monroe's chart exemplifies this.

Marilyn Monroe is featured in *The King's Book of Numerology, Volume 10 – Historic Icons* and in *Destinies of the Rich & Famous – The Secret Numbers of Extraordinary Lives*.

The next example also features a famous figure who shall be revealed later. As a matter of note, there are no voids in this chart.

CHANGES & SHIFTS: SIMPLE FORMAT
DOB: 29 August 1958 – 6 Lifepath

Crown Pinnacle
7

Grand Pinnacle
5

1st Pinnacle	2nd Pinnacle
1	4

1st Epoch – Day: 29	2nd Epoch – Month: 8	3rd Epoch – Year: 1958
2	8	5

1st Challenge	2nd Challenge
6	3

Grand Challenge
3

Crown Challenge
3

The 1 1st Pinnacle address the self, ego, action, independence, genesis and originality. This clashes with the 2 1st Epoch. Furthermore, the 1 LIST in the 1st Pinnacle never repeats for the entire life.

Richard Andrew King

The 8 2nd Epoch addresses connection, interaction, engagement, commerce and business. As an earth sign it integrates well with the 2 1st Epoch and its water element. Therefore, there is no drastic change or shift from the 1st Epoch to the 2nd Epoch. They're both social energies with negative charges.

The only major shift in the LIST energies is from the 4 2nd Pinnacle to the 5 Grand Pinnacle. This represents a change from stability (4) to detachment (5). As we know, the 4-5 pairing is one of three pairs of diametrically opposed dyads. The 1-2 and 7-8 duos represent the other two.

The shift of the 8 2nd Epoch to the 5 3rd Epoch does involve the element of earth (8) to fire (5), which is valid but not as potent as the 4 to 5 shift.

The 5 Crown Epoch reveals changes, movement, motion, freedom, detachment, stimulation, sensuality, excitement, diversity, adventure. It is accompanied by the 7 Crown Pinnacle, which does possess a 16 root (11 transition master of the 29 plus the 5 simple cipher of 1958). Thus, themes of the later life will be freedom and detachment in general (5); isolation, solitude, withdrawal, potential trouble and a fall (16-7).

So far this seems to be a rather simple Life Matrix LIST format. Its numeric energies are very diverse and house every single number of the Alpha-Numeric Spectrum except the 9. However, as we know, simple numbers cannot describe the immense complexities of an individual's destiny, so let's keep digging.

CHANGES & SHIFTS: SPECIFIC FORMAT - A
DOB: 29 August 1958 – 6 Lifepath (33)

Crown Pinnacle
52

Grand Pinnacle
68

1st Pinnacle	2nd Pinnacle
37	31

1st Epoch – Day: 29	2nd Epoch – Month: 8	3rd Epoch – Year: 1958
29	8	23

1st Challenge	2nd Challenge
21 & 6	3 & 15

Grand Challenge
21 & 6

Crown Challenge
21 & 6

Here we see that the Lifepath actually houses a hidden 33 master root. This is generated by adding the 2 simple day of birth (29-11-2) to the 8 of August and the 23 of 1958 (2 + 8 + 23 + 33).

Richard Andrew King

CHANGES & SHIFTS: SPECIFIC FORMAT - B
DOB: 29 August 1958 – 6 Lifepath (33)

	Crown Pinnacle	
	52-7	

	Grand Pinnacle	
	68-5	

1st Pinnacle	2nd Pinnacle
37-1	31-4

1st Epoch – Day: 29	2nd Epoch – Month: 8	3rd Epoch – Year: 1958
29-11-2	8	23-5

1st Challenge	2nd Challenge
21-3 & 6	3 & 15-6

Grand Challenge
21-3 & 6

Crown Challenge
21-3 & 6

The complexity begins to unfold in this Specific Life Matrix format. The next chart with its IR Set Format is telling. The individual associated with this birthday of 29 August 1958 is Michael Jackson, born Michael Joseph Jackson and, my-o-my is it powerful, illuminating why Jackson was such an international musical superstar but troubled soul. To keep the chart from being too cluttered with numbers, simple numbers are used where appropriate so as not to overshadow the master numbers in Jackson's chart.

The King's Book of Numerology, Volume 12 – Advanced Principles

CHANGES & SHIFTS: IR SET FORMAT – 8 EXPRESSION
Michael Joseph Jackson – DOB: 29 August 1958; 33-6 Lifepath

Crown Pinnacle
16-7/(8)/**33-6**

Grand Pinnacle
5/(8)/**22-4**

1st Pinnacle	2nd Pinnacle
1/(8)/**99-9**	sc**22**-4/(8)/3

1st Epoch – Day: 29	2nd Epoch – Month: 8	3rd Epoch – Year: 1958
11-2/(8)/**55**-1	8/(8)/**88**-16-7	5/(8)/**22**-4

1st Challenge	2nd Challenge
3/(8)/**11**-2 & 6/(8)/5	3/(8)/**11**-2 & 6/(8)/5

Grand Challenge
3/(8)/**11**-2 & 6/(8)/5

Crown Challenge
3/(8)/**11**-2 & 6/(8)/

It is in this IR Set format that Jackson's immense success, troubles, rise and fall become clear. This will become more intense when the changes and shifts of his Name and Letter timelines are added to this Life Matrix format.

Of course, the first item popping off the page are the master numbers – one in every Life Matrix component and two in the 1st Epoch!

Richard Andrew King

Another major observation is his 1st E-P-C Triad: 1/(8)/99-9 1st Pinnacle, 11-2/(8)/55-1 1st Epoch and 3/(8)/11-2 and 6/(8)/5 1st Challenge. This was the most powerful time of his life. The 99-9 ROPE in his 1st Pinnacle clearly reveals his public and universal reality. Its LIST is the 1 of self, ego, action, genesis, individuality. More than any other IR Set, it was this 1/(8)/99-9 energy that was responsible for Jackson's fame. As we know, the 9 is the Grand Ruler, Grand Amplifier, Grand Elemental, and the 99 master energy rocketed Jackson's notoriety through the stratosphere.

Notice, however, that the 99-9 appears only in his 1st Pinnacle and nowhere else. In fact, as we look forward, his final E-P-C Triad is problematic, especially with his 16-7/(8)/33-6 Crown Pinnacle. It speaks to turmoil, trouble, darkness, chaos (16-7) in the realm of image, love, sexuality, communication, pleasure and, as is common with the 33-6, drugs. Simply juxtaposing his 1st and 3rd E-P-C Triads tells a story of Jackson's immense early fame and fortune transitioning through his life journey into an eventual state of demise. For those interested, an open-source autopsy report of Jackson's death is located at the end of this section. It is quite revealing.

More than just having fame, Jackson was an original performer; his behavior impossible to control. This is reflected in his 11-2/(8)/55-1 energy field, making him a totally unique artist and revolutionary in his field.

Jackson's life linkage 3/(8)/11-2 and 6/(8)/5 IR Set are quite telling. Jackson was consumed with his looks, image and well-being, having multiple plastic surgeries to change his appearance throughout his life and ultimately becoming enslaved by drugs, especially propofol, as his autopsy validates. Plus, his issues regarding children, having once been arrested on charges of child molestation but found non-guilty, were with him, arguably, for the entirety of his adult life. These are referenced in both the 3/(8)/11-2 and 6/(8)/5 IR Sets, the very issues dominating his public life.

The 6/(8)/5 IR Set further indicates Jackson's family issues, especially with his father. Jackson stated many times that he never had a childhood because his father was pushing his sons into the music world.

The 5 ROPE references changes, detachments and a variety of family and love interests. With the 5 and 6 being sexual in combination, this would explain Jackson's proclivity in sleeping with children, although he denied any untoward behaviors with children.

After Jackson's 1st E-P-C Triad ran its course, the change and shift into his 8/(8)/88-16-7 2nd Epoch was dramatically painful . . . and lethal. It exemplifies how a person can be on top of the world in the first part of his life and have everything subsequently collapse afterwards. This is the timeframe when Jackson's very public problems surfaced. He died at age 50 in this 2nd Epoch 8/(8)/88-16-7 timeline. Had he lived, his life would most likely not have improved, especially with the 16-7/(8)/33-6 IR Set sitting above his chart in the Crown Pinnacle position.

Michael Jackson is one of twelve individuals featured in *The King's Book of Numerology – Volume 10, Historic Icons* and *Destinies of the Rich & Famous – The Secret Numbers of Extraordinary Lives* available at RichardKing.net and online retailers.

Michael Jackson's autopsy follows on the next page. It is interesting to correlate its findings with his numbers.

The Michael Jackson Autopsy:
Insights Provided by a Forensic Anesthesiologist
Richard J. Levy

(Reproduced in full with permission)

https://www.omicsonline.org/the-michael-jackson-autopsy-insights-provided-by-a-forensic-anesthesiologist-2157-7145.1000138.php?aid=2172

Division of Anesthesiology and Pain Medicine, Children's National Medical Center, The George Washington University School of Medicine and Health Sciences, USA

***Corresponding author:** Levy at Division of Anesthesiology and Pain Medicine, Children's National Medical Center, 111 Michigan Ave., NW, Washington, DC USA; 20010, Tel: (202) 476-2025; Fax: (202) 476-4922; E-mail: rlevy@cnmc.org

Received July 10, 2011; **Accepted** October 24, 2011; **Published** October 26, 2011

Citation: Levy RJ (2011) The Michael Jackson Autopsy: Insights Provided by a Forensic Anesthesiologist. J Forensic Res 2:138. doi:10.4172/2157-7145.1000138

Copyright: © 2011 Levy RJ. This is an open-access article distributed under the terms of the Creative Commons Attribution License, which permits unrestricted use, distribution, and reproduction in any medium, provided the original author and source are credited.

Abstract
Based on toxicology findings performed on samples taken at the time of autopsy, the cause of Michael Jackson's death was determined to be acute propofol intoxication with a contributory benzodiazepine effect. The manner of death was determined by the coroner to be homicide. At the center of this case are several anesthetic medications. Insight into the toxicology, review the autopsy results, and summary of the findings are provided from a forensic anesthesiologist's point of view.

Introduction
Michael Jackson was pronounced dead on June 25, 2009 at 2:26 pm in the afternoon at UCLA Medical Center. He died despite two and a half hours of attempted cardiopulmonary resuscitation (CPR). At 12:22 pm, roughly thirty minutes after the 911 call from Mr. Jackson's residence, paramedics found the pop star unresponsive and asystolic. They placed an endotracheal tube in his airway, began chest compressions, and administered epinephrine. Spontaneous circulation was never restored. Mr. Jackson remained unconscious with fixed and dilated pupils. At the direction of Mr. Jackson's physician, Dr. Conrad Murray, the decedent was taken by ambulance to UCLA Medical Center while CPR efforts continued. When they arrived at the hospital, Mr. Jackson remained asystolic. Emergency room physicians placed three central venous catheters and an arterial balloon pump within his aorta in order to attempt to restore coronary perfusion. Death was

officially pronounced at 2:26 pm and was immediately reported to the Los Angeles County Department of Coroner. The death investigation began at 5:20 pm on June 25, 2009. Michael Jackson's autopsy was performed on June 26, 2009 at 10:00 am. Based on toxicology findings, the cause of his death was determined to be acute propofol intoxication with a contributory benzodiazepine effect. The manner of death was determined by the coroner to be homicide. Michael Jackson's personal physician, Dr. Conrad Murray, was charged with involuntary manslaughter; a felony.

On July 22, 2009, a search warrant was issued for the search and seizure of several items from Dr. Murray's self storage unit in Harris County, Texas. The sworn affidavit provided by Detective Orlando Martinez of the Los Angeles Police Department was included in the search warrant to indicate probable cause [1]. The details of the events of June 25, 2009 and the days leading up to that fateful day are detailed in this affidavit. On February 8, 2010, The Smoking Gun posted the death investigation and autopsy findings [2]. It revealed post-mortem details of Michael Jackson's medical conditions and the toxicologic evidence trail of an accidental death. At the center of this case are several anesthetic medications. The trial will focus on two potential scenarios. The prosecution will aim to show that Dr. Murray administered the propofol that killed Mr. Jackson and the defense will argue that Mr. Jackson administered propofol to himself. As a forensic anesthesiologist, I will provide insight into the toxicology, review the autopsy results from a clinician's point of view, and interpret the findings.

The medical findings
Michael Jackson was a 50 year old man. His autopsy demonstrated that he suffered from many common medical conditions. Although none of these illness and findings contributed to his death; they are of interest from a medical curiosity standpoint.

Genitourinary system
Michael Jackson's autopsy demonstrated that he had nodular prostatic hyperplasia. The prostate gland is part of the male reproductive system and the urethra courses through it. When the prostate enlarges, it can constrict the urethra and impede the flow of urine. Such constriction makes initiating the urine stream difficult, results in weak flow, dribbling after urination, the feeling that the bladder is not completely empty, urgency, and frequency [3]. About 50% of all men over the age of 75 will have some of these symptoms [3]. On autopsy, Mr. Jackson's bladder was distended and filled with urine. In life, his enlarged prostate would have resulted in urinary retention and difficulty voiding. At autopsy, a condom-type urinary catheter was found on his genitals. At the time of his death, Jackson was being treated with tamsulosin to alleviate his urinary symptoms. Tamsulosinis an alpha receptor antagonist which relaxes the prostate and alleviates the constriction on the urethra [3].

Gastrointestinal system
Examination of Michael Jackson's gastrointestinal system revealed a 2 mm pedunculated polyp in his sigmoid colon. Histologic evaluation of the polyp identified it as a tubular adenoma. This type of polyp accounts for about 75% of all colon polyps and can potentially become malignant if left untreated [4]. It is likely that Mr. Jackson had no symptoms from this and had no knowledge of it. A routine colonoscopy would have identified the polyp and permitted biopsy and removal.

Citation: Levy RJ (2011) The Michael Jackson Autopsy: Insights Provided by a Forensic Anesthesiologist. J Forensic Res 2:138. doi:10.4172/2157-7145.1000138

The American Cancer Society recommends routine screening colonoscopy beginning at age 50 for both men and women [4]. Follow up evaluations depend on whether or not polyps and malignancies are detected.

Skeletal system

Several x-rays were taken of Mr. Jackson's skeletal system. He had mild degenerative spondylosis of the lower thoracic spine and suffered from degenerative osteoarthritis in several joints including his lower lumbar spine and digits. He also was found to have a small cervical rib on the second to last cervical vertebrae on the right side of his neck (C7). Cervical ribs occur in 5-10% of the population and they can cause thoracic outlet syndrome [5]. It is unknown if Michael Jackson suffered symptoms from his cervical rib. Thoracic outlet syndrome results when the rib compresses or traps the brachial plexus and the subclavian artery that supply the ipsilateral hand and arm [5]. Such compression often results in sharp, burning or aching pain as well as numbness, weakness, and parasthesias in the affected arm.

Pulmonary system

Microscopic examination of Michael Jackson's lungs revealed impressive and long standing abnormalities. Both lungs were markedly inflamed with bronchiolits, chronic interstitial pneumonitis, eosinophilic infiltrates, and there was evidence of fibrocollagenous scarring. In addition, there was widespread congestion in both lungs and patchy areas of hemorrhage. Furthermore, two small arteries had organizing and recanalizing thromboemboli. This means that the arteries clotted off in the past and were in the early stages of re-establishing blood flow. There was also evidence of histiocytic desquamation and focal desquamation of the respiratory lining with squamous metaplasia. This means that cells were sloughing off of the inner lining of his airways within each lung and there was a change in cell type. These findings are very abnormal. In life, such pathology could cause shortness of breath and difficulty breathing as well as a chronic cough. Michael Jackson's lung pathology would have made it difficult for him exert himself physically and probably caused him to fatigue easily.

Teeth, Skin, and Hair

Dental examination revealed a root canal along with endosseal implants and metallic and ceramic restoration of many different teeth. His skin demonstrated patches of dark pigmented and lighter less pigmented areas consistent with vitiligo. Mr. Jackson also had dark tattoos in his eyebrows and had tattooed his eyelids to look like eyeliner. He also had tattooed both of his lips pink. He was wearing a black wig kept in place by an adhesive substance. Underneath the wig, his own hair was short and tightly curled with frontal balding. Hair loss could have been the result of the incident in which Mr. Jackson's hair caught fire during the 1984 filming of a cola commercial. He had several surgical scars around the face and neck likely from prior plastic surgical procedures.

A Serious Medical Diagnosis

The combination of vitiligo, arthritis, and lung inflammation raises the concern for an autoimmune disease. In fact, in 1986, Michael Jackson was diagnosed with systemic lupus erythematosus (SLE). SLE is a serious and potentially life threatening disease that can occur at any age [6]. It affects women more commonly than men and African Americans and Asians more commonly than other races [6]. Symptoms vary widely and often flare or go into remission frequently. Common symptoms include chest pain, fatigue, fever, hair loss, skin rash, swollen lymph nodes, sensitivity to sunlight, and mouth sores [6]. Complications from SLE include thrombosis, hemolysis, pleural and pericardial effusions, stroke, and vasculitis [6]. There is no cure for SLE and treatment usually consists of ant-inflammatory medications and steroids. Although Michael Jackson had received treatment for lupus in the past, he was not on any such therapy at the time of his death. His SLE was reportedly in remission, however, the pulmonary findings suggest that it had caused significant lung injury. Although none of the medical findings in Michael Jackson's autopsy contributed to his death, they certainly indicate that the singer suffered from both SLE and prostatic hyperplasia.

The Death Investigation

Witness statements:
On June 27, 2009, a detective from the Los Angeles Police Department interviewed Dr. Murray in the presence of his attorneys. Murray provided the following information. Dr. Murray, a cardiologist, began treating Michael Jackson as his personal physician for insomnia six weeks prior to June 25, 2009. Each evening, he would administer propofol mixed with lidocaine to Mr. Jackson. Murray stated that he injected Mr. Jackson with 50 mg of propofol via an intravenous catheter (iv). The lidocaine was added in an attempt to prevent the painful stinging sensation associated with propofol injection. Dr. Murray stated that, at the time, he believed Mr. Jackson was developing an addiction to propofol. In the days prior to Mr. Jackson's death, Murray attempted to wean him off of the anesthetic. On June 22, 2009, Murray administered 25 mg of propofol, lorazepam (a long acting benzodiazepine), and midazolam (a short acting benzodiazepine) to Michael Jackson. On June 23, 2009, Murray only gave Mr. Jackson lorazepam and midazolam and did not inject propofol. At 1:00 am on June 25, 2009, Michael Jackson called Dr. Murray, complaining of dehydration and insomnia. At 1:30 am, Murray gave Mr. Jackson a 10 mg tablet of diazepam (a long acting benzodiazepine). This did not help Mr. Jackson fall asleep. Murray then injected 2 mg of lorazepam thirty minutes later. Dr. Murray stated that he was monitoring Michael by using a pulse oximeter connected to Jackson's finger. This device measures oxygen saturation in the blood and is a standard of care when administering sedatives in a variety of clinical settings. At 3:00 am, Murray gave Mr. Jackson 2 mg of midazolam. Mr. Jackson remained awake. Murray then gave a subsequent 2 mg dose of lorazepam at 5:00 am. At 7:30 am, Dr. Murray injected Michael with 2 mg of midazolam. Mr. Jackson remained awake and repeatedly asked for and demanded a propofol injection. At 10:40 am, Murray injected 25 mg of propofol mixed with lidocaine. According to Murray, Mr. Jackson finally fell asleep. Dr. Murray then left the bedroom to use the restroom. He stated that he was away from Mr. Jackson for no more than 2 minutes. Upon his return, Michael Jackson was unconscious and apneic. In the interview, Murray did not mention what Mr. Jackson's oxygen saturation was at the time or if the monitor had been alarming. He then pulled Mr. Jackson's body onto the bedroom floor and initiated CPR by himself. Murray stated that, at this time, he gave 0.2 mg of flumazenil (a benzodiazepine reversal agent) to try to reverse the effect of the lorazepam and midazolam. He called Mr. Jackson's security detail by cell phone for help. They did not respond. Murray then stopped CPR, left Michael Jackson's bedside, and ran downstairs to ask Jackson's chef to send Jackson's eldest son in to help him. When Murray returned, he continued CPR. It is unclear how long he was gone for. The security detail finally arrived shortly after and called 911.

Citation: Levy RJ (2011) The Michael Jackson Autopsy: Insights Provided by a Forensic Anesthesiologist. J Forensic Res 2:138. doi:10.4172/2157-7145.1000138

Murray told investigators that he was not the first doctor to administer the anesthetic, propofol to Michael Jackson. According to Murray, Mr. Jackson admitted that two doctors in Germany had previously administered Jackson the drug. In addition, in March or April of 2009, Mr. Jackson convinced Murray to arrange for an office based anesthesiologist to administer propofol to Jackson. In January of 2009, Michael Jackson met a nurse practitioner who was providing care for his three children. Mr. Jackson told her that he was fatigued. She diagnosed him with borderline-hypoglycemia. She placed Michael on a nutritional diet with a supplemental protein drink. On April 12, 2009, Mr. Jackson visited the nurse practitioner again and complained of insomnia. He asked if she was familiar with the drug propofol. She was not. Michael tried to convince her that it was safe. The practitioner subsequently read about propofol and warned Mr. Jackson not to take the medication. Michael then asked if she could obtain some propofol or if she knew of someone who could. According to the nurse practitioner, Mr. Jackson offered to pay her or anyone else whatever they wanted in exchange for it. She refused and that was the last time she saw Michael Jackson.

The death scene
Investigators went to Michael Jackson's 2-story mansion in the Bel-Air section of Los Angeles at 7:10 pm on June 25, 2009. They found the home to be clean and in order. They went directly to second floor bedroom where Dr. Murray was administering care to Mr. Jackson. The room was furnished with a queen sized bed, several tables and chairs, a dresser, and a television. The bed was in disarray. On the bed, there was an impression in the sheets where Michael Jackson slept and a blue pad was present (in case of accidental voiding). Near the foot of the bed, there was a tube of toothpaste, a string of beads, and a bottle of urine. On the other side of the bed, there was a book, a pair of glasses, and a laptop computer. Several empty orange juice bottles were on a nearby table. An oxygen tank rested on the side of the bed. This tank was empty when examined on July 13, 2009. A self-inflating ventilation bag along with face mask (that was not attached to the oxygen tank) was found near where Mr. Jackson received CPR along with latex gloves, disposable needles, alcohol pads, and a box of iv catheters. There was no mention of a pulse oximeter monitor at the scene. It is unknown if the emergency responders brought the oxygen tank and ventilation bag or if these were Dr. Murray's. An iv fluid setup was found consisting of a 1-liter bag of clear fluid, connection tubing, and a short Y-connector. A short section of iv tubing attached to the Y-connector contained yellow tinted fluid. Two 10 mL syringes with some residual white fluid and multiple opened bottles of propofol were also found. Eight bottles of propofol in all were recovered. The iv setup and syringes were collected as evidence. Multiple vials of lidocaine, lorazepam, midazolam, and flumazenil were also found. Several bottles of prescription pills were in the home. These medications included clonazepam, trazodone, diazepam, lorazepam, tamsulosin, temazepam, and tizanidine. The diazepam, tamsulosin, lorazepam, and temazepam were prescribed by Dr. Murray, the clonazepam and trazodone were prescribed by a different general practitioner, and the tizanidine was prescribed by Jackson's dermatologist. Each of these medications, except for the tamsulosin, was prescribed to treat insomnia.

The witness accounts indicate that Michael Jackson craved propofol and demonstrated drug seeking behavior. His pattern of visiting various different physicians and medical caregivers in order to obtain propofol and other prescription sleep-aids is a clear example "doctor shopping". When a particular caregiver refuses or ceases to give a patient the medication they are seeking, they simply try to find another caregiver that will. It is common for such patients to reach out to several different medical providers in a variety of different specialties. These actions are classic drug addiction behavior.

The Autopsy and Toxicology

The external examination of Michael Jackson at the time of autopsy revealed gauze pads on the right side of his neck, in the antecubital region of his left and right arms, and on his left forearm. These were presumably sites where placement of iv catheters during CPR was attempted. Three large central venous catheters were in place: one in his left jugular vein and one in each femoral vein. An arterial balloon pump was in the appropriate position within the aorta through the left femoral artery and an endotracheal tube was present within the decedent's airway. These had been successfully placed by the Emergency Room team at UCLA Medical Center during the resuscitation. In the center of his chest, Mr. Jackson had a large bruise and abrasion. His sternum and several ribs were fractured. These were undoubtedly as a result of chest compressions during CPR. There were also several puncture sites in both arms, one on his left knee and one on his right ankle. It is unclear if any of these represented sites where intravenous medications were administered by Dr. Murray. The anesthesiology consultant for the case stated that an iv catheter was noted in Mr. Jackson's left leg, however, the autopsy report did not mention such a catheter.

Of note, the blood within Michael Jackson's heart was unclotted at the time of autopsy. The autopsy was performed on June 26, 2009 at 10:00 am; roughly 20 hours after the time of death. Finding unclotted blood at the time of autopsy is consistent with hypoxia. This is often seen in cases of asphyxia and sudden infant death syndrome, for example [7]. It suggests that Mr. Jackson was apneic prior to his death, resulting in a critical decline in oxygen saturation and subsequent asystole.

Toxicology was performed by the coroner's office on Michael Jackson's blood (samples drawn at UCLA Medical Center and at the time of autopsy), vitreous, liver, stomach contents, and urine (the bottle collected at the scene and taken from his bladder during the autopsy). In addition, tests were performed on the 10 mL syringes and iv fluid setup and tubing. These results were critical to determining the cause of Michael Jackson's death (table). Propofol was detected in his blood, vitreous, liver, stomach contents, and in both urine samples. The levels of propofol found in each sample of blood were within the therapeutic range. This means that there was enough propofol in his system at the time of death to render him unconscious. Lidocaine was also detected in each specimen except for the vitreous. Three different benzodiazepines along with a metabolite of diazepam (nordiazepine) were detected in Mr. Jackson's blood. Midazolam was also present in his urine. These findings indicate that Michael had either taken or was given diazepam, lorazepam, and midazolam within hours prior to his death. Ephedrine was detected in the two urine samples. The two 10 mL syringes found at the scene each contained a small amount of white fluid (0.19 grams and 0.17 grams). Propofol and lidocaine were detected in one syringe and propofol, lidocaine, and flumazenil were detected in the other. The short section of iv tubing attached to the Y-connector that contained yellow tinted fluid was tested and was also found to contain propofol, lidocaine, and flumazenil. No drugs were detected in the rest of the intravenous tubing or 1-liter bag with clear fluid. These fluids were presumably saline or some other routine medical delivery solution.

Citation: Levy RJ (2011) The Michael Jackson Autopsy: Insights Provided by a Forensic Anesthesiologist. J Forensic Res 2:138. doi:10.4172/2157-7145.1000138

In order for an accurate interpretation, it is important to review some important pharmacologic properties of propofol.

Propofol
Propofol is a potent anesthetic drug that rapidly causes sedation and unconsciousness when intravenously injected [8,9]. Since 1986, it has been used world-wide in clinical settings and has become the anesthesiologist's drug of choice to induce general anesthesia and to provide sedation for a variety of procedures [9,10]. Propofol is administered as a single injection to induce unconsciousness or as a continuous infusion to maintain a desired level of sedation [11]. It is a very short acting drug and patients rapidly awaken following injection if an infusion is not initiated [11].

In 2009, propofol was not a controlled substance scheduled by the U.S. Drug Enforcement Agency. However, today, the drug is in the process of being reclassified. Hospitals usually have policies to restrict propofol use to specific areas within the hospital and limit those capable of administering it to qualified personnel such as anesthesiologists and critical care physicians. In addition to being clinically indicated for anesthesia and sedation, propofol has also been used to treat seizures, migraine and tension headaches, severe alcohol withdrawal and delirium tremens, and has been used to facilitate narcotic detoxification [8,11]. It has never been indicated to treat insomnia. Propofol is insoluble in water and the current formulation is an emulsion of soybean oil, glycerol, and egg lecithin. This lipid formula gives the drug its characteristic and unique white color [8]. In his interview with investigators, Dr. Murray told investigators that Michael Jackson craved propofol and called it "his milk" (because of the white color). Certain preparations of propofol will turn yellow when exposed to air for 6 to 7 hours. Propofol causes a burning pain when it is injected, so many anesthesiologists will attempt to anesthetize the vein with lidocaine, a local anesthetic. This can be done either by injecting lidocaine into the vein prior to propofol administration or by mixing lidocaine with propofol in the syringe. According to Murray, Mr. Jackson was well-versed in the use of lidocaine to limit or prevent propofol's pain on injection. Propofol induces unconsciousness rapidly. Loss of consciousness occurs 100 seconds following a 2.5 mg per kilogram injection and lasts for 5-10 minutes [8]. It blunts the respiratory drive and relaxes oropharyngeal muscle tone, potentially resulting in airway obstruction. Without proper management by an experienced provider, a single injection of propofol can result in apnea, hypoxia, and death [8]. Furthermore, injection of 2.5 mg per kilogram results in a 25-40% reduction in blood pressure [8]. This decrease in blood pressure is more pronounced in dehydrated patients. These effects make propofol potentially dangerous and lethal when injected by inexperienced personnel or self administered. Following injection, propofol is rapidly eliminated by the body. It is metabolized in the liver and excreted into the urine by the kidneys [8]. Thus, propofol does not accumulate in the body.

The abuse potential of propofol was not recognized until 1992. Since then, 38 cases of propofol abuse have been published [10]. Propofol has increasingly become a drug of abuse largely because it is easily accessible, it has a rapid onset of action, and the duration of action is ultra-short without long term side effects [10].Medical professionals and healthcare workers represent the largest group of known propofol abusers [10]. Of these personnel, anesthesiologists and nurse anesthetists are the most common offenders. The most likely rationale for this is familiarity with the drug and previously unregulated access to it. Recent studies suggest that propofol diversion and abuse are on the rise [12].

The majority of cases of propofol abuse involve use of the drug for recreational purposes, stress relief, and to alleviate insomnia. In one report, propofol dependency was described in a lay person following a propofol prescription for the treatment of tension headaches [11]. The average age of known propofol abusers is about 30 years of age and most abusers are male [13]. In most cases, propofol was used in addition to other drugs of abuse and the user had a history of drug dependency [13].

Physical dependence has not been described in propofol abusers, however, psychological dependence is quite common [10,13]. This is because propofol can cause euphoria, stress and tension relief, sexual fantasies and dreams, and sexual disinhibition [10,13]. These effects of propofol lead to drug craving and loss of control over the amount and frequency of drug injected as well as continued use of propofol despite adverse consequences. Chronic propofol abuse can result in tolerance and repeated injections exceeding 100 times per day have been reported [14].

Propofol abuse and recreational use often result in death because of the rapid onset of unconsciousness and apnea following injection [10]. Thirty-seven percent of the 38 published cases of abuse were fatal [10]. The majority of these propofol related deaths resulted from accidental overdose or suicide. Recently, the first case of first degree murder with propofol was reported [10].

Blood levels of propofol in most propofol related deaths are usually within the therapeutic range (1.3 – 6.8 µg/mL). This means that propofol induced unconsciousness and the cause of death was likely due to apnea with subsequent hypoxia. As with other drugs of abuse, a specific "lethal level" may not be necessary to conclude that death was caused by propofol injection. Simply detecting it in blood indicates it was injected prior to death and at least contributed to if not caused the death.

Several accidental propofol related deaths have been reported. A 26 year old male ICU nurse who was a known propofol abuser was found dead in his apartment surrounded by several empty and partially empty propofol vials along with two syringes [15]. His autopsy demonstrated several recent and partially scarred needle marks on his arms, wrists, and hands. Propofol was detected in his hair, blood, urine, brain, and liver.

A 27 year old male nurse anesthetist was found dead at his home with three empty propofol vials next to him [16]. Unopened propofol bottles were found in his car. Several needle marks in his skin suggested chronic abuse. His autopsy revealed pulmonary hemorrhage and inflammation of the pancreas. Propofol was detected in his blood, bile, and urine.

A 44 year old female nurse anesthetist was found dead at her home with an empty vial of midazolam and a syringe near her body [17]. Toxicology revealed propofol, midazolam, and alcohol in her blood. Analysis of her hair demonstrated propofol and midazolam in several segments indicating repetitive abuse for 6 months prior to her death. A 21 year old male lay person purchased propofol online using an internet bidding system [18]. He was found with an iv catheter *in situ* that he had placed in order to inject propofol several times a day. Propofol was detected in his blood.

Richard Andrew King

A 38 year old known propofol abusing female anesthesiologist was found dead in a hospital on call room [19]. She was kneeling on the floor facing downward with three empty vials of propofol and two used syringes next to her. Autopsy demonstrated numerous needle marks with recent and older hemorrhages in both arms, two iv catheters secured in each wrist, and pulmonary edema. Propofol was detected in her blood.

Seven other accidental propofol related deaths have been reported in members of anesthesiology residency programs [10]. Six of the victims were anesthesiology residents and one was an anesthesia technician. All were propofol abusers. Two suicides have also been reported in which propofol was used to operationalize the plan. In the first case, a 29 year old female radiologist committed suicide by self-administering propofol [20]. Propofol was detected in her blood and liver.

In another case, a 37 year old male medical doctor committed suicide with propofol after he recently broke off an extra-marital affair [21]. He was found dead, lying on his back on the bed of a rented room. Two needles had been inserted into the dorsum of his left and right hands. Each was attached to an iv fluid delivery system. Eight empty propofol vials were found at the scene. His body was moderately decomposed and autopsy findings were fairly unremarkable. Propofol was detected in his blood, liver, kidney, and brain. It was calculated that he self-administered about 1600 mg of propofol. Of note, Dr. Murray claimed that he only gave Michael Jackson 25 mg of propofol the day he died.

To date, there has only been one case of murder by propofol injection [10]. The details are as follows. A 24 year old University of Florida student was found dead in her house in 2005 near Gainesville. Syringes, needles, and 2 empty propofol vials were found in grocery store bags outside of her house next to her garbage cans. Autopsy demonstrated a pinpoint puncture wound in the crease of her left elbow with hemorrhage directly over a superficial vein. Toxicology assessment detected propofol in her blood. The medical examiner concluded that the woman's death was homicide caused by a lethal dose of propofol administered by a person skilled in iv injection. Investigation of the propofol bottle lot numbers found at the crime scene indicated that the vials were obtained from a University of Florida hospital. Upon further investigation it was determined that the propofol bottles had been removed from the hospital by a male ICU nurse. He had acquired the propofol approximately 5 to 6 days prior to the murder.

Thorough questioning of the nurse's former roommate revealed important details and a potential motive. The roommate had previously introduced the nurse to the victim. The male nurse soon became infatuated and obsessed with the victim. After learning that the victim had gotten engaged to her boyfriend of 4 years, the nurse became enraged and planned to kill her. Detectives learned that the victim suffered from chronic migraine headaches. She apparently trusted the nurse and he convinced her that he would relieve her symptoms with propofol. One week after her engagement, the male nurse injected the victim with the lethal dose of propofol. The nurse left the country and a few weeks later he was apprehended in the West African Republic of Senegal. He was escorted to the Alachua County Department of the Jail by the US Marshall's Service and was ultimately tried

and convicted of first degree murder. He was sentenced to life in prison without parole. Jackson's death has also been determined to be a homicide. This is because the coroner concluded that:
1. Propofol and benzodiazepines were administered by another person.
2. Propofol was injected in a non-hospital setting without appropriate medical indication.
3. The standard of care for administering propofol was not met.
4. There was no evidence that Michael Jackson administered propofol to himself. The prosecution's case will hinge on the evidence that Dr. Murray administered the medications to Mr. Jackson. The defense will try to demonstrate that Mr. Jackson may have possibly administered propofol to himself prior to his death. Is this a homicide, suicide, or accidental death?

Whodunnit?

The prosecution's scenario:
Dr. Murray administered benzodiazepines and propofol mixed with lidocaine to Michael Jackson in the pop star's bedroom. After Mr. Jackson lost consciousness, Murray left his patient to go to the bathroom. During the time that Murray was out of the room, Michael either became apneic or his airway became obstructed. He soon became hypoxic and asystolic. When Murray returned to the bedside, he recognized that Mr. Jackson was not breathing. He drew up flumazenil in the same syringe that previously had propofol and lidocaine in it and injected the medication to try to reverse the benzodiazepine effect. Nothing happened. Murray then began CPR.

Evidence that supports this theory is Murray's own testimony. He admitted that he gave Mr. Jackson benzodiazepines and propofol with lidocaine. The objective evidence that supports the prosecution's theory is that the amounts of propofol, lidocaine, and benzodiazepines in Michael Jackson's blood confirm that these medications were given in the hours prior to death. Furthermore, the amount of propofol in the blood was within the therapeutic range. Thus, it is likely that propofol caused apnea or an obstructed airway.

There is a problem with this version of the story, though. Dr. Murray stated that he only administered 25 mg of propofol to Mr. Jackson. At the time of death, Michael weighed approximately 60 kilograms. The 25 mg dose, less than 0.5 milligrams per kilogram, is incredibly small. Although some patients may have a mild sedative effect from this propofol dose, they would not become unconscious unless there were extremely hypovolemic or had significant cardiac dysfunction. Jackson had neither of these conditions. Also, this small dose of propofol would not result in the blood levels that were detected in the toxologic analysis. Furthermore, since Michael was receiving propofol almost every night, he would have likely developed some tolerance to the drug. So, something doesn't add up. The prosecution would say that Dr. Murray is not being truthful about the dose of propofol he used. He must have administered more. The total injected dose was probably in the 120 mg to 180 mg range (2-3 mg per kilogram). The lidocaine concentrations found in the blood are consistent with a 2 mg per kilogram injection about one hour prior to Michael's death [22]. Most anesthesiologists combine 40 mg of lidocaine with J Forensic Res Volume 2 • Issue 8 • 1000138 ISSN: 2157-7145 JFR, an open access journal

Citation: Levy RJ (2011) The Michael Jackson Autopsy: Insights Provided by a Forensic Anesthesiologist. J Forensic Res 2:138. doi:10.4172/2157-7145.1000138

180 mg of propofol in a syringe when they mix the two for injection. The toxicology suggests that Michael received between 60 and 120 mg of intravenous lidocaine. Depending on how Murray mixed the two drugs, if he had only given 25 mg of propofol, then he would have only given about 5.5 mg of lidocaine. This would have been barely detectable in the blood. On the other hand, an intravenous injection of 60 mg of lidocaine equates to a dose of roughly 270 mg of propofol (more than 5 mg per kilogram) when using a standard lidocaine/propofol mixture. Such a dose of propofol would have been more than adequate induce unconsciousness and apnea.

The defense's scenario:
Dr. Murray administered benzodiazepines and propofol mixed with lidocaine to Michael Jackson in the pop star's bedroom. After Mr. Jackson fell asleep, Murray went to the bathroom. During the time that Murray was out of the room, Michael Jackson, in a semi-awake state, administered the lethal dose of propofol to himself. He either injected propofol into his iv catheter himself, attempted to drink propofol, or both. The defense is essentially arguing that Mr. Jackson's death was an accidental death caused by his own actions. What is the evidence to support this theory? First, the blood levels of propofol would certainly reflect a potentially lethal dose of propofol regardless of who injected it. Could Michael Jackson have injected propofol into his own vein? It may be possible. He had seen the procedure enough times in the past so that he would have understood the logistics. The anesthesiology consultant to the coroner stated that, because the injection port in the iv tubing setup was 13.5 cm from the tip of the iv catheter in his left leg, self-injection would be awkward and unlikely. The consultant never stated that it was impossible. How about ingestion of propofol as a contributor?

The evidence to support this is that his stomach contents contained both propofol and lidocaine. The only way these drugs could have entered his stomach prior to death is if they were ingested. Only 0.13 mg of propofol was detected in the 70 mL of stomach contents. This is an extremely small amount of propofol. However, the fact that both drugs were detected indicates that they came from the same syringe in which both medications were mixed. Proving that Michael Jackson injected himself with propofol or drank from the syringe is very difficult. One possible technique would have been to perform fingerprint analysis on the propofol bottles and syringes. Certainly, finding the decedent's fingerprints on the syringes would not rule out the possibility that he handled these earlier in the day or that someone placed them in his hands after he died. However, to my knowledge, fingerprint analysis was never done. The defense will argue that oral ingestion of propofol can result in sedation and unconsciousness. What is the evidence? There are only two related publications on the matter. In the first study, propofol absorption via rectal suppository (55 mg per kilogram) in 6 week old piglets was evaluated [23]. None of the piglets became sedated with rectal propofol and blood levels of propofol were 100-fold lower than those achieved following intravenous injection. The second relevant study assessed propofol absorption following oral administration in rats [24]. In this work, propofol was shown to undergo extensive metabolism in the intestine and only 10% of the ingested dose reached the circulation. As with rectal absorption, the resultant blood levels of propofol following oral administration were 100 times less than parenteral injection. Thus, in order to become unconscious from propofol ingestion, Michael Jackson would have had to drink about 12,000 mg of propofol (over 1-liter in volume). This is a very unlikely scenario.

It is possible, however, that Mr. Jackson attempted to drink the drug. Furthermore, one cannot rule out the possibility that he may have intravenously administered propofol himself. Another scenario is that someone else may have deliberately injected the contents of a syringe of propofol into the decedent's esophagus in the peri-mortem period to make it appear as if Mr. Jackson ingested the drug. This would imply that the person: 1. knew that the coroner would check stomach contents for medications, 2. knew that finding propofol in the stomach would provide an alibi, and 3. attempted to divert blame to the decedent.

Neither of these scenarios addresses the ephedrine in Mr. Jackson's urine or why flumazenil was detected in the same syringe as propofol and lidocaine. Ephedrine is a stimulant. In the US, ephedrine is controlled by the FDA and they have put strict limits on maximum daily dosage. It is unknown how ephedrine was taken by or administered to Mr. Jackson. It is quite possible that he was using this stimulant to help him work through exhaustion and lethargy as he prepared for his upcoming concert tour. Of note, patients who take or receive ephedrine while taking serotonin-reuptake inhibitors, such as trazodone, could have a fatal reaction (Michael Jackson was taking trazodone). Since there was no ephedrine detected in the decedent's blood, it played no role in his death and was not given to him that evening. So it is unclear how ephedrine fits in to the story.

Flumazenil is a pharmacologic agent used to reverse the effects of benzodiazepines. It is strictly avoided in patients who have been chronically taking benzodiazepines because it can result in seizures, withdrawal, or life threatening arrhythmias. Thus, it is would have been contraindicated for Mr. Jackson. Furthermore, if a clinician wanted to reverse the sedative effect of benzodiazepines, they certainly would not inject flumazenil along *with* propofol. This is because additional propofol administration would only deepen the level of sedation and would antagonize the situation. Finding flumazenil mixed with propofol likely indicates that Dr. Murray hurriedly prepared the reversal agent in a syringe that he had previously used for propofol injection.

Drug	Heart blood	Hospital blood	Femoral blood	Vitreous	Liver	Stomach contents (in 70 mL)	Urine	Urine at the scene
Propofol	3.2	4.1	2.6	<0.40	6.2	0.13 mg	0.15	<0.10
Lidocaine	0.68	0.51	0.84	-	0.45	1.6 mg	present	present
Diazepam	<0.10	present	-	-	-	-	-	-
Nordiazepam	<0.05	-	-	-	-	-	-	-
Lorazepam	0.162	-	0.169	-	-	-	-	-
Midazolam	0.0046	-	-	-	-	-	0.0068	0.025
Ephedrine	ND	-	-	-	-	-	present	present

Levels are presented in µg per mL or µg per gram. mL; milliliters, mg; milligrams, ND; not detected.

Table 1:
Summary of Toxicology Findings.

Citation: Levy RJ (2011) The Michael Jackson Autopsy: Insights Provided by a Forensic Anesthesiologist. J Forensic Res 2:138. doi:10.4172/2157-7145.1000138

Richard Andrew King

Summary

There is no question that Dr. Murray was irresponsible, medically negligent, and did not follow the standard of care. However, were his actions criminal? Did he inject the lethal dose or did Michael Jackson? It will be up to the legal system and the jury to determine if Dr. Murray is guilty of involuntary manslaughter. Regardless of the outcome of the trial, the Michael Jackson death case will forevermore provide a high profile example of drug addiction, manipulation, and the dangers of the anesthetic, propofol.

References

1. http://i.cdn.turner.com/cnn/2009/images/08/24/murray.search.warrant.affadavits.pdf. Accessed September 14, 2011.
2. http://www.thesmokinggun.com/documents/crime/michael-jackson-autopsyreport. Accessed September 14, 2011.
3. Lepor H (2011) Medical treatment of benign prostatic hyperplasia. Rev Urol 13:20-33.
4. Winawer SJ, Zauber AG, Fletcher RH, Stillman JS, O'brien MJ, et al. (2006) Guidelines for colonoscopy surveillance after polypectomy: a consensus update by the US Multi-Society Task Force on Colorectal Cancer and the American Cancer Society. CA Cancer J Clin 56:143-159.
5. Loscertales J, Congregado M, Jiménez Merchán R (2011) First rib resection using videothorascopy for the treatment of thoracic outlet syndrome. Arch Bronconeumol 47: 204-207.
6. Ben-Menachem E (2010) Review article: systemic lupus erythematosus: a review for anesthesiologists. Anesth Analg 111:665-676.
7. Goldwater PN (2003) Sudden infant death syndrome: a critical review of approaches to research. Arch Dis Child 88:1095-1100.
8. Marik PE (2004) Propofol: therapeutic indications and side-effects. Curr Pharm Des 10:3639-3649.
9. Abad-Santos F, Gálvez-Múgica MA, Santos MA, Novalbos J, Gallego-Sandín S, et al. (2003) Pharmacokinetics and pharmacodynamics of a single bolus of propofol 2% in healthy volunteers. J Clin Pharmacol 43:397-405.
10. Kirby RR, Colaw JM, Douglas MM (2009) Death from propofol: accident, suicide, or murder? Anesth Analg 108:1182-1184.
11. Schneider U, Rada D, Rollnik JD, Passie T, Emrich HM (2001) Propofol dependency after treatment of tension headache. Addict Biol 6: 263-265.
12. Wischmeyer PE, Johnson BR, Wilson JE, Dingmann C, Bachman HM, et al. (2007) A survey of propofol abuse in academic anesthesia programs. Anesth Analg 105:1066-1071.
13. Roussin A, Montastruc JL, Lapeyre-Mestre M (2007) Pharmacological and clinical evidences on the potential for abuse and dependence of propofol: a review of the literature. Fundam Clin Pharmacol 21:459-466.
14. Soyka M, Schutz CG (1997) Propofol dependency. Addiction 92:1369-1370.
15. Iwersen-Bergmann S, Rösner P, Kühnau HC, Junge M, Schmoldt A (2001) Death after excessive propofol abuse. Int J Legal Med 114:248-251.
16. Roussin A, Mirepoix M, Lassabe G, Dumestre-Toulet V, Gardette V, et al. (2006) Death related to a recreational abuse of propofol at therapeutic dose range. Br J Anaesth. 97:268.

17. Cirimele V, Kintz P, Doray S, Ludes B (2002) Determination of chronic abuse of the anaesthetic agents midazolam and propofol as demonstrated by hair analysis. Int J Legal Med 116:54-57.
18. Strehier M, Preuss J, Wollersen H, Madea B (2006) Lethal mixed intoxication with propofol in a medical layman. Arch Kriminol 217:153–160.
19. Kranioti EF, Mavroforou A, Mylonakis P, Michalodimitrakis M (2007) Lethal self administration of propofol (Diprivan). A case report and review of the literature. Forensic Sci Int 167:56-58.
20. Drummer OH (1992) A fatality due to propofol poisoning. J Forensic Sci 37:1186–1189.
21. Chao TC, Lo DS, Chui PP, Koh TH (1994) The first fatal 2,6-di-isopropylphenol (propofol) poisoning in Singapore: a case report. Forensic Sci Int 66:1-7.
22. Tsai PS, Buerkle H, Huang LT, Lee TC, Yang LC, et al. (1998) Lidocaine concentrations in plasma and cerebrospinal fluid after systemic bolus administration in humans. Anesth Analg 87:601-604.
23. Cozanitis DA, Levonen K, Marvola M, Rosenberg PH, Sandholm M (1991) A comparative study of intravenous and rectal administration of propofol in piglets. Acta Anaesthesiol Scand 35:575-577.
24. Raoof AA, Augustijns PF, Verbeeck RK (1996) In vivo assessment of intestinal, hepatic, and pulmonary first pass metabolism of propofol in the rat. Pharm Res 13:891-895.

Richard Andrew King

Our next example is very interesting. What can you surmise about the destiny of this individual? Notice the flow of energies? The 22-4 Lifepath is a major clue.

CHANGES & SHIFTS: SIMPLE FORMAT
DOB: 1 April 1961 – 4 Lifepath (22)

Crown Pinnacle
9

Grand Pinnacle
8

1st Pinnacle	2nd Pinnacle
5	3

1st Epoch – Day: 1	2nd Epoch – Month: 4	3rd Epoch – Year: 1961
1	4	8

1st Challenge	2nd Challenge
3	4

Grand Challenge
1

Crown Challenge
7

Here is a fuller look. No definitive clues, however.

CHANGES & SHIFTS: SPECIFIC FORMAT – A

DOB: 1 April 1961 – 4 Lifepath (22)

Crown Pinnacle
18

Grand Pinnacle
26

1st Pinnacle	2nd Pinnacle
5	21

1st Epoch – Day: 1	2nd Epoch – Month: 4	3rd Epoch – Year: 1961
1	4	17

1st Challenge	2nd Challenge
3	13

Grand Challenge
10

Crown Challenge
16

Richard Andrew King

If by this time you've noticed the latter life houses an 8 Grand Pinnacle, 8 Crown Epoch and 9 Crown Pinnacle you're doing well. With 8 being the most powerful social number and 9 being the Grand Elemental, this destiny started slowly, gained steam in its 8 Grand Pinnacle and then blossomed onto the public stage in its 9 Crown Pinnacle. As we know, no two numbers combined are more powerful than the 8 and 9.

CHANGES & SHIFTS: SPECIFIC FORMAT - B

DOB: 1 April 1961 – 4 Lifepath (22)

Crown Pinnacle
18-9

Grand Pinnacle
26-8

1st Pinnacle	2nd Pinnacle
5	21-3

1st Epoch – Day: 1	2nd Epoch – Month: 4	3rd Epoch – Year: 1961
1	4	17-8

1st Challenge	2nd Challenge
3	13-4

Grand Challenge
10-1

Crown Challenge
16-7

Let's add more clues. This person has an 11-2 Expression (the Life Matrix Filter). Combined with the 22 Lifepath (the Name and Letter Timeline Filter), a 33 PE is generated. Obviously, this is a powerful Umbrella. The 22 Lifepath is, arguably, the Lifepath creating the most power and wealth; the 33 PE is the most formidable energy of words and communication. What this chart reveals is a destiny that started small and ended big. The next page reveals who the person is. Any guesses?

CHANGES & SHIFTS: IR SET FORMAT – 11-2 EXPRESSION
DOB: 1 April 1961; 22 Lifepath; 33-PE
Voids: 8 and 9, noted

Crown Pinnacle
9v/(11-2)/11-2

Grand Pinnacle
8v/(11-2)/19-1

1st Pinnacle	2nd Pinnacle
5/(11-2)/16-7	3/(11-2)/14-5

1st Epoch – Day: 1	2nd Epoch – Month: 4	3rd Epoch – Year: 1961
1/(11-2)/3	4/(11-2)/6	8v/(11-2)/1

1st Challenge	2nd Challenge
3/(11-2)/14-5	4/(11-2)/15-6

Grand Challenge
1/(11-2)/3

Crown Challenge
7/(11-2)/9v

Richard Andrew King

This Life Matrix is that of Susan Boyle, a Scottish singer who came to fame and resulting fortune after appearing in *Britain's Got Talent*, singing "I Dreamed a Dream" from *Les Misérables*. The show aired on 11 April 2009.

Boyle was born Susan Magdalane Boyle on 1 April 1961. If you haven't heard of her, check her out on the web. She has a phenomenal story and a glorious voice that propelled her to a multi-million dollar fortune in her later life.

Notice in her chart that the 9 Grand Elemental sits at the top of her chart in the Crown Pinnacle position as the LIST energy. The 9 anchors her life in the ROPE Crown Challenge position. The Grand Ruler energy was nowhere present until the latter part of her life. With her 8 Grand Pinnacle, 8 Crown Epoch and her 11-2/(22-4)/33-6 Umbrella, her fame was cemented when the energies came together in her late forties.

As we see from these few examples, single numbers do not, cannot, nor ever will tell the story of an individual's destiny as it pertains to the Life Matrix. We must consider all available data to derive at a reasonable assessment. This said, what single numbers do is reveal a flow of energies from life's beginning to its end. Too many complex numbers in the beginning of the analysis process can be confusing. Therefore, we start with the simple and conclude with the complex.

The Life Matrix, however, is only one half of the destiny picture. The other half contains the Name and Letter Timelines, so let's take a look at some examples and how they reveal the shifts and changes of one's destiny.

NAME & LETTER TIMELINE – MATRIX SHIFTS & CHANGES

After analyzing the Life Matrix, the next step is to examine the Name and Letter Timelines to determine if there are any corroborating energies to the Life Matrix which would create more power than that of the Life Matrix.

For example, Susan Boyle's Name Timeline adds more potency to her latter life fame. First, her Lifepath is a 22, which means that every name and letter will filter through the Master Builder to generate an outcome.

NAME TIMELINE: SUSAN MAGDALANE BOYLE		
Susan	**Magdalane**	**Boyle**
11-2 LIST	31-4 LIST	23-5 LIST
(22 Filter)	(22 Filter)	(22 Filter)
33-6 ROPE	53-8 ROPE	45-9 ROPE
11-2/(22)/33-6	53-8/(22)/75-3	23-5/(22)/45-9
Timeline: birth thru age 11	Ages 12 thru 42	Ages 43 thru 65

Notice the IR Set of *Susan*? Its 11-2/(22-4)/33-6 resonates perfectly with her 11-2/(22-4)/33-6 Umbrella creating stacking for the first eleven years of her life. This explains her desire to sing and express herself musically but lacking 8 or 9 energy prevents any public attention.

Her middle name, *Magdalane*, generates an 8/(22)/3 IR Set (in a simple format). Here we see her connection and interaction with less powerful energies than her first eleven years but still focused on her engagement (8) with singing (3) from ages 12 through 42.

Her surname of *Boyle* (age 43 to 65) generates a 5/(22)/9 ROPE. Bingo! This 9 ROPE resonates with her 9 Crown Pinnacle LIST and 9 Crown Challenge ROPE, creating stacking and cementing her public persona and fame in the latter phase of her life.

Richard Andrew King

Susan Boyle's fame took off like a rocket on 11 April 2009 with the airing of her performance on *Britain's Got Talent*. This was during her NTL of *Boyle* and its 5/(22)/9 energy field. It was also ten days after she turned 48, three years before her Crown PC Couplet with its 9 LIST Pinnacle and 9 Crown Challenge ROPE became active, further strengthening her global presence and fame.

On that most fortuitous day – 11 April 2009, Boyle was transiting the "O" Letter Timeline from age 45 through 50. Its IR Set was a 6/(22)/1.

Two important factors to note in Boyle's chart are her dual Umbrella Filters of a 22 Lifepath and 11 Expression. Every LIST number in her Life Matrix filtered through her 11 Expression master number, and every letter and name filtered through her 22 Lifepath. These cannot be ignored for the part they played in her destiny.

The other major factor are the 8s and 9s. No matter how talented someone is, unless the 9 is present there will be no mass public exposure; hence, no fame. Without any 8s, there will be no energy of engagement with others in a social paradigm. For Susan Boyle, the energies of her destiny all came together to vault her and her talent into fame and fortune.

What if Susan Boyle had been able to see her future via her numbers when she was a young girl? By her own admission during her *Britain's Got Talent* episode, she wanted to be a professional singer at a high level. Would she have been spared any concerns or worries in her early and mid-life as to her desires if she had known what her future held for her? She does have a 3 Soul and 3 Material Nature which, along with her 33 PE, confirm her singing ambitions. At any rate, it makes no difference in the long run. Karma will always lead us down the road of destiny. Fortunately for Susan Boyle, her deepest desires were fulfilled as she and her famous vocal talent graced the world.

Interestingly, the song Boyle sang during *Britain's Got Talent* was "I Dreamed a Dream," the last line of which is, " Now life has killed the dream I dreamed." Thankfully, for Susan Boyle her life's dream was realized in the latter phase of her life.

The saga of Tiger Woods was covered in *Chapter 2 – The Numerology of Betrayal*. Let's assess the numeric changes and shifts in his life via both his Life Matrix and Name Matrix.

CHANGES & SHIFTS: SIMPLE FORMAT
ELDRICK TONT WOODS; DOB: 30 December 1975 – 1 Lifepath
Voids Notated: 7 and 8

Crown Pinnacle
7v

Grand Pinnacle
4

1st Pinnacle	2nd Pinnacle
6	7v

1st Epoch – Day: 30	2nd Epoch – Month: 12	3rd Epoch – Year: 1975
3	3	4

1st Challenge	2nd Challenge
9	1

Grand Challenge
1 & 8v

Crown Challenge
1 & 8v

What jumps out is the early life of ease and notoriety with the 3s in both his 1st and 2nd Epochs and the 9 in his 1st Challenge. Also of note are the 7v and 8v in his later life. The three 1s in his 2nd, 3rd and 4th Challenges reveal issues with his ego and identity. Pretty telling already.

Richard Andrew King

CHANGES & SHIFTS: SPECIFIC FORMAT - A
ELDRICK TONT WOODS; DOB: 30 December 1975 – 1 Lifepath
Voids: 7 and 8

Crown Pinnacle
52

Grand Pinnacle
76

1st Pinnacle	2nd Pinnacle
42	34

1st Epoch – Day: 30	2nd Epoch – Month: 12	3rd Epoch – Year: 1975
30	12	22

1st Challenge	2nd Challenge
18	19

Grand Challenge
19 & 8v

Crown Challenge
19 & 8v

The 18 in his 1st Challenge contains a 7 Subcap. Both the 7 and 8 are void in his chart. This is problematic. Also, the 19, which represents individual power, contains an 8v Subcap which stacks with his single cipher 8 void. This clearly reveals that his identity and power (19) will unravel from his 2nd Challenge until the end of his life. Combine this with his 7v 2nd Pinnacle and 7v Crown Pinnacle and the horizon for Woods would never be like his early superstar life. Quite the contrary.

The King's Book of Numerology, Volume 12 – Advanced Principles

CHANGES & SHIFTS: SPECIFIC FORMAT - B
ELDRICK TONT WOODS; DOB: 30 December 1975 – 1 Lifepath
Voids Notated: 7 and 8

Crown Pinnacle
52-7v

Grand Pinnacle
76-4

1st Pinnacle	2nd Pinnacle
42-6	34-7v

1st Epoch – Day: 30	2nd Epoch – Month: 12	3rd Epoch – Year: 1975
30-3	12-3	22-4

1st Challenge	2nd Challenge
18-9	19-1

Grand Challenge
19-1 & 8v

Crown Challenge
19-1 & 8v

Richard Andrew King

CHANGES & SHIFTS: SIMPLE IR SET FORMAT – 9 EXPRESSION
ELDRICK TONT WOODS; DOB: 30 December 1975 – 1 Lifepath
Voids Notated: 7 and 8

Crown Pinnacle
7v/(9)/16-7v

Grand Pinnacle
4/(9)/4

1st Pinnacle	2nd Pinnacle
6/(9)/15-6	7v/(9)/16-7v

1st Epoch – Day: 30	2nd Epoch – Month: 12	3rd Epoch – Year: 1975
3/(9)/3	3/(9)/3	4/(9)/4

1st Challenge	2nd Challenge
9/(9)/9	1/(9)/1

Grand Challenge
1/(9)/1 & 8v/(9)/8v

Crown Challenge
1/(9)/1 & 8v/(9)/8v

The destiny of Tiger Woods, as far as his Life Matrix is concerned, clearly shows his fame and success during his 1st E-P-C Triad, the most dominant energy field being his 9/(9)/9 1st Challenge. No IR Set is more powerful, universal and public than the 9/(9)/9. The only problem is that after his 1st PC Couplet runs it course (ending at age 35), his Cinderella life ends. The 9/(9)/9 is gone, not to return. What remains is a much different life, sadly different.

The King's Book of Numerology, Volume 12 – Advanced Principles

At age 36, Woods 2nd Pinnacle 7v/(9)/16-7v kicked in, accompanied by a 1/(9)/1 Challenge. This time period, active through age 44, was during his great Humpty Dumpty fall from grace when his global, illusory, wholesome, family man image was shattered, and the world of golf went wanting in the disgraced wake of its #1 fallen star.

The 1/(9)/1 IR Set indicates a struggle with one's image, ego, self and personal power and remains active for the rest of his life. The 7v/(9)/16-7v reemerges at age 52 when it, too, will be active until the end of his life.

Woods' Name and Letter Timelines compounded his troubles.

NAME TIMELINE: ELDRICK TONT WOODS		
Eldrick	**Tont**	**Woods**
35-8 LIST	15-6 LIST	22-4 LIST
(1 Filter)	(1 Filter)	(1 Filter)
36-9 ROPE	16-7v ROPE	23-5 ROPE
35-8v/(1)/36-9	15-6/(1)/16-7v	22-4/(1)/23-5
Timeline: birth thru age 35	Ages 36 thru 50	Ages 51 thru 72

Woods' Name Timeline of *Eldrick* corroborated his 1st E-P-C Triad energy. Likewise, his Name Timeline of *Tont* with its 15-6/(1)/16-7v energy corroborated his fall. The timing between his 2nd PC Couplet of 7v/(9)/16-7v and his 2nd NTL of *Tont* was eerily perfect, creating a double dose of 16-7v energy in the ROPE position and a 16-7v tristack with the 7v LIST 2nd Pinnacle.

To make matters worse, the Letter Timeline "O" in *Tont* generated a 15-6/(1)/16-7v IR Set from age 38 through 43! This created internal stacking or stacking within stacking – a 15-6/(1)/16-7v Letter Timeline housed within a 15-6/(1)/16-7v Name Timeline. All this lends credence to the saying, "The bigger they are, the harder they fall." For Tiger Woods his life, at one time, couldn't have been bigger; his ultimate fall from grace any harder.

Richard Andrew King

Let's do one more full celebrity example illustrating the changes and shifts in one's life.

CHANGES & SHIFTS: SIMPLE FORMAT
DOB: 29 January 1954 – 4 Lifepath (22)
Voids: 2 and 4

Crown Pinnacle
3

Grand Pinnacle
5

1st Pinnacle	2nd Pinnacle
3	2v

1st Epoch – Day: 29	2nd Epoch – Month: 1	3rd Epoch – Year: 1954
2v	1	1

1st Challenge	2nd Challenge
1	9

Grand Challenge
1 & 8

Crown Challenge
1 & 8

There's not much change in this chart; certainly nothing dramatic. The only major shift is from the 2v 1st Epoch to the 1 2nd Epoch. However, the 2 1st Epoch shares time with the 1 1st Challenge. This 2v-1 duo existed from birth through age 41, so there was a familiarity with both the 2 and 1 but never an unfamiliar change. Plus, the 1 life linkage speaks to numeric constancy of the destiny, not diversity.

Here's a slightly expanded look. Not much more to comment on.

CHANGES & SHIFTS: SPECIFIC FORMAT – A
DOB: 29 January 1954 – 4 Lifepath (22)
Voids: 2 and 4

Crown Pinnacle
48

Grand Pinnacle
50

1st Pinnacle	2nd Pinnacle
30	20

1st Epoch – Day: 29	2nd Epoch – Month: 1	3rd Epoch – Year: 1954
29	1	19

1st Challenge	2nd Challenge
28	18

Grand Challenge
10 & 17

Crown Challenge
10 & 17

Richard Andrew King

CHANGES & SHIFTS: SPECIFIC FORMAT – B

DOB: 29 January 1954 – 4 Lifepath (22)

Voids: 2 and 4

Crown Pinnacle
48-3

Grand Pinnacle
50-5

1st Pinnacle	2nd Pinnacle
30-3	20-2v

1st Epoch – Day: 29	2nd Epoch – Month: 1	3rd Epoch – Year: 1954
29-11-2v	1	19-1

1st Challenge	2nd Challenge
28-1	18-9

Grand Challenge
10-1 & 17-8

Crown Challenge
10-1 & 17-8

Now we're getting somewhere with the IR Sets and the inclusion of the 7 Expression. To avoid confusion, the IR Sets have been kept simple.

CHANGES & SHIFTS: IR SET FORMAT – 7 EXPRESSION
DOB: 29 January 1954 – 22-4 Lifepath; 11-2 PE
Voids Notated: 2 and 4

Crown Pinnacle
3/(7)/55-1

Grand Pinnacle
5/(7)/66-3

1st Pinnacle	2nd Pinnacle
3/(7)/1	2v/(7)/9

1st Epoch – Day: 29	2nd Epoch – Month: 1	3rd Epoch – Year: 1954
11-2v/(7)/9	1/(7)/8	1/(7)/8

1st Challenge	2nd Challenge
1/(7)/44v-8	9/(7)/16-7

Grand Challenge
1/(7)/8 & 8/(7)/33-6

Crown Challenge
1/(7)/8 & 8/(7)/33-6

So who is this person with life linkage of the 1/(7)/8 IR Set, a 3/(7)/55-1 Crown Pinnacle IR Set, 5/(7)/66-3 Grand Pinnacle and 8/(7)/33-6 Grand and Crown Challenges? There's massive lifetime entrepreneurial energy in this chart via the 1/(7)/8 energy, as well as strong energies of

Richard Andrew King

communication via the 33 and 66 masters? This destiny is that of Oprah Gail Winfrey, born on 29 January 1954.

The most powerful energy in Winfrey's Life Matrix is the 1/(7)/8 life linkage, a LIST energy of leadership, action, independence and genesis (1) playing itself out in a ROPE of business, commerce, social integration and engagement (8). Without a break in this energy field, Oprah's destiny allowed her to keep building her business acumen into a billion dollar empire. However, her Name Timeline housed a major shift from a life of constant television exposure to one of, well, "Where's Oprah?"

NAME TIMELINE: OPRAH GAIL WINFREY		
Oprah	**Gail**	**Winfrey**
31-4 LIST	20-2 LIST	46-1 LIST
(22 Filter)	(22 Filter)	(22 Filter)
44-8 ROPE	33-6 ROPE	77-5 ROPE
4/(22-4)/8	2/(22-4)/6	1/(22-4)/5
Timeline: birth thru age 31	Ages 32 thru 51	Ages 52 thru 97

As the chart reveals, Winfrey's NTL of *Oprah* from birth through age 31 was solid earth in its elemental structure. This 4/(22-4)/8 energy pattern established a foundation for her life.

At age 32 she moved into her *Gail* NTL for twenty years. Its 2/(22-4)/6 IR Set is relationship oriented with water, emotion and female energy (2) serving as the LIST, with water, emotion, nurturing and love (6) being the ROPE. This was perfect for her talk show and media endeavors.

However, beginning at age 52 her NTL of *Winfrey* generated a 46 year period of action and independence (1) focused on change, detachment, freedom (5). Its 1 LIST fire element resonates with the 5 ROPE fire element – very different from the elemental structure of her life up through age 51. This is the exact period she left major network television and went on her own, literally, creating the Oprah Winfrey Network (OWN). This change/shift in her life was enormous and, frankly, defined the latter years of her destiny as being more obscure and less commercially visible.

LIFE NOTES: SHIFTS & CHANGES

This chapter has laid the ground work for assessing the changes and shifts in one's destiny, changes and shifts that may create confusion in one's mind as to, "What happened?" We may ask, "How could life be one way and suddenly change to another way?" "Why could things be so good and then so bad?" Or, "Why were things so bad and now they're great?" Or, "Why doesn't my life ever change?" Or, "Why does my life keep changing?" The "Whys" are endless.

As we see from the evidence presented, there is an obvious pattern of destiny to life. The shifts and changes in our lives are quite obvious when we study the science of numbers, of numeric energies, and move beyond the delusion that life is uncertain and unknowable. This is one of the great benefits of numerology – being able to forecast changes and shifts before they arrive, thus allowing us to manage our lives better and never be blindsided and thrown into a helter-skelter frenzy of imbalance, confusion and uncertainty.

When assessing changes and shifts in the destiny, here are twelve questions to keep in mind to get the ball rolling:

1. Are there changes/shifts of direct numeric opposites: the 1-2, 4-5 or 7-8 pairings?
2. Are there major elemental shifts: fire to water, air to earth, water to air, fire to earth, etc.?
3. Is there an absence or presence of voids, and if so, what are their locations?
4. Are there differences between the Life Matrix, Name and Letter Timeline Matrices?
5. Do numbers move from a positive to a negative vibration or negative to positive?
6. Is the early life different from the latter life? If so, why? What numbers were involved?
7. Is there stacking anywhere in the chart?
8. Is there life linkage or partial linkage in the chart?
9. How do changes/shifts in the destiny blend or not blend with Basic Matrix components?
10. Is there a saturation or dominance of either positive or negative numbers in the Matrices?
11. Is there a cluster of one or two numbers in the Matrices?
12. What is the general numeric flow of the Life Matrix from beginning to end?

Richard Andrew King

Every life, every destiny, has changes; some are more drastic than others. Answering the questions above gives us a base line from which to work and draw reasonable conclusions as to the blueprint of destiny and its flow, whether smooth or rough or both. We should start the process with our own charts first, as normal, and then proceed to other destinies and their life designs.

CHAPTER 9

VOIDS, VACUUMS & KARMIC SCALES

Voids have been a major focus of the King's Book of Numerology™ series, and for good reason. As we have been studying, voids can be highly problematic in a chart. Yet, they have their purpose in the grand scheme of things.

Like all numbers, voids have two sides – one positive, one negative. How voids are perceived is a matter of personal perspective and attitude. Is the glass half empty or is it half full? Not to be forgotten is the old adage: "Sometimes, the greatest blessings are unanswered prayers." What we cannot overlook, however, is that if there is a void or voids in a chart there is a reason for it or them to be there. Our lives are not random happenings. Our destinies are no accident. They are perfectly designed to the nth degree. Why they are designed the way they are is known only to God.

VOIDS AS VACUUMS

One way to look at voids is to consider them as a vacuum or black hole of sorts drawing, even sucking, the missing numeric energy they represent into them, much like a black hole sucks everything into it.

In this sense, voids can create obsessions and addictions, forcing the individual to learn or seek the very aspects or knowledge attributed to their voids. As an example of this phenomenon, take a look at the Basic Matrices of three of the greatest scientists of all time: Isaac Newton, Nikola Tesla and Albert Einstein.

Richard Andrew King

ISAAC NEWTON: Born 4 January 1643							
BASIC MATRIX							
LP	Exp	PE	Soul	MS	Nature	MN	Voids
1	7	8	4	5	3	4	4-7-8

NIKOLA TESLA: Born 10 July 1856							
BASIC MATRIX							
LP	Exp	PE	Soul	MS	Nature	MN	Voids
1	2	3	4	5	7	8	4-7-8

ALBERT EINSTEIN: Born 14 March 1879							
BASIC MATRIX							
LP	Exp	PE	Soul	MS	Nature	MN	Voids
6	9	6	7	4	2	8	4-6-7-8

What do you see in these three charts? Look at their voids. Every one of these great minds had the same 4-7-8 Voided Triad in their Basic Matrix! Einstein also had a 6 void. This is remarkable – three of the most prodigious scientists of all times with the same 4-7-8 voids. Amazing.

What does this triune combination of voids in the charts of these extraordinary men tell us? Answer: a great deal. The 4 and 7 together equate to *structural analysis*. The 8 involves *integration*, *connection*, *interaction* and *engagement*. All three of these famous scientists were deeply *engaged* in the pursuit of the *structural analysis* of the universe for their entire lives. Is it by accident that they each had a 4-7-8 Voided Triad in their charts? Answer: No.

Here's another interesting point: the 4-7-8 voids are present in their Basic Matrices. Newton had a 7 Expression, an 8 PE, 4 Soul and 4 Material Nature. Tesla had a 4 Soul, 7 Nature and 8 Material Nature. Einstein had a 7 Soul, 4 Material Soul, 8 Material Nature, 6 Lifepath and 6 PE.

Upon seeing such interconnectivity of these three most auspicious intellects, one has to ponder the specific relationship between intelligence and the 4-7-8 Voided Triad, especially when the voids are included in the Basic Matrix. The voids by themselves don't necessarily create intelligence, but when they appear in the Basic Matrix one has to stop and ponder as to why? Nothing is coincidental in the universe. All is by design. Therefore, when three historically vaunted icons of the scientific community all have the same 4-7-8 Voided Triad appearing in their Basic Matrices, the question arises, "Why?"

Another observation: Newton had a 4 Soul; Tesla also had a 4 Soul; Einstein had a 4 Material Soul. In other words, they each possessed a dominant desire for order, organization, structure, detail, foundation, design. Too, they each had a 7 in their Basic Matrix. It's a given that individuals with some combination of 4 and 7 in their name are involved with *structural analysis* of some sort to some degree. Scientists, engineers, programmers, architects, accountants, mechanics, builders, even numerologists, (yes, numerologists) are excellent candidates for having the 4-7 in their charts. The 4 focuses on structure and order; the 7 on analysis, study and examination.

Newton, Tesla and Einstein also had the 8 energy in their charts. The 8 has critical importance because it connects the dots of all the working parts. Without 8 energy there would be no ability to integrate the order of the 4 and the analysis of the 7. The 8 ties them all together and relates one to the other.

So what is the purpose of the 4-7-8 being voided? Answer: to generate an obsession or addiction in order to solve the problems related to order, analysis and integration. It's fair to say that Newton, Tesla and Einstein were addicted and obsessed with finding answers to physics, life and creation. Why else would they have devoted their entire lives to such a pursuit? Each of them was drawn to seeking and finding answers, just as iron is attracted to magnets.

So here's a valid question? What is the difference between voids which have a Basic Matrix connection compared to voids which have no Basic Matrix connection? Are there other factors to consider? Let's look at the Basic Matrix of naturalist, geologist and biologist Charles Darwin.

Richard Andrew King

Like Newton, Tesla and Einstein, Charles Darwin has a 7 void. However, he has no 7s in his Basic Matrix. Rather, it houses two 2s, two 5s, two 6s and one 9.

CHARLES ROBERT DARWIN: 12 February 1809							
BASIC MATRIX							
LP	Exp	PE	Soul	MS	Nature	MN	Void
5	6	2	9	5	6	2	7

Darwin's work is renowned, especially regarding his contributions to the science of evolution, but a 7 void by itself would not generate the level of research associated with Darwin and his work. So why was he driven to the scientific exploration of evolution?

Here's the answer. Although his Basic Matrix is devoid of 7 energy, his Life Matrix is not. Darwin's 1st Challenge is a 1/(6)/7v. His 2nd Challenge contains a 7v/(6)/4 IR Set, and his 3rd Pinnacle is also a 7v/(6)/4. Thus, Darwin had 7v linkage in one form or another up to age 50 in his Life Matrix, thus causing him to seek answers to evolution – the subject for which he is most famous.

Too, when any timeline associated with a 1 LIST energy filtered through his 6 Expression serving as the Filter, a 7v ROPE would be generated. This includes his Annual Cycle Patterns, Decade Timelines, Monthly Timelines, Cycle of 9s, and so forth. When such timelines became active, they would create stacking up to age 50 because of the aforementioned Life Matrix IR Sets.

Because of his 5 Lifepath, the letters "B" and "T" in *Robert* would create a 2/(5)/7v energy during each of their two year reigns. His three names, however, would not. *Charles* and *Darwin* both generate a 3/(5)/8 IR Set; *Robert* generates a 6/(5)/2 IR Set.

This is quite spooky, but do you know who was also born on the same day Charles Darwin was born, 12 February 1809; whose Basic Matrix is exactly like that of Darwin and who also has a 7 void? Answer: the 16th President of the United States, Abraham Lincoln!

ABRAHAM LINCOLN: 12 February 1809							
BASIC MATRIX							
LP	Exp	PE	Soul	MS	Nature	MN	Void
5	6	2	9	5	6	2	7

Looks familiar, doesn't it? If the previous paragraph didn't announce the natal relationship between Darwin and Lincoln, you may have thought a mistake was made. Yet, there is no mistake. These two esteemed historic icons were, indeed, born on the same day (12 February 1809) and their Basic Matrices are identical. Both their Umbrellas house a 5 Lifepath, 6 Expression, 2 PE. Both Soul numbers are a 9; Material Souls are a 5; Natures are a 6 and Material Natures are a 2!

Being born on the same day with the same 6 Expression, their Life Matrices would also be identical! Lincoln's 1st Challenge, like Darwin's, is a 1/(6)/7v. His 2nd Challenge is a 7v/(6)/4 and his 3rd Pinnacle is also a 7v/(6)/4. Both have a 3/(6)/9 Crown Pinnacle, 9/(6)/6 Crown Epoch and a 6/(6)/3 Crown Challenge. All the other LM components are identical.

Their Name Timelines are different, however. *Abraham* is an 8, which generates an 8/(5)/4 IR Set. This was active from birth through age 26. *Lincoln* is a 7, generating a 7v/(5)3 NTL IR Set for 34 years, which would have been active from age 27 through age 60. It was during his *Lincoln* Name Timeline when his political career and the Civil War were most active. Lincoln died at age 56.

As with Darwin, Lincoln's destiny forced him to be a thinker, introspective, reflective and studious. Their 7 voids drove them deeply into issues of great concern to both of them, each in a different way, obviously. And, of course, both men will remain great historic icons of civilization.

Richard Andrew King

The destiny of General George Patton Jr., born George Smith Patton, Jr., on 11 November 1885, offers an interesting study of the 3 void – the energy of communication, words, self-expression, ego, narcissism.

GEORGE SMITH PATTON JR.: 11 November 1885								
BASIC MATRIX								
LP	Exp	PE	Soul	MS	Nature	MN	Void
8	6	5	5	4	1	9	3

Featured in *The King's Book of Numerology, Volume 10 – Historic Icons* and *Destinies of the Rich & Famous – The Secret Numbers of Extraordinary Lives*, Patton's words could inspire his troops to do the impossible. Yet, his words often got him in trouble, and at one point in World War II almost cost him his career for verbally dressing down and slapping a soldier named Charles Kuhl, whom Patton felt was acting cowardly while other brave men were courageously fighting, even dying in battle.

Although George Patton has no 3s in his Basic Matrix, both his 2nd Pinnacle and 4th Pinnacle house a LIST 33-6 IR Set. When ciphered showing the void, the IR Set becomes a 33v-6/(6)/12-3v or, more exactly, a 3v3v/(6)/12-3v (both cipherings are acceptable). Patton loved to read and he loved words, but his blue-flamed flamboyant rhetoric, although inspiring, could sometimes be quite problematic. Having a 3v3v/(6)/12-3v Crown Pinnacle with its energies raining down from the highest part of his chart served as a two-edged sword for "Old Blood and Guts," as he was known.

Following and reprinted from KBN10 and *Destinies of the Rich & Famous* (DRF) is the incident involving Charles Kuhl.

FIERY WORDS, INSPIRATIONAL SPEECHES & COLORFUL LANGUAGE

Patton was no stranger to language that both inspired and inflamed, often drawing praise, criticism and censure. What numbers in his chart reflect this aspect of his life and destiny?

The basic number of communication is the 3. Patton's 2nd Pinnacle and 4th (Crown) Pinnacle are a 33-6/3. This is a positive energy of supportive and personal communication. The problem is that in Patton's chart the 3 is void. Therefore, the 33-6/3 could be written as 3v3v-6/3v to reflect the problematic issues with communication. Still, the energy is there in his chart, so it served Patton well when energizing and inspiring his troops, but contrarily was active in creating harsh, critical, blue-flamed speech which caused him problems throughout his career.

The most famous incident involving the negative expression of Patton's 3 void was the slapping and berating incident of Charles Herman Kuhl, born on 6 November 1915 [Wikipedia], a soldier whom Patton felt was playing ill in order to avoid fighting when other soldiers were bravely placing their lives on the line in combat. Although Kuhl was subsequently diagnosed with malaria after the fact, Patton became irate in the moment, called the soldier a coward, slapped and kicked him. This created an uproar. Patton was forced to apologize to the soldier publicly and was temporarily relieved of his command.

Since this slapping incident was such a scurrilous scar on Patton's career, and since there are no coincidences in the universe, there had to be some numeric connection to it all involving the number 3, and indeed there was. The following bullet-point list highlights the "3 Connections" between Patton, Kuhl and the day of the incident.

Patton & Kuhl – Relationship with the number 3

- The name *Charles* is a 3
- Patton had a 3 void in his chart
- *Old Blood and Guts* is a 57-3 energy
- Patton was 57 years old at the time [57 is a 3 in reduction]
- Patton was a 3 star Lieutenant General at the time of the incident

Richard Andrew King

- The PE of Charles Herman Kuhl's Basic Matrix is a 3
- The Lifepath of Charles Kuhl [6 November 1915] is a 33-6
- The Incident occurred on a 3 calendar day [3 August 1943]
- The incident happened in Patton's 4th Pinnacle: 3v3v-6/3v
- Newspaper columnist Drew Pearson related the story publicly on his radio program on 21 November 1943, another 3 calendar day
- The name *Drew Pearson* is a 57-3—same as *Old Blood and Guts*

Skeptics may argue the amalgam of 3 instances in the Patton striking incident of Charles Kuhl is merely coincidental. This work takes the viewpoint that nothing is coincidental in this universe and that everything is constructed perfectly by powers beyond our understanding and that such construction is based in numbers and the energies they represent.

The facts in the Patton case are the facts. This concept of *stacking* has been shown already in the lives of both Amelia Earhart's disappearance and Elvis Presley's death. The purpose of relating these *stacking* examples is to show, once again, the relationship between life's events and numbers, which are nothing more than labels for energy fields. Life is not random, and the whole purpose of this book is to present the evidence and let you, the reader, decide for yourself, keeping in mind observations made by two of the greatest scientists in history.

As Pythagoras said,

> *Numbers rule the universe; everything is arranged according to number and mathematical shape.*

And as Newton stated,

> *God created everything by number, weight and measure. It is the perfection of God's works that they are all done with the greatest simplicity. He is the God of order and not of confusion.*

And so it is with life and its events, whether they are slapping incidents, disappearances, deaths or whatever they may be. Numbers tell the tale. (finis)

The King's Book of Numerology, Volume 12 – Advanced Principles

Oprah Winfrey offers another excellent example of how voids can create positive addictions and obsessions, albeit subconscious. Known as the "Queen of Media," Oprah Gail Winfrey was born on 29 January 1954. She is also featured in KBN10 and DRF.

OPRAH GAIL WINFREY: 29 January 1954							
BASIC MATRIX							
LP	Exp	PE	Soul	MS	Nature	MN	Void
4	7	2	2	6	5	9	2 & 4

What is obvious with Winfrey's Basic Matrix is that her 2 & 4 voids appear in her PE and Soul as a 2 energy and in her Lifepath as a 4 energy. Additionally, her Lifepath houses a 22 master root. Therefore, Oprah's 2 and 4 voids were the substance of her life's script (22-4 LP), the role she was to give on the great life stage (2 PE) and as her primary need, want, desire and motivation (2 Soul).

Including the void in the ciphering, her Lifepath would be 2v2v-4v; her PE an 11-2v, and her Soul would also be an 11-2v. This would certainly create a vacuum for the 2 and 4.

Furthermore, what one word describes the essence of Oprah's career? Answer: *relationships*, especially relationships with females and all things Yin. Her talk show and magazine are based in the 2 energy. For example, how many males have ever been shown as part of the audience of one of her talk shows?

Oprah's 1st Epoch is a 29-11-2v/(7)/9. The 29 is important because it references "power in relationship" more than any other binary. Her 2nd Pinnacle is also a 2v/(7)/9. Her 1st Challenge is a 1/(7)/44-8 or 1/(7)/4v4v-8. These IR Sets reveal the difficulty of Oprah's early life, which she has talked about often.

Even though Oprah's 2 and 4 voided energies were filled through her work, and she has had a longtime partner in Stedman Graham, she never married. This resonates with her 2 and 4 void. The 2 governs close personal relationships and the 4 rules the structure of relationships, even confinement. Thus, she shies away from such commitment. Plus, her 7 Expression, 5 Nature, Crown Pinnacle 55-1 ROPE and life linkage of the 1/(7)/8 energy all but guarantee her sense of solitude (7), freedom (5), and independence (1). Frankly, with such numbers anyone would rebel against the thought of being tied down or constricted in any way. Remember, no three numbers together reveal being separate and alone more than the 1-5-7 Disunited Triad. Add a 2 and 4 void to the mix and marriage becomes virtually impossible. Therefore, Oprah's non-marital condition is no mystery. It is in perfect consonance with the science of numbers.

On a personal note, this brings to mind an event in the early history of The King's Numerology[tm] in which I was asked to do brief readings for partygoers, all of whom had at least two of the Social Quatrain 2-4-6-8 missing in their charts. Most had three of the four numbers missing. When querying the hostess upon leaving the party as to what type of party it was, she said a "singles party." Bingo! It makes total sense. The 2 rules relationship; 4 governs the order and structure of relationship; 6 is the love and nurturing in the relationship, and 8 involves the management and integration of the relationship. When 50% or more of the Social Quatrain numbers are voided, the odds of being involved in a serious, committed, confined relationship become challenged. Add the 1-5-7 Disunited Triad of independence, freedom and solitude to the mix and the result is a state of not being in a relationship, at least a structured and consistent one.

There are exceptions to this rule, which we've discussed before. If a person with voids marries a person whose numbers fill those voids, then a successful marriage is possible. In fact, the filling of voids through marriage or partnership is quite common and recommended. Still, if the 1-5-7 energies are dominate in a person's chart, the probability of a conventional marriage is questionable.

The 6 void poses issues of love, romance and family. Individuals with a 6 void will have love issues to some degree. They may hunger for love, seek love, have love conflicts, a plethora of romantic liaisons and assignations, domestic problems and so forth but unless they find a partner to fill their 6 void they will most likely remain unfulfilled and feeling abandoned by love. In many ways a 6 void generates an addiction to love. Individuals may seek it but never find it; want it but never have it; have it but never keep it. For them, the 6 void makes love illusive, unattainable.

In attempting to solve the 6 void love problems, individuals may find themselves in careers and occupations where love from them, not to them, is required, such as the medical and dental fields, education and teaching jobs, caring for others such as the elderly, homeless or physically handicapped and so forth. By generating love, we fulfill love, even in ourselves. Maybe this is the reason as to why people have a 6 void in the first place – to learn to love rather than be loved; to nurture rather than be nurtured; to give rather than to take.

What we can learn from voids is salient. Although we may consider voids problematic in many cases, they also have a positive aspect. The emptiness created by a void or voids generates a magnetism of sorts drawing the energy of the void to the individual so, perhaps, the individual can then radiate the voided energy back into the universe.

What we see in Oprah's chart is similar to the other examples. Her 2 and 4 voided energies became a major focal point of her life, just as the 7v was fundamental to Newton, Tesla, Einstein and Darwin, and the 3v rooted in the destiny of Patton. In their own way, they each tried to fill their void(s) up with the very energy the void represented.

Think of your void or voids if you have them. Are your life script and its actions reflective of the voided energy in some way? Next, assess people you know who have voids. Most people do. How are their voids related to their lives? Do their voids appear in the Basic Matrix? Are their voids occupying a Challenge position in the Life Matrix?

VOIDS – NAME & LETTER TIMELINES

Voids can be found in the Name Timeline but never in the Letter Timeline, which is why they're voided. Voids represent missing letters (and their corresponding numeric values) so it's impossible to have a void in the LTL. If the letter is absent it's inactive. However, it's different in the NTL. A person could have no 4s in their name (no Ds-Ms-Vs), creating a 4v, but still have a 4 Name. For example, the name *Ali* is a 4 with roots of 13 and 22 but it contains a 4v (no Ds-Ms-Vs).

Richard Andrew King

A positive aspect of having a void is that its missing energy cannot create havoc in someone's life. For example, say a person has a 1 Lifepath and a 6 void – no Fs, Os or Xs in the natal name. Since the energy of the 6 is missing, there is no possibility of a 16-7 showing up in a ROPE position in the entire life as far as the Letter Timeline is concerned. If the natal name had an F, O or X, then the 6 would filter through the 1 Lifepath to generate a 7, which may have a 16 root.

Although a person with a 6 void is not in jeopardy of having a 7 in the LTL ROPE position, there may be a 7 ROPE in a Name Timeline position. For example, the name *Mara* is a 6 with roots of 15 and 33. With a 1 Lifepath the name *Mara* would create a 7 NTL ROPE (6 +1 = 7).

Contrastingly, the name *Koy* generates a 6 Name Timeline (roots of 15 and 51) as well as containing a 6 Letter Timeline with the "O". When the Lifepath 1 energy mixes with the name *Koy* as well as the "O," a 16-7 will emerge in both the NTL and LTL ROPE. The timeline for the name *Koy* is 15 years; the timeline for the letter "O" is 6 years. Stacking of the 6/(1)/7 ROPE would occur in the six year period when the "O" is active, which would be year 3 through year 8 of the NTL for *Koy*. Thus, between the names *Mara* and *Koy*, the most problematic is *Koy* because it generates a dual stack 16-7 ROPE energy when a 1 Lifepath is the filter – one 16-7 in the NTL and another in the LTL.

Another scenario would be if a 6 void appeared in the Life Matrix of a person with a 1 Expression. For example, take the birth date of 3 March 2002. The simple Epoch structure forming the Lifepath is a 3-3-4. The 1st Pinnacle would be a 6 void; its IR Set would be a 6v/(1)/7. It would be the same if the day of birth were a 12, 21 or 30 and the month was December.

There are many combinations to consider when analyzing voids in a chart. Where they occur means there will be issues and problems related to them, whether they are located in the Life Matrix, Name Timeline, Letter Timeline, Decade Timeline, Monthly Timeline, Cycles of 9 and so forth. Think of voids as generating a magnetism or a vacuum, drawing energies of the void into the person's environment. Remember, though, voids have both a positive and negative aspect, so they should not generate despair but an opportunity to learn, fulfill our destiny and potentially reconcile our karmas.

VOIDS AS KARMIC SCALES

We've talked extensively about karma in this volume. It is *the* law of this dimension, albeit almost universally ignored. What karma tells us is that there are no victims in this world. What numerology tells us is that our numbers are *Karmic Scales* representing the reconciliation of our actions of past lives.

Numerology is the numeric manifestation of the architectural design of life and destiny. This is why it is a divine science. Individuals who have been a student of The King's Numerology[tm] and applied its knowledge to their own lives deeply understand the truth and accuracy of the science of numbers. This "knowing" allows for the expansion of human consciousness beyond the mundane world of phenomena to the mystical world of Divine Reality.

Factually, all numbers represent karma. Voids, however, seem to be the energies bringing back into balance the negative or untoward actions of previous lives. They force us to pay attention to them or, as we've previously discussed, act as magnets drawing ourselves to them.

Voids do create discomfort in us. We have to pay the piper sometime for past sins, and although paying our debts is uncomfortable, it is necessary to balance the karmic books and return us to a state of wholeness and centeredness.

Therefore, voids can be considered as *Karmic Scales of Justice*. We would be wise to consider them as such, rather than railing against them as some harbingers of turmoil, stress and trouble. If voids occur in our charts, they're there for a divine reason. They are not there by accident, and we err greatly for cursing them. Rather, we should be grateful for them, embrace them, work with them and learn from them because, ultimately, they are meant for our highest and best good.

Furthermore, we can't overlook the possibility that voids represent subjects and tests we must engage and pass if we're to move up the ladder of life. Only God knows exactly why our destinies are designed as they are. We would be well-served to always focus on the positive, strengthen our negatives, and continue to advance because if we do not, who's to say we won't recede into less

Richard Andrew King

than what we are now. Just because we're human in this life is no guarantee we will remain human in a future life. We must, therefore, be diligent, vigilant and wise, ever conscious of our ephemeral state of being and make the most of what we've been given, i.e., a human form and the opportunity it offers for spiritual ascent.

CHAPTER 10

LIFE MATRIX DIAMOND

The Life Matrix Diamond (LMD) is a simple snapshot of destiny from its beginning energy fields to its ending energy fields. The LMD features the 1st and 3rd Epochs and the Crown PC Couplet.

LIFE MATRIX DIAMOND – SCHEMATIC

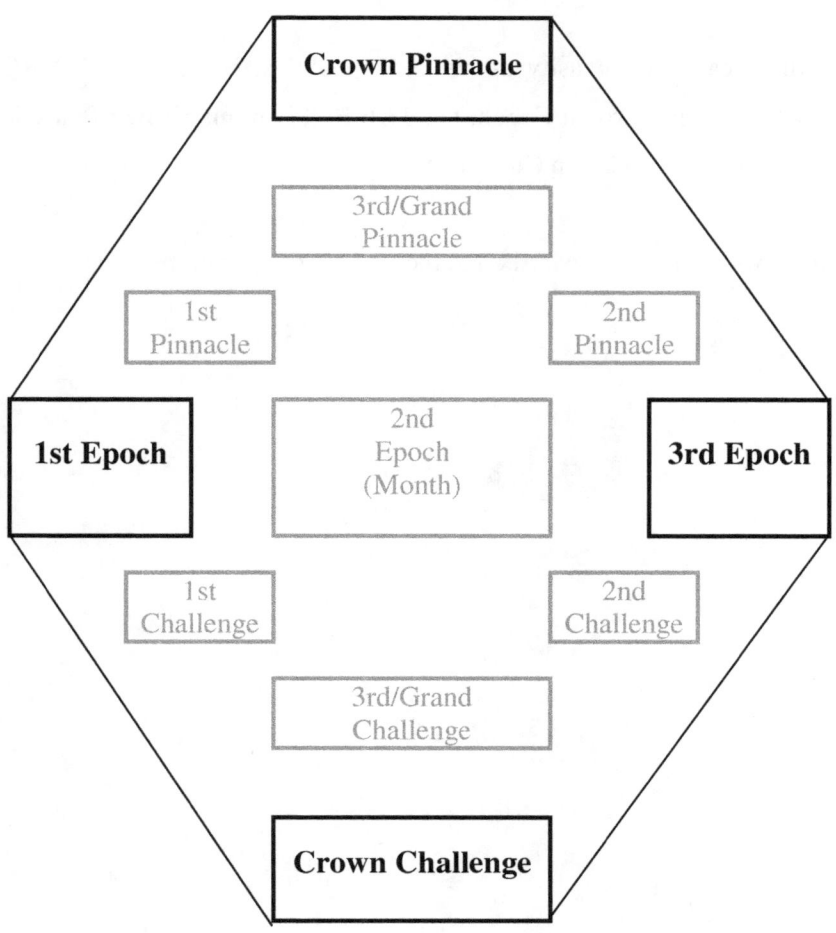

Richard Andrew King

We've discussed Michael Jackson extensively in this volume. Following is a visual depiction of his Life Matrix Diamond in four diagrams: 1. Simple ciphers; 2. Simple ciphers with a little more detail; 3. Simple IR Set; 4. Extended IR Set.

As you look at the first LMD example, review the meanings of the simple numbers and how they change as his life progresses.

In the second LMD diagram, we see more telling clues regarding his life's journey, starting with the 11-2 energy in his 1st Epoch with a final 16-7 Crown Pinnacle, a 23-5 Crown Epoch of change and detachment, and dual Crown Challenges of 3 and 6 – all LIST energies.

The third design of simple IR Sets reveals the ROPES of his Life Matrix Diamond.

The fourth pattern reveals the intensity of his LMD realities. Notice the 55-1 ROPE in the 1st Epoch, the 22-4 ROPE in his Crown Epoch, the 33-6 ROPE in his Crown Pinnacle, and the dual ROPES of 11-2 and 14-5 in his Crown Challenges.

The fifth pattern shows the full Life Matrix and the IR Sets of each component.

Michael Joseph Jackson – DOB: 29 August 1958; 33-6 Lifepath; 8 Exp

LIFE MATRIX DIAMOND – Example #1

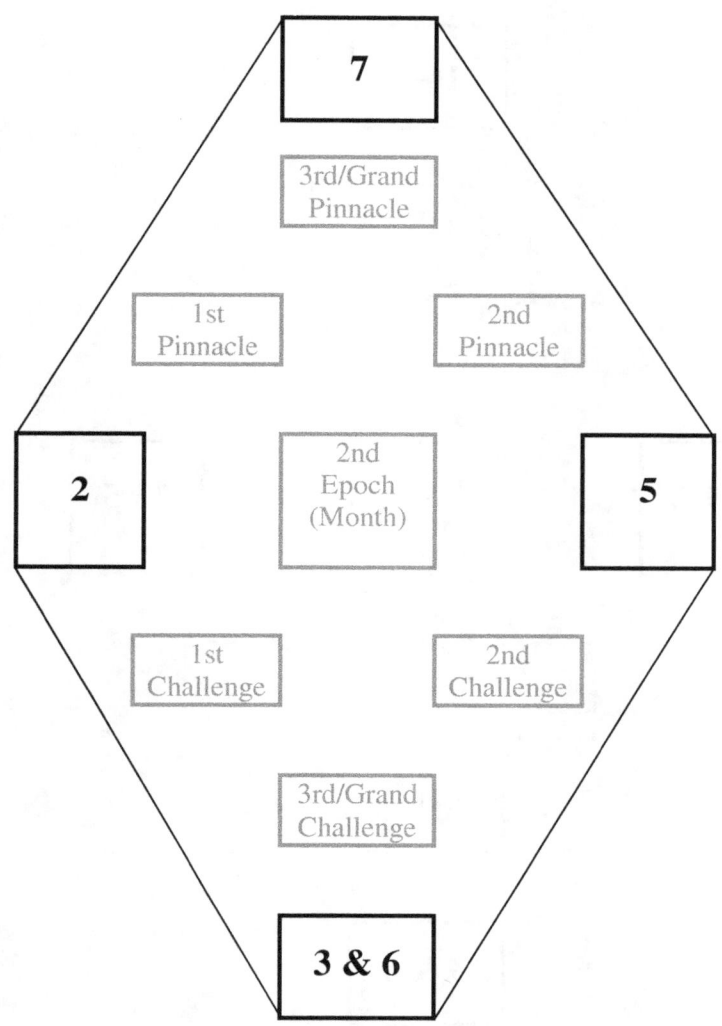

Michael Joseph Jackson – DOB: 29 August 1958; 33-6 Lifepath; 8 Exp

LIFE MATRIX DIAMOND – Example #2

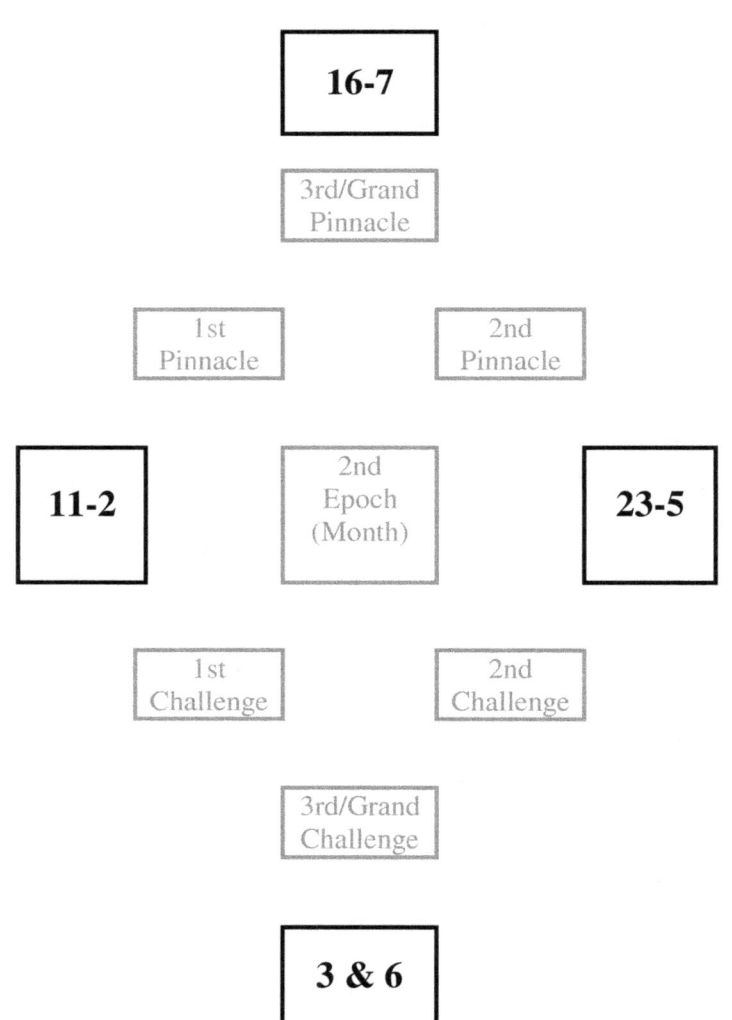

Michael Joseph Jackson – DOB: 29 August 1958; 33-6 Lifepath; 8 Exp

LIFE MATRIX DIAMOND – Example #3: Simple IR Set

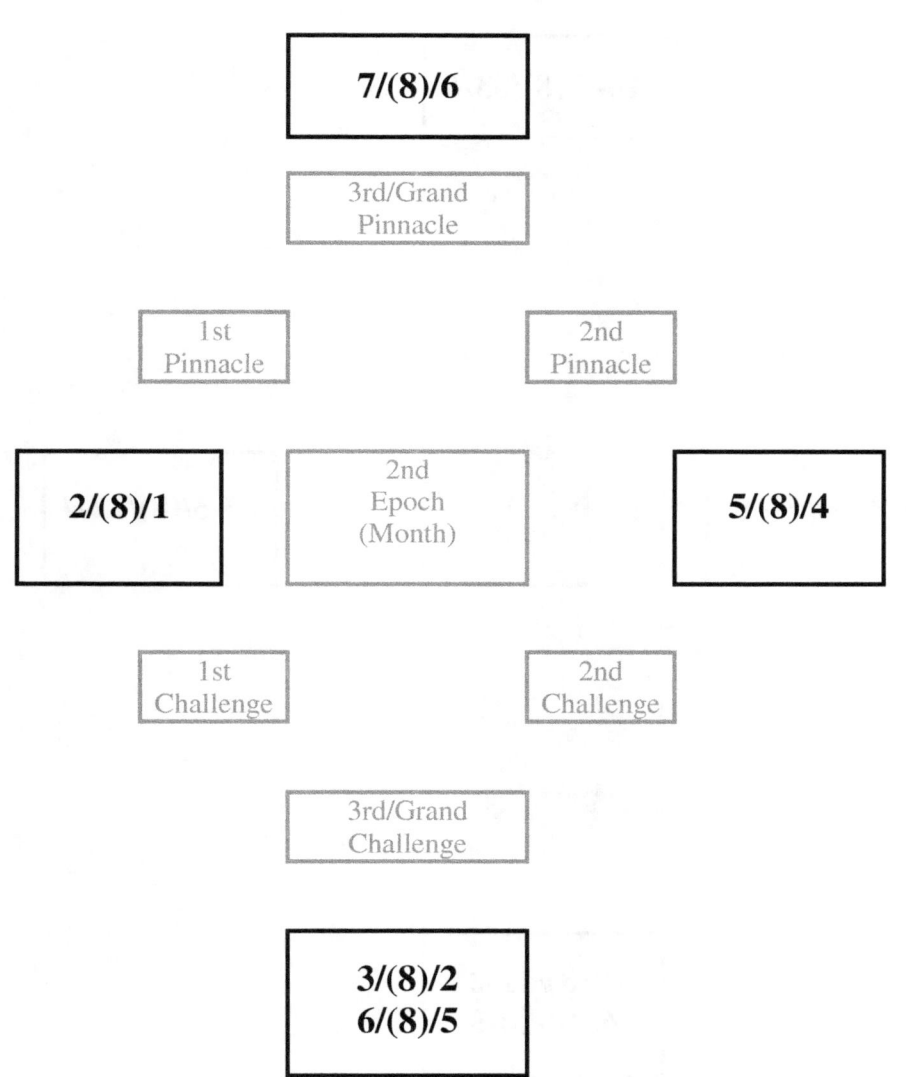

Richard Andrew King

Michael Joseph Jackson – DOB: 29 August 1958; 33-6 Lifepath; 8 Exp

LIFE MATRIX DIAMOND – Example #4: Extended IR Set

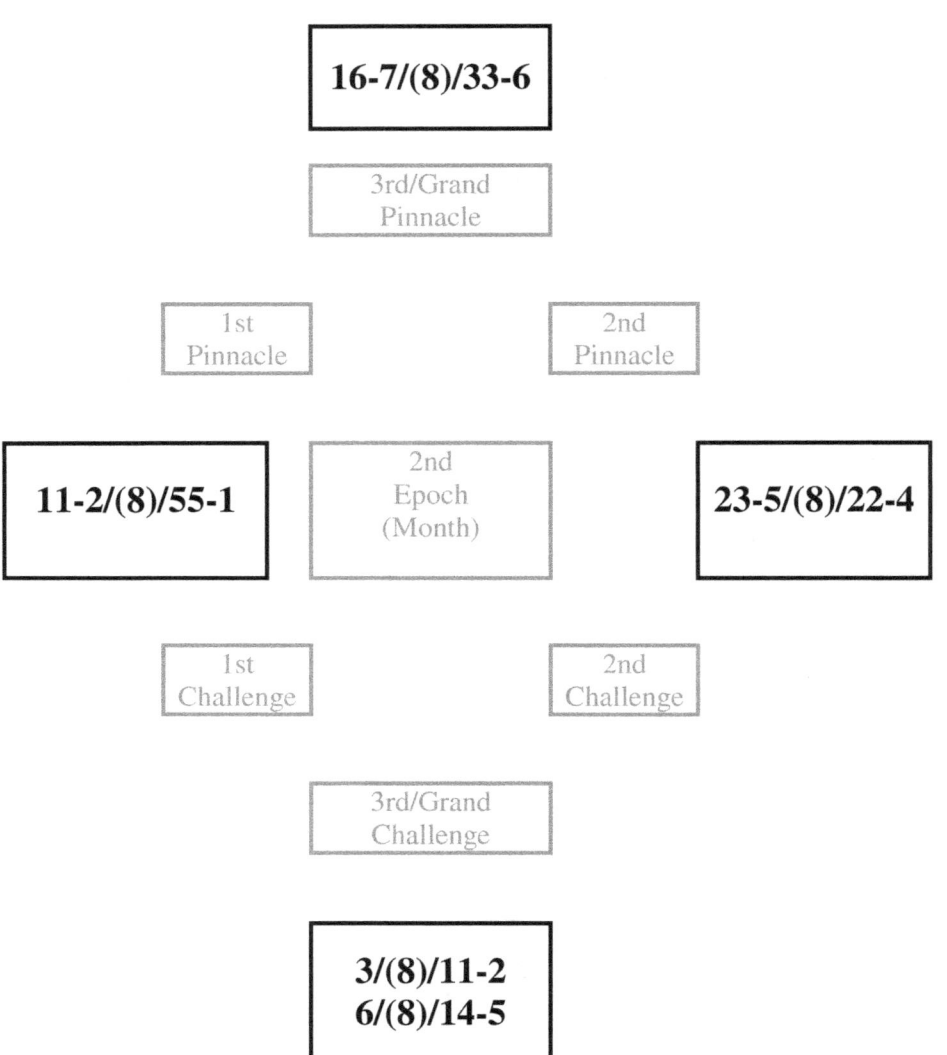

These four LMD charts start with simple energies and fill in Jackson's destiny. This fourth chart reveals the intensity of relationships (11-2) and extreme originality (55-1) of his early life, ultimately culminating with the Great Purifier 16-7 LIST and its 33-6 ROPE in his Crown Pinnacle. His Crown Challenge ROPES reveal continued tension (11-2) and loss (14-5); his Crown Epoch 5 LIST indicates change/freedom with the 22-4 ROPE of power and wealth.

The King's Book of Numerology, Volume 12 – Advanced Principles

Michael Joseph Jackson – DOB: 29 August 1958; 33-6 Lifepath; 8 Exp

LIFE MATRX

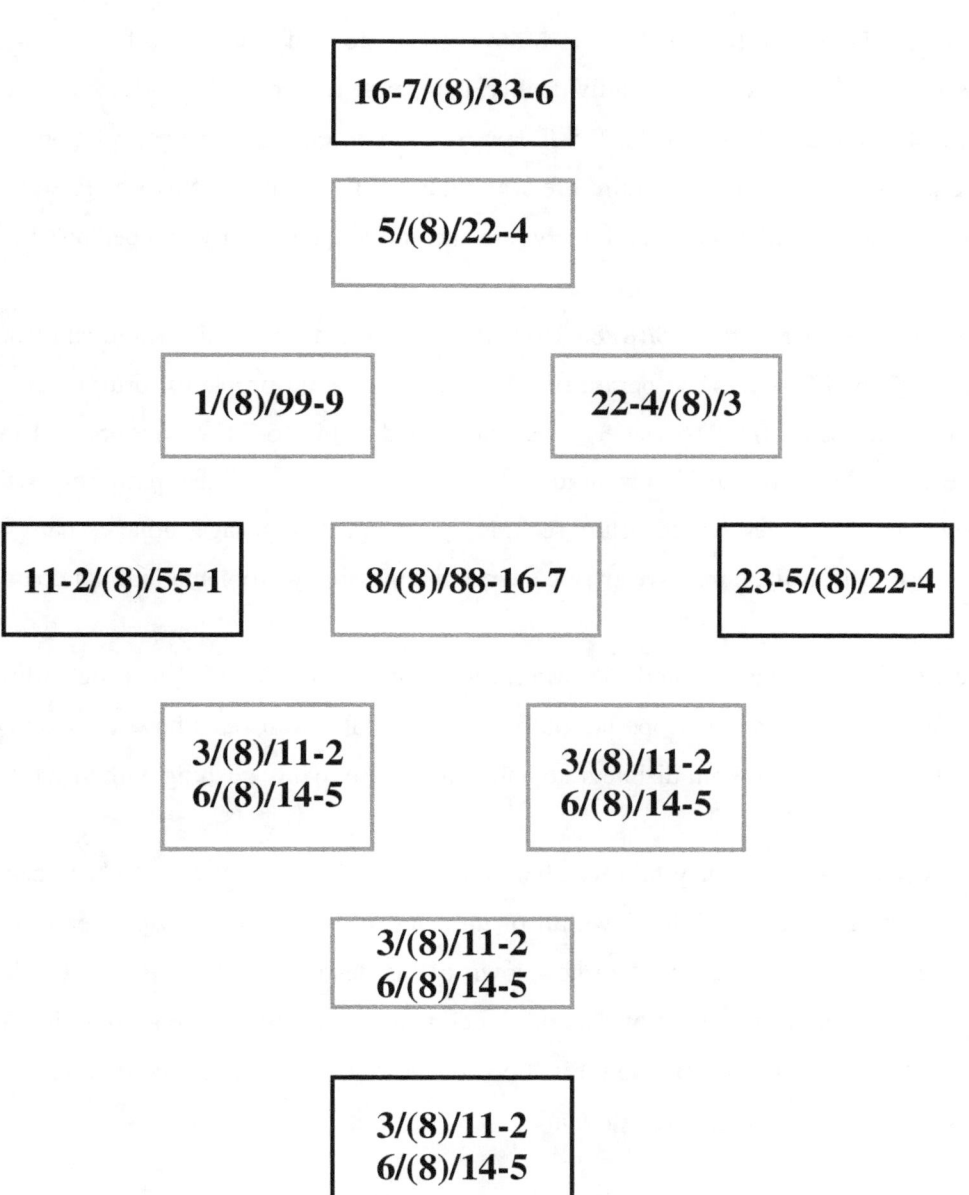

As we've observed, the simple Crown Diamond gives us a general idea of one's destiny but hardly the full picture. As we add the different layers, the richness and fullness of the destiny becomes quite clear.

Beyond the LMD, Michael Jackson's Life Matrix tells a story of massive early fame with his 1st Pinnacle of 1/(8)/99-9. His extreme individuality, independence, creativity and original persona are reflected in his 1st Epoch of 11-2/(8)/55-1. His issues with children, image, relationship, family and detachment are active for his entire life with dual 3/(8)/11-2 and 6/(8)/14-5 IR Sets. Such life linkage dual Challenge IR Sets are extremely rare and add to the intensity of a person's life.

Jackson's middle Epoch with its 8/(8)/88-16-7 IR Set presaged powerful turmoil and trouble from age 28 through 54. This was the period of his child molestation problems, drug usage, fall from grace and death. The 8/(8)/88-16-7 energy was intensified by his 16-7 Crown Pinnacle LIST and its 33-6 ROPE. As we know, the 33-6 is, arguably, the most dangerous of the master binaries because of its potential for excessive pleasure seeking, partying, drug usage, image, narcissism and concupiscence. It is, truly, a massive artistic energy but massively problematic if not controlled.

From the Life Matrix Diamond and Life Matrix it is obvious that Michael Jackson's life would be intense, powerful, universal in scope but ultimately tragic. It also reveals how a person's early life can be incredibly successful but disintegrate into a nightmare reality gushing with turmoil.

To some people, ignorance may be bliss, but ignorance can be devastating. It has been said that ignorance is the root cause of the downfall of the soul. It is interesting to ponder what Michael Jackson's life would have become had he known of his destiny early in his life. Could he have mitigated the impact of the tumult of his 2nd Epoch and its 8/(8)/88-16-7 energy field? It's a moot question, isn't it? For Michael Jackson, his life was one of extreme fame and extreme pain with a sad and ignominious end to his life's drama.

This next LMD series is that of Oprah Winfrey. Notice the energy of relationship (2) to begin her life. Her 3 Crown Pinnacle indicates image, media and communication; the 1 & 8 Crown Challenge energies involve self/independence and social integration/involvement/engagement.

Oprah Gail Winfrey – DOB: 29 January 1954; 22-4 Lifepath; 7 Exp

LIFE MATRIX DIAMOND – Example #1

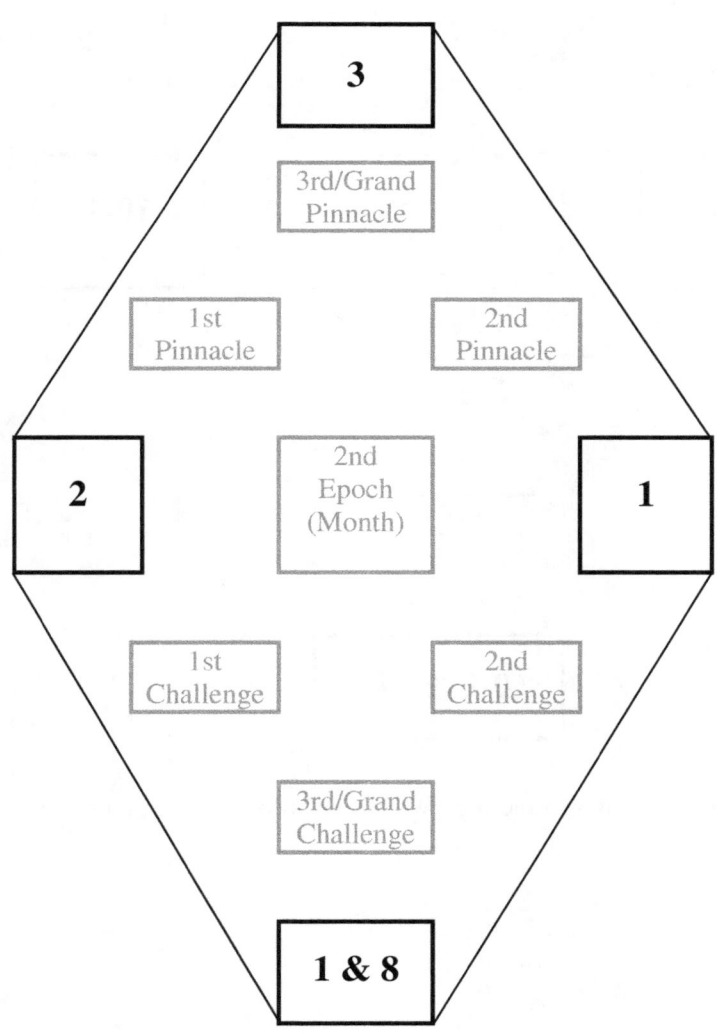

Richard Andrew King

Oprah Gail Winfrey – DOB: 29 January 1954; 22-4 Lifepath; 7 Exp

LIFE MATRIX DIAMOND – Example #2

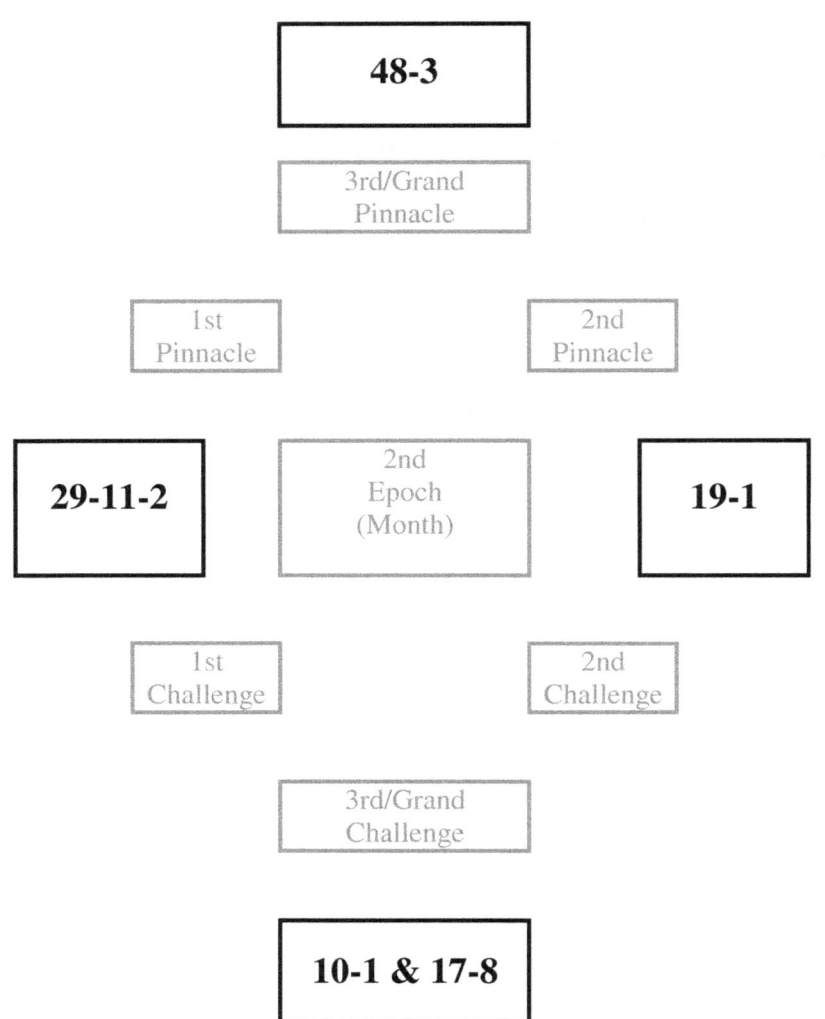

(Note: the 17 was derived by subtracting 29 from 1954 to get 1925, reducing to a 17-8)

Oprah Gail Winfrey – DOB: 29 January 1954; 22-4 Lifepath; 7 Exp

LIFE MATRIX DIAMOND – Example #3

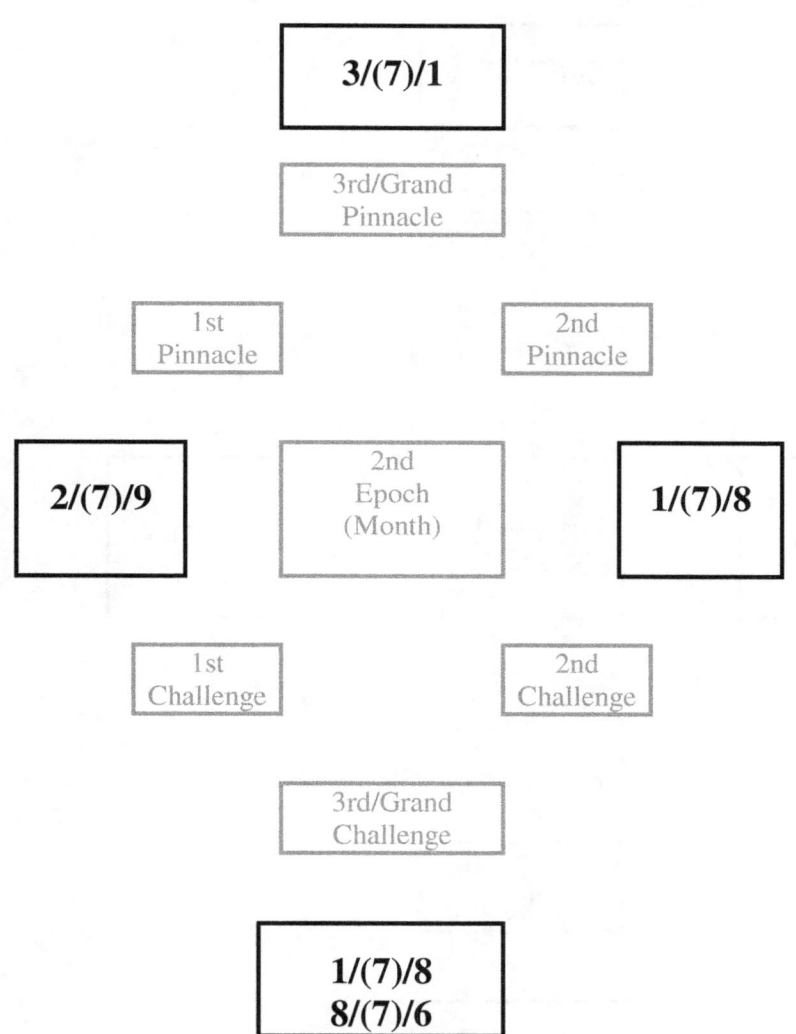

Richard Andrew King

Oprah Gail Winfrey – DOB: 29 January 1954; 22-4 Lifepath; 7 Exp

LIFE MATRIX DIAMOND – Example #4

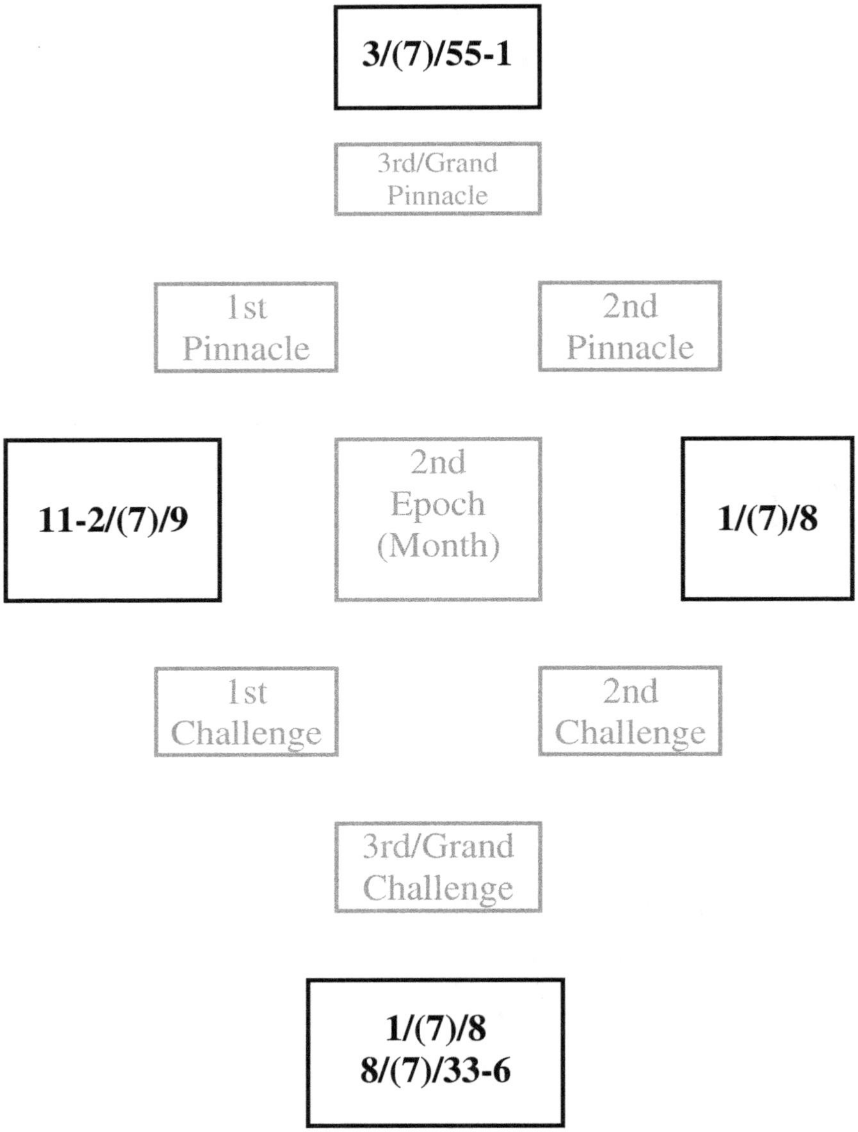

	3/(7)/55-1

3rd/Grand Pinnacle

1st Pinnacle

2nd Pinnacle

11-2/(7)/9

2nd Epoch (Month)

1/(7)/8

1st Challenge

2nd Challenge

3rd/Grand Challenge

1/(7)/8
8/(7)/33-6

Oprah Gail Winfrey – DOB: 29 January 1954; 22-4 Lifepath; 7 Exp

LIFE MATRX

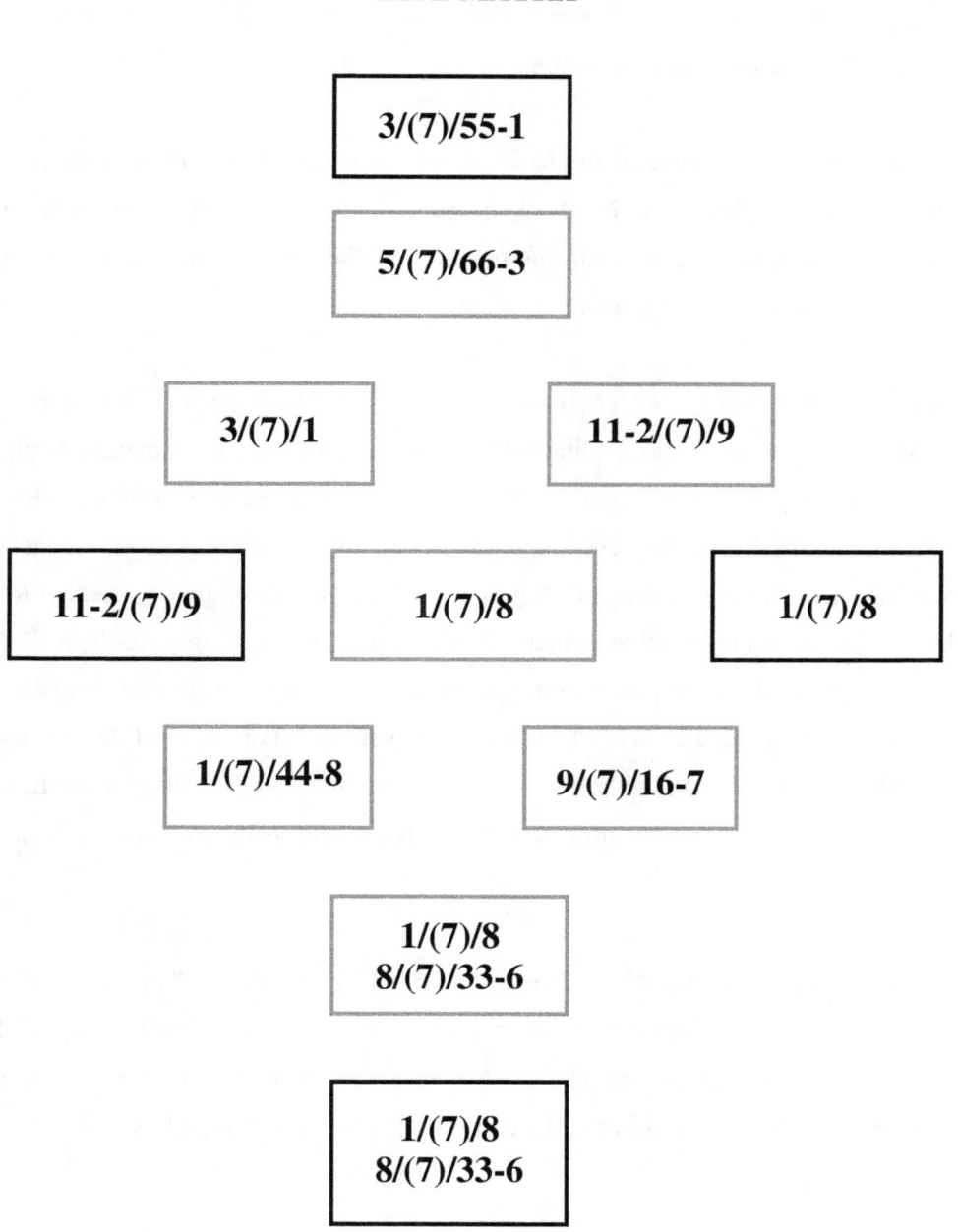

Of particular note in Winfrey's Life Matrix is life linkage of the 1/(7)/8 IR Set. It is located in her 1st Challenge, 2nd Epoch, 3rd Epoch, Grand Challenge and Crown Challenge. It is this 1/(7)/8 life linkage energy that is primarily responsible for her massive success in life. It began the instant she was born and will only terminate at her death.

This 1/(7)/8 pattern is very common in charts of entrepreneurs, managers, executives and other individuals who are individually involved in some activity requiring interconnection and engagement. Because the number 8 is a business vibration, the 1 energy often propels the person to go into some type of business or commercial enterprise.

Another major energy is Winfrey's 5/(7)/66-3 Grand Pinnacle. The 5 governs all people, as it is the *Number of Man*. The 7 Filter brings qualities of introspection, analysis, examination, thought, study and perception into the mix which generates a 66-3 outcome – an energy identifying a love of talk, communication, words, image, joy and happiness. It is this 5/(7)/66-3 Grand Pinnacle energy, coupled with her dual Grand Challenge IR Set of 1/(7)/8 and 8/(7)/33-6 that caused her to focus on people, business and communication, which all of her activities certainly do. The 33-6 and its mirror 66-3 sibling are the most potent communication and artistic master duo there is. We must remember, too, that the Grand Pinnacle/Challenge Couplet is the core of the Lifepath. Everything centers around it because it is the only number pattern that incorporates all three of the birth date data – day, month and year. We've discussed this early on in The King's Book of Numerology^{tm} series.

The other major energy is her 3/(7)/55-1 Crown Pinnacle. Here we see the 3 again. It is also located in her 1st Pinnacle. The difference is that the 55-1 is far more dominant than the simple 1 ROPE of her early life, which makes sense. The 55-1 shows that Winfrey grew into a unique and independent person, which she was not in her early years – budding but not blooming.

This third example is that of General George Patton, of whom General Dwight D. Eisenhower (later becoming the 34th President of the United States) stated: *George Patton was the most brilliant commander of an army in the open field that our or any other service produced* (*Patton: A Genius for War* – Carlo D'Este). Patton's Life Matrix Diamond clearly reveals such dominance. In fact, his LMD could be labeled as a Life Matrix Master Diamond because it houses only master numbers, the acronym for which is LMMD.

George Smith Patton, Jr. – DOB: 11 November 1885; 44-8 Lifepath; 6 Exp

LIFE MATRIX DIAMOND – Example #1

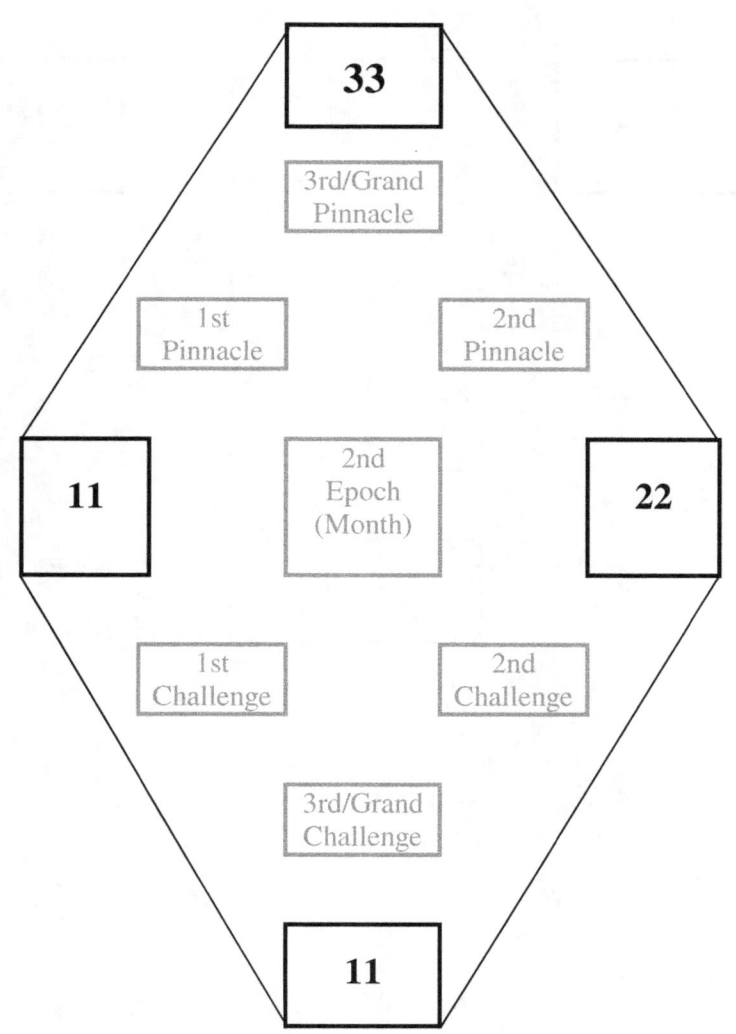

Richard Andrew King

George Smith Patton, Jr. – DOB: 11 November 1885; 44-8 Lifepath; 6 Exp

LIFE MATRIX DIAMOND – Example #2

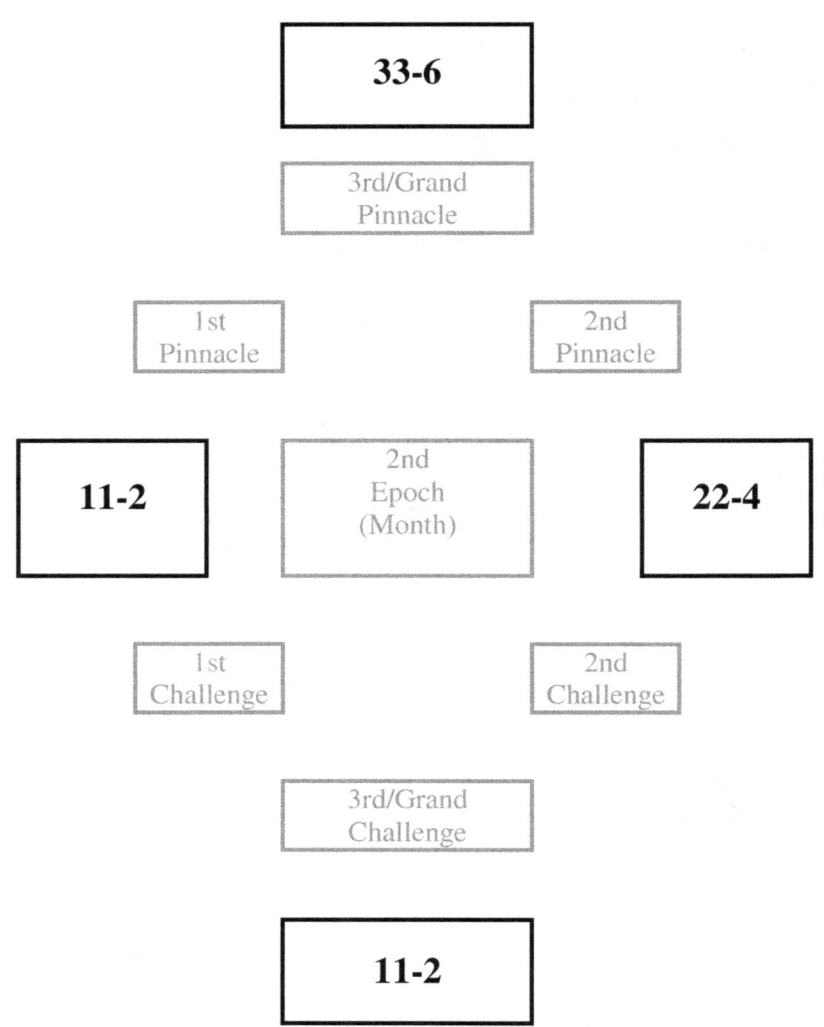

George Smith Patton, Jr. – DOB: 11 November 1885; 44-8 Lifepath; 6 Exp

LIFE MATRIX DIAMOND – Example #3

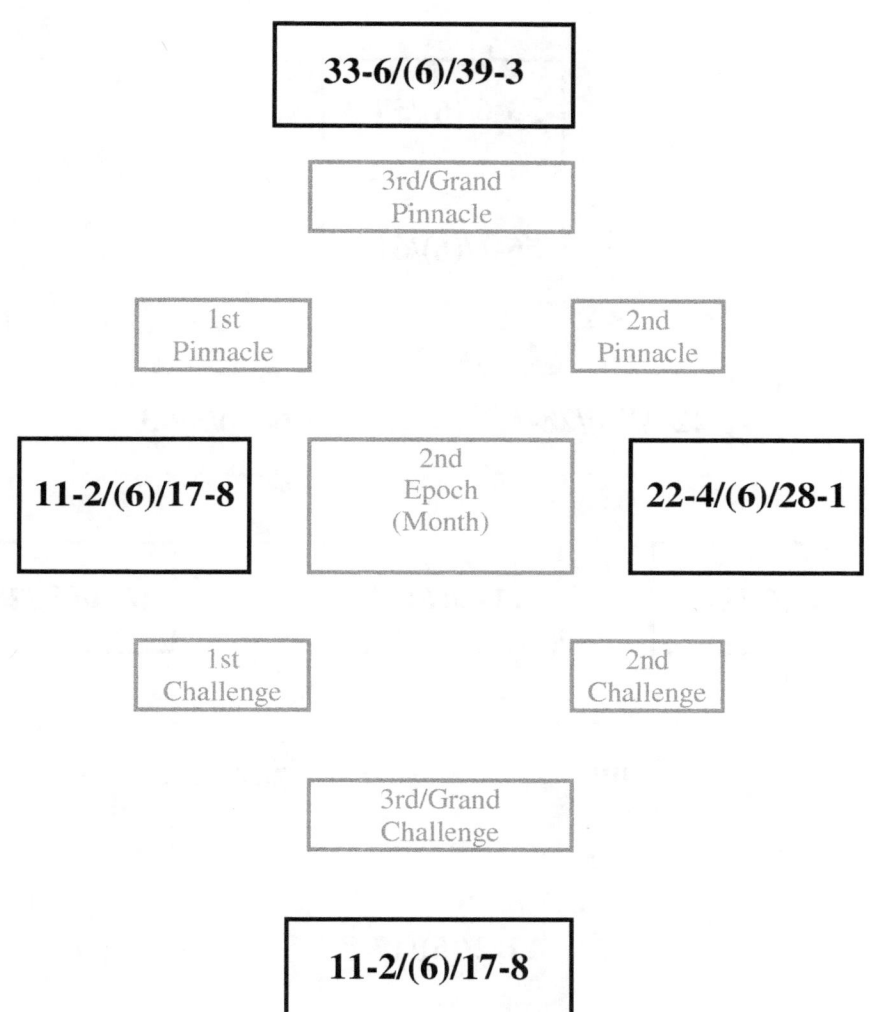

The IR Sets of Patton's Life Matrix Master Diamond (LMMD) reveal ROPES of two 8s stemming from the 11-2 energy (1st Epoch & Crown Challenge); one 1 (Crown Epoch from the 22-4) and one 3 (Crown Pinnacle from the 33-6). The 1 ROPE is fire and independence; the one 3 is air and communication; the two 8s are earth, management and engagement.

Richard Andrew King

George Smith Patton, Jr. – DOB: 11 November 1885; 44-8 Lifepath; 6 Exp

LIFE MATRIX

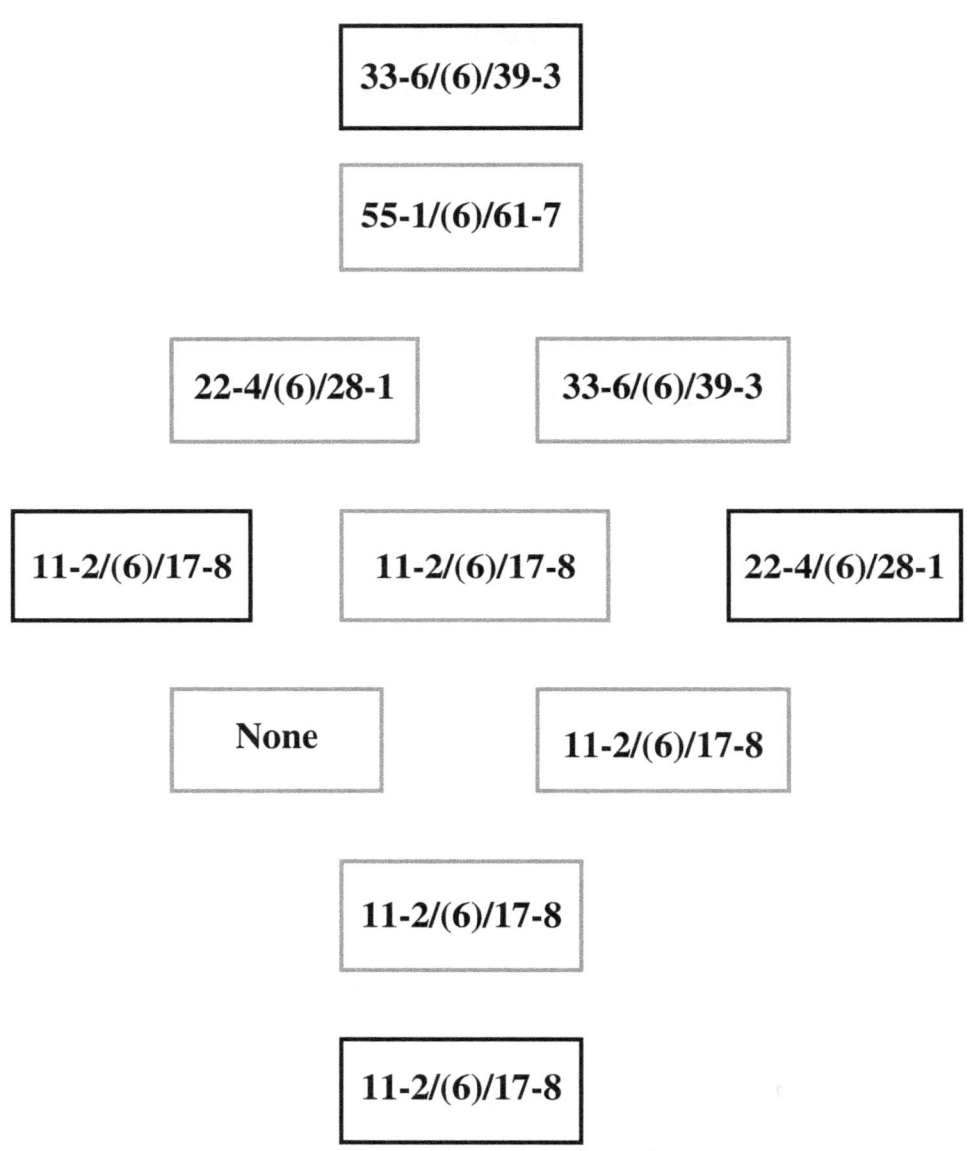

The King's Book of Numerology, Volume 12 – Advanced Principles

Patton's Life Matrix Master Diamond (components are: 11-22-33) reveals how powerful a full Life Matrix can be because it spawns other master energies in the chart. Extraordinarily, with the exception of his 1st Challenge, every component of Patton's Life Matrix features a master number in the LIST position! It is no wonder General Dwight D. Eisenhower stated that Patton was the greatest field commander in World War II. His numbers obviously corroborate this truth, but they should. A powerful life is the manifestation of powerful numbers. Without exception, this truth has been verified time and time again through The King's Book of Numerology™ series as well as The King's Numerology™ system, its articles and teachings.

Another powerful factor in Patton's Life Matrix is life linkage of the 11-2/(6)/8 IR Set which, in one phase, represents *team management*. We must remember that Patton's 44-8 Lifepath is one of generalship and executive ability. His Life Matrix is the internal structure of this 44-8 LP energy. How much more powerful can a general of military stature be?

This life linkage 11-2/(6)/8 IR Set is manifested in Patton's own words:

An army is a team. It lives, sleeps, eats and fights as a team.

Team is a function of the number 2. *Lives, sleeps, eats and fights* represent the number 8 and its process of interaction, engagement, management, connectivity.

Here's another great Patton quote, one which speaks to the destiny revealed through the science of numbers:

A man must know his destiny ... if he does not recognize it, then he is lost.

This fundamental truth which Patton so succinctly stated represents the very purpose of numerology. It allows us to know our destiny, and if we refuse to recognize it, then we are lost, truly.

General Patton is featured in *Destinies of the Rich & Famous – The Secret Numbers of Extraordinary Lives* and in *The King's Book of Numerology, Volume 10 – Historic Icons, Part 1.*

Richard Andrew King

This chapter on the Life Matrix Diamond has revealed a simple process of knowing the general run of one's life. After the LMD is established, the other Life Matrix components can be added to fill in the full picture of the Life Matrix.

So this brings us to you. What is your Life Matrix Diamond? Those of your parents, children, extended family members, friends, associates?

For those of us who are professional numerologists, it gives us a simple tool to begin a life analysis. It sets the framework of the puzzle of destiny. From that framework, we then proceed to fill in the remaining puzzle pieces to reveal the full destiny, at least as far as the Life Matrix is concerned.

CHAPTER 11

PROFESSIONAL CHART ANALYSIS

A professional chart analysis consists of many parts, many components, many layers, many timelines, many puzzle pieces. This chapter offers a partial checklist of what needs to be assessed in order to arrive at a competent conclusion in understanding any chart and the individual's destiny associated with it.

The components of the following chart analysis are not listed in any particular order. Nor do they encompass the entirety of a chart analysis. Continued numerology research will, no doubt, add new items to the puzzle-analysis process. Still, the following list will generate a massive amount of knowledge creating a substantial energetic picture and puzzle of one's life and destiny.

CHART ANALYSIS COMPONENTS

Natal Data
It may seem commonplace but make sure the full name and birthdate of the individual are correct. If you're working through the web in regard to historic or public figures, check multiple sites. Blog sites, celebrity sites, movie sites such as IMDB (International Movie Data Base), etc., often give common names but not full birth names. Wikipedia is a fairly good source for accuracy. Biography sites are good, too. Be thorough in your initial research gathering. Incorrect data will not give you the appropriate information to generate an accurate assessment of destiny.

When working with clients, it's not unusual for people to get their data wrong. Therefore, double check with the client before doing any work. Once you have their natal data, resend it to them asking them to verify its correctness, informing them that any charts created by their mistake will have to be redone. This will take your time and effort, so they will have to remunerate you for your time in redoing charts. Be clear about this to avoid any misunderstandings.

Also, be careful during Mercury Retrogrades. Communication problems abound during these times, so research their dates annually. There are usually three Retrogrades each year. Always double check, even triple check, your work and data during a Mercury Retrograde.

Let your clients know that your fees are based on one name and one birth date. Additional names require an additional fee, unless you're working for free and have no concern about your everyday expenses, bills, etc. The laborer is worthy of his hire, of his reward (Bible: Luke 10: 7, 1). There is nothing wrong in getting paid for your skill and knowledge. We all have to work to make a living, so make sure your needs are taken care of appropriately and professionally.

Regarding multiple names, sometimes people will give you a birth name; you establish a fee but then they tell you multiple names were given to them at birth and they don't know which name to use. Result: a problem arises. Now you'll have to do more work to ascertain which name carries the blueprint of destiny. That will require more time and an increased fee. To avoid such a problem, be very clear up front with the client about getting everything exactly right before you begin your work. Honesty and clarity are critical to one's professional reputation and success.

Birthdates can be confusing. For example, is 1/2/2000 the 1st of February or January 2nd? Is 5/6/1985 the 5th of June or the 6th of May? American protocol is to place the month first and the day second. The European method, which The King's Numerology^{tm} promotes and has proven through thousands of charts and real life analyses to be the absolute correct method in the forecasting process, is to place the day first and month second (day/month/year). This was specifically covered in KBN2-Forecasting, Part 1. The simple solution is to always ask the client to spell out the month when forwarding his/her natal data to avoid confusion.

The bottom line regarding natal data is do your homework and get it right the first time. You've probably heard the saying, "If you don't get it right the first time, how much time, effort and money will it take you to get it right the second time?" Avoid the calamity. Get it right the first time.

Basic Matrix

As we know, the Basic Matrix is the most centric instrument describing an individual. An entire book could be written on any individual based on its information. It also gives us a quick analysis of the individual, and it only takes a few minutes to generate. The Basic Matrix is the first numeric device in a King's Numerology™ report.

When analyzing a Basic Matrix, start with the simple single numbers of each of its components: Lifepath (LP), Expression (Exp), Performance/Experience (PE), Soul, Material Soul (MS), Nature and Material Nature (MN). Notate the voids.

King's Numerology™ BASIC MATRIX								
Roots ⇩	LP	Exp	PE	Soul	M/S	Nature	M/N	Voids
Simple #s								
Master #s								
General								
Specific								
Transition								

Analysis Aspects

Go through the simple numbers in each component. Review their characteristics, attributes and meanings. Are there duplicate numbers – the same cipher in different components?

Are the Lifepath and Expression ciphers the same? If so, they create dual Filters, and the person's entire life will be colored in their energy. Dual Filters generate internal stacking. The greater the stacking, the more intense the destiny.

What is the dispensation of the numbers in the Basic Matrix? For example, the Umbrella of Elvis Presley (Elvis Aaron Presley; born 8 January 1935) consists only of 9s – 9 Lifepath, 9 Expression, 9 PE. Every Basic Matrix component of Garth Brooks (Troyal Garth Brooks; born 7 February 1962) consists only of 9s! The Basic Matrix of Queen Elizabeth II (Elizabeth Alexandra Mary;

born 21 April 1926) only houses two numbers – the 7 and 9. Such saturation of one or a few numbers equates to a life that is uncommon and concentrated in a few energies. Such lives and destinies are not "normal." The Basic Matrix of most people consists of a variety of numbers, which, in a sense, creates more balance than those that are heavily laden with one or two numbers.

What is the elemental relationship of the Basic Matrix components? Fire (1 and 5)? Water (2 and 6)? Air (3 and 7)? Earth (4 and 8)? Is there saturation of one or more elements? Is there a diversity of elements? Is there a clashing of elements? For example, a lot of fire and water? Is there a harmony of elements? For example, water and earth? Air and fire?

What is the distribution of polarities of the components? All negative charged ciphers (2-4-6-8) or positive charged ciphers (1-3-5-7)? Is there a dominance of one polarity over the other? A mixture?

Is the Basic Matrix social or separate? The 2-4-6-8 are all social numbers, which means the individual's energies will involve other people and relationships. On the other hand, when the numbers 1-5-7 occupy the Basic Matrix, the individual will manifest energies of independence, freedom, detachment, reclusion, introversion, solitude.

Is there Soul Release through the Umbrella? If so, the individual will experience some degree of fulfillment in their life? If there is no Soul Release, the potential of fulfillment is doubtful unless it can be achieved through a life partner, business or some other entity whose numeric energy matches the Soul of the individual. Keep in mind that Soul Release can be achieved through various timelines in the Life Matrix, Name and Letter Matrices, Decade timelines, 9 Cycle timelines and so forth, but these will be temporary depending on the length of the timeline.

Does the Soul number match the Expression number? If so, the individual will be extremely comfortable with himself or herself because their Expression is exactly what they need and desire?

Does the Soul number clash with the Expression number? As an example, is the Soul a 1 energy but the Expression a 2? This combination will generate internal conflict because the 1 Soul wants to be the star, to be independent and the center of attention, but the 2 Expression speaks to being dependent and a supporter or follower. As we know, the 1 and 2 are exact opposites, so this combination will never be comfortable. The same would go for a 4 Soul and 5 Expression or a 7 Soul and 8 Expression.

A comparable dilemma exists between the Expression and the PE. For example, a 1 Expression person is highly self-oriented but a 2 PE demands attention to others in a support capacity. Hence, an internal struggle exists between the individual and his/her role in life for the entire life. The same goes for the 4-5 and 7-8 combinations.

A similar situation exists between the Expression and the Lifepath. A 1 Expression wants to be independent and the star but the 2 Lifepath forces it to focus on Lessons, Influences, Subjects and Themes (LIST) regarding others and their interests.

Such oppositions can also exist between the Soul and Nature. This will be evident in the SNO – Soul/Nature Overview. What a person needs, wants and desires (Soul energy) may be contrapuntal to the individual's basic personality (Nature). For example, what if a person's Soul is a 4 but their Nature is a 5? The 4 Soul seeks stability but the 5 Nature exudes adventure, risk-taking and change. The 9 Expression is the result of this 4 Soul/5 Nature combination. Since the 9 is the Grand Elemental housing all numbers, the individual would most likely be able to adjust to the 4/5 opposition.

Another example. What if the SNO consisted of an 8 Soul and an 8 Nature? The Expression would be a 16-7, thus generating an 8-8-7 opposition. The 8 Soul seeks social integration. The 8 Nature is itself social, but the 7 Expression is private, reclusive and solitary.

In contrast, what are the harmonies between the Basic Matrix components? A 4 Expression with a 4 Lifepath and 8 PE will create harmony because the 8 is a derivative of the 4 and these two numbers are both earth signs carrying a negative charge. Individuals with a 5 Expression coupled with a 5 Lifepath will experience a 1 PE, which should create a sense of harmony in their lives because the 1 and 5 are both fire signs carrying a positive charge. The point of the previous examples highlights the necessity of looking for harmonies and inharmonies in the components of the Basic Matrix.

Then, of course, voids have to be taken into account. How many are there? What is the composition of each as to elemental structure and polar charge? Evidence seems to suggest that if the voided letter is situated in the Soul or Nature its negative effects will be mitigated to some degree.

This is especially true of the Soul. For example, let's say a person has a 7 void but also has a 7 Soul or 7 Material Soul. Since the Soul energies drive a person's passions, they (the 7's energies) will be filling up the individual's missing 7 energy. Normally, a person with a 7 void has no interest in the deeper aspects of life, in pondering destiny, in being reclusive, introspective, imaginative, inquiring. Yet, people with a 7 Soul or 7 Material Soul are often hungry for knowledge and understanding. Therefore, they will not be victimized by a voided 7 as much as a person with a 7 void who has no 7s in their Basic Matrix. This is pretty much true for all numbers. If they're voided but exist in a Basic Matrix component, their negative effects will be mitigated.

After the single numbers of the Basic Matrix are analyzed, begin checking the root structures of each component. These are critical because they color how the single number (crown) manifests. For example, a 1 Lifepath indicates lessons of independence, identity, leadership, instigation, genesis, self, ego, courage, will, creativity, being solo, a lone wolf, a maverick. Yet, having a General root of 28 in a 1 Lifepath is much different from a 37, 46 or 55. The 28 speaks to others, relationship and engagement; the 37 indicates creativity, thought, imagination; the 46 focuses on the house, home, domicile, being a nurturer and head of household; the 55 is the rebel, renegade, the free spirit, lone wolf. Still, they all carry a 1 crown. As we see, crowns create conditions which are generally alike but roots reveal how they are specifically different.

This process of analyzing root structures goes for every crown in the Basic Matrix. Too, be aware of the polarity of the numbers forming the roots. A 28 root includes only a negative charge while the 37 holds a positive charge. Binaries associated with the 1 crown will always carry one charge, which will be the same for each single number of the root.

However, it's different for a 2 crown. Its binary roots are: 11-20-29-38-47-56-65-74-83-92. The numbers 38 to 83 are composed of single ciphers with opposite charges. Their elements are also different. The same process involves trinary roots, even quaternary root structures.

When analyzing the root systems of each of the Basic Matrix components we have to be aware of the subcaps of each root. These play a major function in understanding destiny. Subcaps (aka Subcap Challenges) indicate the hidden challenges people will face in their lives. They are critical aspects of a chart. They should not be ignored.

To simplify the Basic Matrix data, the Lifepath is the script of the individual. The Expression is the person playing the part of the actor or actress. The PE is the performance they will give on the great life stage in *this* incarnation. The Soul Layers (Soul and Material Soul) are the drivers, the engine, the force behind all that the actor/actress does. The Nature Layers (Nature and Material Nature) form the personality and the way the person does things. Voids are absences of energy demanding attention.

The Inclusion (House of Letters)

There are two main things to look for in the House of Letters: master numbers and the percentage of each genera to the whole. The 1 genera consists of A-J-S; the 2 genera of B-K-T and so forth.

Master numbers in the Inclusion reveal an intensity of their energy in the specific genera. For example, a 22 master in the first House of Self reveals the strength of the individual and his/her rootedness, even stubbornness. If the 22 is in the 2nd House of Others and Relationships, it signals strength among others and relationships. The 11 in the 2nd House of Others indicates inspiration for others. The 33 master in the 3rd House of Communication or in the 5th House of Versatility almost invariably occurs in charts of famous orators, actors, media personalities, singers, writers, etc. A 44 master anywhere indicates strong managerial skills and social power.

Master numbers can occur in any of the nine Houses of the Inclusion. Be aware of them. They represent a major key to one's personality.

Richard Andrew King

The other factor to note in the Inclusion is the percentage of one House to the whole Inclusion. If the 1st House of Self has a high percentage, say 30% or so, this reveals a strong personality. A low percentage reveals an individual who may be lacking in self-esteem. This can be dangerous because a person may work to overcome his feelings of inadequacy by being imperious, arrogant, extremely domineering or overcompensating in other areas. Adolf Hitler (born 20 April 1889) is one such personality. His 1st House of Self was only .91% of his Expression, while 84% was located in four Houses – 2nd, 3rd, 6th and 9th: 18.18% in his 2nd House of Others; 21.82% in his 3rd House of Image, Words and Communication; 19.09% in his 6th House of Home and Homeland; 24.55% in his 9th House of Mankind and the Universal Stage.

Billionaire Warren Buffett (Warren Edward Buffett; born August 30, 1930) is another. His 1st House of Letters housed only .93% of his Expression, while 80% of his Expression was centered in the 2nd, 5th and 9th Houses (19.63% in his 2nd House; 35.05% in his 5th House and 25.23% in his 9th House). Buffett's compensatory behavior was to become super rich.

One of the scariest examples is that of notorious serial killer, Ted Bundy (Theodore Robert Cowell; born 24 November 1946). Bundy had voids of 1 and 7. This meant his sense of self was zero, nothing, nada, nil, 0.00% in his 1st House of Self. His 7 void meant he had no energy of depth, thought, discretion or wisdom, as well as a potential lack of feeling and remorse.

Part of Bundy's scary "serial killer puzzle" is that he had a 1 Lifepath, which was void, so every Name and Letter Timeline filtered through a 1v energy field, i.e., an empty (0) energy field! Furthermore, his *Theodore* Name Timeline was a 9/(1v)/1v! It would have lasted for 45 years but he died at age 42 by electrocution in Florida State Prison. It was during this NTL of *Theodore* in which he did all of his barbarous crimes.

To note: the rarest voids are the 1 and 5. To be quite clear, very few people who have a 1 void are serial killers, but this said, there will be some type and degree of issues involving one's self and ego when the 1 is void in a chart. The disturbing fact of Bundy's life was his 1 voided Lifepath and its function as the Filter for every Name and Letter of his natal name. In this regard, the two "Os" in *Theodore* (ages 16 -21 and 26-31) generated a 15-6/(1v)/16-7v IR Set! Dark, dark, dark!

The Influence/Reality Set Formats

There are two primary Influence/Reality Set formats – one in which the Lifepath is the Filter and the other in which the Expression is the Filter. The 81 IR Sets are applicable to each. IR Sets have been fully addressed in *The King's Book of Numerology 2: Forecasting, Part 1* and *The King's Book of Numerology 5: IR Sets – Level 1*

IR Sets are centric to the forecasting process via their LIST/(FILTER)/ROPE formula (LFR). The data presented in KBN2 and KBN5 only scratch the surface of what these structures reveal about life and destiny but they're a start. Continued study of IR Sets is a lifelong process.

KBN5 used single numbers for the L/(F)/R components for simplicity purposes. As we become more advanced in our numerological acumen, we can begin to expand the L/(F)R pattern to include binary numbers, as has been done many times heretofore. Even trinary numbers can be used but unless one is extremely advanced in the science of numbers, binaries will be adequate in the analysis process.

When "reading" an IR Set it is important to consider the elemental and polar attributes of each number. How do the three components react one to the other? What are the harmonies and/or inharmonies? Opposites? Voids? Master numbers? Duplicates of a number within the set? Are there any correlations with the individual's Basic Matrix? Umbrella? What about the Life Matrix components? Name and Letter timelines? Are there shifts between the early life versus the latter life? Are there duplicates in the Epochs, Pinnacles and Challenges? Is the energy flow from beginning to end positive or negative? Does the Great Purifier 16-7 show up in the IR Sets anywhere in the entire chart? Do master numbers occupy one or more of the three components? If so, is the master root voided? What about its crown? Is there a Grand Voided Master anywhere in the chart? Do the IR Sets house any Grand Voided Challenges? Grand Voided Pinnacles? Grand Voided Epochs? These are important questions to address in a professional analysis.

Following are the two primary IR Set formats in a King's Numerology^{tm} chart.

Richard Andrew King

LIFE MATRIX IR SET FORMAT

Life Matrix IR Set Format: Filter is the Expression, i.e., the full natal name. This IR Set format will be used for each of the Life Matrix components, Decade Timeline, Monthly Timeline, Lifetime Monthly Timeline, the 9 Cycles Timeline, Annual Cycle Patterns, etc. The only timelines it is not used for are the Name and Letter Timelines.

LCP	L/(E)/R		Filter: Expression						
Influence/Cause-L	1	2	3	4	5	6	7	8	9	LIST
[+ Expression-E]	+E	+E	+E	+E	+E	+E	+E	+E	+E	[+ Expression]
Outcome/Effect-R	R	R	R	R	R	R	R	R	R	ROPE

NAME & LETTER IR SET FORMAT

Name and Letter IR Set Format: Filter is the Lifepath, i.e., the birth date. This pattern will not be used with any other timeline.

LCP	L/(LP)/R		Filter: Lifepath						
Influence/Cause-L	1	2	3	4	5	6	7	8	9	LIST
[+ Lifepath-LP]	+LP	+LP	+LP	+LP	+LP	+LP	+LP	+LP	+LP	[+ Lifepath]
Outcome/Effect-R	R	R	R	R	R	R	R	R	R	ROPE

Following is the Author's Introduction to KBN5. It's offered here as a useful reminder of IR Sets.

Author's Introduction to KBN5

Influence/Reality Sets are the crux, core and substance of numerology forecasting, indispensable to the King's Numerology^{tm} system and to anyone choosing to know where they've been, where they are now and where they're headed. They are obligatory for any serious student of numerology.

There are 81 IR Sets. *The King's Book of Numerology 5: IR Sets – Level 1* contains over 700 examples of real life case studies, offering a general explanation of each of the 81 IR Sets in order to create a foundation on which to build a greater understanding of how life's events affect us.

Serving as an excellent reference source for Influence/Reality Sets, KBN5 is a starting point from which to grow greater knowledge of one's self and destiny.

IR Sets give us a general blueprint of the varying lessons, influences, subjects, themes, events and situations of our lives as we travel down and navigate the highways and byways, mountains and valleys, meadows and deserts of our destiny. They inform us as to how we will generally respond to such lessons, influences and situations, giving us a forewarning so we can prepare, adjust and remain balanced. IR Sets empower us with knowledge we can use to manage our lives successfully on a daily basis, knowledge without which we are traveling blind through a journey filled with twists and turns, unknown circumstances, potential storms and mine fields.

Regardless of our age, IR Sets allow us to see a full picture of our life – past, present and future. Seeing our past validates our experiences of that time, allowing us to understand them and let go of what has been, to forgive and move on. Knowing our present helps us manage daily circumstances efficiently, and having a glimpse of the future allows us to prepare and adjust beforehand so we don't get blind-sided and sucker-punched by the blows and strikes, slings and arrows, tumults and tempests of life.

It takes courage to see the blueprint of one's life, but what's the alternative? Traveling blind and unprotected on a journey where we have no idea what to expect? Our destinies are not unknown. We can know them if we choose and be grateful recipients of such knowledge. We can know life on levels we never knew existed, levels which will lift us into higher realms of consciousness and reality, for with every step we take up the mountain, reality changes. When we see the whole picture from higher vantage points we gain a state of knowing that can only benefit us in our journey.

As a note, please remember that no one IR Set exists in a vacuum. Every IR Set is a piece of the numeric puzzle that is our life. Voids and Challenges play a major role in how each IR Set is manifested. Stacking and linkage create intensity and continuity – major factors determining the effect of any Influence/Reality pattern.

Richard Andrew King

Make no mistake. IR Sets are a gift for those willing to receive them, study them and apply their vast level of knowledge to make our lives more understandable, manageable, easier, better, whole.

The Life Matrix (LM)

The Life Matrix is the internal structure of the Lifepath. Therefore, all the Epochs, Pinnacles and Challenges must be analyzed in context with the Lifepath energy. Multiple people with the same Expression could have the same IR Set in any combination of Life Matrix components but have different Lifepaths. Therefore, it is important to always consider the Lifepath energy when interpreting a Life Matrix IR Set.

For example, John and Mary both have a 6 Expression. John's birthdate is 1 March 1992, generating a 7 Lifepath. Mary's birthdate is 1 July 2007, generating an 8 Lifepath. Both of their 1st Epochs house a 1/(6)/7 IR Set. See the problem?

Since John's Lifepath is a 7, his 1/(6)/7 1st Epoch creates stacking, which we know generates intensity. Mary's Lifepath is an 8, so her 1/(6)7 1st Epoch won't be as severe. Therefore, we must interpret the 1/(6)/7 energy differently in both cases. To assess them equally would be incorrect. John's 7 Lifepath is one of internalization, isolation, introspection, solitude – all things internal. Mary's 8 Lifepath is one of externalization, socialization, engagement, flow – all things external. Both individuals will experience problems with the father or issues with loneliness and solitude, even turmoil, potential alcohol or drug abuse, maybe divorce because of the 1/(6)/7, but John will feel them more intensely because of his 7 Lifepath.

Although this example of John and Mary is simple, it highlights the relationship between the Lifepath and any IR Sets within the Life Matrix. How does one number or number pattern interact, resonate or clash with others? Is stacking involved? Does the IR Set repeat itself in other components of the Life Matrix? Is it a one off? Does it exist by itself? Is there life linkage of an IR Set? Does such life linkage match the LIR Umbrella (Lifepath/(Expression)/PE? This would create intensity of the same issue for the entire life.

When analyzing all the IR Sets within the eleven components of the Life Matrix, be sure to consider voids and their location in the IR Set as LIST, Filter or ROPE. Do any of the IR Sets appear in any of the three main components – Epochs, Pinnacles, Challenges? If so, are they Grand Voided, i.e., containing a number that is missing from the Basic Matrix? Are there multiple voided numbers in an IR Set? This would create a heavier and more complex manifestation of energy.

To be thorough, we must also check the roots of the Epochs, Pinnacles and Challenges. Are they common binaries? Problematic binaries such as the 15-6 or 16-7? Master numbers? Are any of the binaries voided, wholly or partially?

For example, let's say a person is born on 22 November, generating a 33-6 1st Pinnacle. Let's also ascribe a 3 void to the individual. If we were to only use single numbers, the LIST energy of the 1st Pinnacle would be 6. However, with the 3 being voided, the 1st Pinnacle would more precisely be a 33v-6, which tells us that the 6 is negatively aspected and would not be as loving, kind, nurturing and positive as it would be if the 33 were not voided. A 3 void generally indicates an acerbic, bitter, negative, caustic, unhappy energy. Therefore, with a voided 33 the 6 would not, could not, be whole. This is another example of why we must explore the root systems of single numbers if we want to achieve a level of excellence in our work.

As we've discussed earlier, we need to ascertain the flow of the Life Matrix timelines. If there are changes, how do they change? Do they resonate with the Lifepath or any of the Basic Matrix components? Do they start in a positive way and end in a negative way? We've already seen charts of individuals who were riding high in life in the early years of their life but took a Humpty-Dumpty fall from grace in their latter years. There are people whose destinies began in difficult circumstances but finished in happy and fruitful experiences.

When analyzing changes in the Life Matrix, do any of the ROPES match the Soul or Material Soul? If so, this will generally be a time of fulfillment for the individual because the ROPE energy will then generate Soul Release. If the ROPE is in a Challenge position, the individual can expect to be forced to concentrate on it. If it's voided, that may create challenges.

Richard Andrew King

One of the major focal points to assess in the Life Matrix is linkage, especially life linkage because it reveals a life saturated with a major energy field that keeps growing and growing. Linkage can also be comprised of three components, such as the 2nd, 3rd and 4th Challenges. It's not uncommon to see a two component linkage, such as the 1st and 2nd Epochs or 2nd and 3rd Epochs. Same thing goes for Pinnacles. Linkage creates continuity, whether the IR Set is positive or negative.

A major focal point involves stacking. As we know, stacking creates intensity, whether it's positive or negative. If stacking combines with linkage, the destiny will be strong and continuous. We must always look for stacking and linkage in a chart because of the power they generate.

Another key to look for in the Life Matrix involves the Grand Pinnacle/Challenge Couplet (Grand PC Couplet). It is the centerpoint of the Life Matrix and, arguably, of the Lifepath itself. Princess Diana, Elvis Presley and Howard Hughes, Jr. all had charts centered in a Grand PC Couplet. Diana's was a 5/(4)/9; Presley's was a 1/(9)/1 and Hughes' was a 9/(7)/7.

The Name Timeline Matrix (NTL)

The Life Matrix tells us a great deal about one's destiny, but so does the Name Matrix (Expression) and each of its separate names. In fact, the Name Timeline Matrix often reveals facts about a person's destiny which the Life Matrix does not. Just think of serial killer Ted Bundy, professional golfer Tiger Woods, entertainer Michael Jackson, President John F. Kennedy, Elvis Presley, Oprah Winfrey. The list goes on and on of people whose Name Timelines hold secrets of their destinies which their Life Matrices do not. Therefore, the NTL in toto cannot be ignored. It deserves as much attention as the Life Matrix. The two combined (LM and NTL) are the two most critical treasure chests of the blueprint of destiny.

When considering the NTL, what is the IR Set of each name? How long is its timeline? Do any of its numbers or number patterns match the Basic Matrix or Life Matrix components? Are there voids in the names? Do different names have the same IR Sets, which would create linkage? Do any of the Names match the Soul or Material Soul? Nature or Material Nature? Lifepath? Expression itself? PE? What are the roots of the Names? Subcaps of the roots? Stacking with other chart components? What is the elemental composition and polarity of each name? How does each name blend or not blend with names coming before or after it? Do two names in succession generate one of the three natural opposition duos: 1-2, 4-5, 7-8?

The Letter Timeline Matrix (LTL)

The Letter Timeline is just as valuable as the NTL and its parts. Many secrets of destiny are contained in the LTL just as they are in the NTL. For example, the letters A-J-S always create a new beginning or action for one year, especially the A because it is the first and purest letter of the alphabet and the number 1. The J and S have binaries (the 10 and 19 respectively) attached to them, so they're not as pure – more complex but not as pure as the A's 1.

Do these 1-charged letters stack with the name? In other words, is the name that houses them also a 1? For example, take the name Adam. It is a 1 Expression and it contains two As (the 1-based letter). Hence, stacking and the intensity that goes with it are created at age 1 and 6. Plus, what if the full natal Expression were a 1? What if the Lifepath were a 1 as well? What would you guess would happen in a 1 Age Timeline or in a 1 Month? There would be massive stacking which would have a dramatic effect on the person's life in the area of new beginnings, action, initiation, self. The reality of such new beginnings would be determined by the ROPE created when the 1 energy (LIST) filtered through the Lifepath number/energy.

Another question: does the same letter generate linkage in the name? For example, the name *Jennifer* contains three 5s in a row (e-n-n). Its energy of change, detachment, freedom and loss covers a period of fifteen years. The NTL of *Jennifer* is a 9 lasting for forty-five years. When the solo E is added to the "e-n-n" string, we see that twenty years of her forty-five years would involve change of some type. The I and R would create eighteen total years of 9-based energy.

The name *Jenner* has four 5s in a row (e-n-n-e) – a massive amount of change during a twenty year period. In fact, when Olympic champion Bruce Jenner changed his persona to *Caitlyn Marie Jenner* it was during this four letter linkage of the 5 energy during its twenty year timeline. Bruce Jenner was born William Bruce Jenner on 28 October 1949. His Lifepath is a 7. The IR Set associated with any E, N or W in his name generates a 5/(7)/3 energy pattern indicating change (5) of his image (3). The name *Jenner* is a 3 in reduction, creating a 3/(7)/1 IR Set. So here we see the energy of image – the 3, in both the LIST of ROPE positions during the time of his transformation. Jenner's life story, especially his gender change, is a perfect example of the power of the Letter Timeline and Name Timeline in combination.

Another example. The name *Anne* has a three letter linkage string of the 5 (n-n-e). *Anne* is a 16-7. The two Ns comprise a ten year period of 14-5 energy. Obviously, this is problematic. If the Lifepath associated with *Anne* is a 9, the NTL LIST and ROPE will be 16-7s – 16-7/(9)/16-7 with ten years of detachment, loss and freedom as a result of the two interior Ns. Other Lifepaths will generate different ROPES, of course, but the 14-5 and 16-7 together in a NTL will create challenges for the individual.

Tri-letter linkage strings in a single name are quite common and are generally associated with genera which include at least one vowel. Genera lacking a vowel are hard pressed to create more than a two letter string. Example: the 2nd genera of B-K-T, the 4th of D-M-V and the 8th of H-Q-Z have no vowels. All the other genera do have a vowel. Examples of names which house a three letter string are *Asa*: 1-1-1 (1st genera), *Lucky*: 3-3-3 (3rd genera), *Benny*: 5-5-5 (5th genera), *Foxy*: 6-6-6 (6th genera), *Peppy*: 7-7-7 (7th genera) and *Iris*: 9-9-9 (9th genera).

It is possible, however, to have longer letter strings when two names are juxtaposed in which the final letter(s) of the first name are in the same genera as the initial letters of the following name. For example, the name *Ben Newton* contains a five letter string of the 5 energy: e-n-n-e-w. This generates a twenty-five year period of LIST energy involving change, freedom, loss, detachment, exploration, adventure, etc.

The name *Charles Jackson* contains a three letter string: s-j-a, generating a three year 1-1-1 LIST energy field. There would be lots of new beginnings or action-oriented experiences in this time period. The name *Sam D'Mond*e houses a tri-letter string of the m-d-m. Its twelve year reign will be quite stable, rooted and ordered with its 4-4-4 LIST.

Twin identical letter strings are very common. Examples are *rabbit, holly, boon, feet, mommy, nanny, pepper,* etc.

Letter strings of the same genera can not only be intense (because of stacking) but continuous (because of linkage).

Here are a few sample questions to ask ourselves regarding the Letter Timeline. How do the letters interact with the name in which they are housed? Do they create stacking? Do they match any component of the Basic Matrix or Life Matrix? Is there any opposition between sequential letters in a name (1-2, 4-5 or 7-8)? Is there harmony in the letters of a name? Disharmony? Does the letter energy clash with the name energy? What do the letter IR Sets reveal? If letter linkage exists, how does it interact with other parts of the chart?

The Decade Timeline (DTL)

Running sequentially, Decade Timelines are easy to forecast. Their IR Set energies may stand alone or be part of a stacked group with other timelines. The first year of a DTL is marked with a gestation cipher: 10, 20, 30, etc. These gestation binaries house three identical IR Sets – one for the root, one for the addcap and one for the subcap. Thus, they house a tristack of one IR Set.

For example, individuals with a 2 Expression, while transiting their 50s Decade will, during their 50th year, experience a tristack of 5/(2)/7 energy. Invariably, the Expression will have an 11 transition root and the 7 will have a 16 root, so the IR Set can be ciphered as 5/(11)/16-7. Clearly, this should raise yellow flags for 2 Expression people, not simply for their 50th year but for the entire 50s Decade because the ROPE will be the Great Purifier.

No one escapes the 16-7. Following is a breakdown of the Decade generating a 16-7 ROPE for each Expression. In this case the Decade will become the Nemesis number for each Expression. We must remember that a Nemesis timeline, although potentially challenging, offers excellent potential for internal development and spiritual growth. It is not a time to be feared but embraced and utilized appropriately for one's edification.

Decade Timelines/(Expression)/16-7 ROPE		
Decade/Nemesis #	**Expression**	**16-7 ROPE**
Teens-10s	6	16-7 ROPE
20s	5	16-7 ROPE
30s	4	16-7 ROPE
40s	3	16-7 ROPE
50s	2	16-7 ROPE
60s	1	16-7 ROPE
70s	9	16-7 ROPE
80s	8	16-7 ROPE
90s	7	16-7 ROPE

As with all chart components, questions should focus on how each Decade integrates with every other chart component. Does the DTL match the Soul Layer ciphers? Other Basic Matrix parts, Life Matrix parts, timelines, and so forth.

The Cycle of 9s

Like the Decade Timelines, the 9 Cycles run sequentially. They begin at age 1 and conclude at age 9. The 1st *Grand 9 Cycle*, which houses the first grouping of 9 Cycles 1 through 9, starts at age 1 and ends with the 81st year. Age 82 begins the 2nd Grand 9 Cycle and the pattern continues in perpetuity. All 9 Cycles start in a 1 year and terminate in a 9 year.

The 9 Cycle Timelines/(Expression)/16-7 ROPE		
9 Cycle/Nemesis #	**Expression**	**16-7 ROPE**
1st 9 Cycle – age 1 thru 9th year	6	16-7 ROPE
2nd 9 Cycle – age 10 thru 18th year	5	16-7 ROPE
3rd 9 Cycle – age 19 thru 27th year	4	16-7 ROPE
4th 9 Cycle – age 28 thru 36th year	3	16-7 ROPE
5th 9 Cycle – age 37 thru 45th year	2	16-7 ROPE
6th 9 Cycle – age 46 thru 54th year	1	16-7 ROPE
7th 9 Cycle – age 55 thru 63th year	9	16-7 ROPE
8th 9 Cycle – age 64 thru 72nd year	8	16-7 ROPE
9th 9 Cycle – age 73 thru 81st year	7	16-7 ROPE
(Cycle pattern repeats)		

9 Cycle & Decade Sequences

As we study the 9 Cycle and Decade Timeline charts, we see that a sequence emerges between a particular 9 Cycle and its namesake Decade. For example, the 1st 9 Cycle begins at age 1 and completes its cycle at the end of the 9th year (every 9 Cycle begins in a 1 year and ends in a 9 year). The Teens Decade Timeline (marked by the 1 LIST energy in each binary 10 thru 19) begins at age 10 and concludes at age 19. These two timelines are sequential and inform us that linkage occurs between them.

Since we've been discussing the 16-7 ROPE in relation to both these timelines, individuals with a 6 Expression will experience a 16-7 energy for 19 years, beginning from age 1 and ending at age 19 when the 1st 9 Cycle is linked with the Teens Decade. The IR Set is 1/(6)/16-7, assuming the Expression carries a 16-7 energy in its root system, which is most likely. This would help explain why 6 Expression individuals often have challenging early lives, especially if the 1, 6 or 7 are voided or even Grand Voided.

Likewise, for 5 Expression individuals their 2nd 9 Cycle, which begins at age 10, concludes at age 18. It houses a 16-7 ROPE and a 2/(5)/16-7 IR Set, assuming the Expression contains a 14 root. The 2nd Decade begins at age 20 and ends at age 29. For 5 Expression individuals it, too, houses a 16-7 ROPE. Therefore, with the exception of one year at age 19, 5 Expression individuals will feel the 16-7 ROPE energy continually from age 10 through age 29 – a 19 year period.

It is the same for 4 Expression people whose 3rd 9 Cycle and 3rd Decade generate a 16-7 ROPE. The 3rd 9 Cycle begins at age 19 and ends at age 27, generating a 3/(4)/16-7. The 4 would have to have a 13 root but, once again, this carries a high probability. The 30s Decade for the 4 Expression individual begins after a two year respite during ages 28 and 29 and houses a 3/(4)/16-7 ROPE. Therefore, from age 19 through 39, except for ages 28 and 29, 4 Expression people will experience linkage of the 16-7 ROPE.

Following is a chart showing 9 Cycle/Decade linkage of the 16-7 ROPE for all nine Expressions. The linkage timeline may be slightly split, creating *split-linkage* to account for the years in which the linkage is broken or split.

The 9 Cycle/Decade Linkage of the 16-7 ROPE

(Linkage may be "split-linkage" rather than "pure linkage")

("Split-Linkage" timeframe is noted)

9 Cycle	Decade	Split Linkage	Exp	IR Set
1st 9 Cycle (1-9)	Teens Decade (10-19)	none	6	1/(6)/16-7
2nd 9 Cycle (10-18)	2nd Decade (20-29)	1 year	5	2/(5)/16-7
3rd 9 Cycle (19-27)	3rd Decade (30-39)	2 years	4	3/(4)/16-7
4th 9 Cycle (28-36)	4th Decade (40-49)	3 years	3	4/(3)/16-7
5th 9 Cycle (37-45)	5th Decade (50-59)	4 years	2	5/(2)/16-7
6th 9 Cycle (46-54)	6th Decade (60-69)	5 years	1	6/(1)/16-7
7th 9 Cycle (55-63)	7th Decade (70-79)	6 years	9	7/(9)/16-7
8th 9 Cycle (64-72)	8th Decade (80-89)	7 years	8	8/(8)/16-7
9th 9 Cycle (73-81)	9th Decade (90-99)	8 years	7	9/(7)/16-7
(Cycle pattern repeats)				

Lifetime Monthly Timeline (LMT)

The Lifetime Monthly Timeline is the tool describing the exact number of months an individual has been alive. When forecasting or analyzing an event it is just as important as components of the Life Matrix or Name and Letter matrices. In fact, it's not uncommon for the LMT to hold the keys to understanding an event. It can also be an integral facet of stacking.

Months are important in the forecasting process because they are, arguably, the most practical indicator of events in regarding blocks of time. Weeks, days and hours move very fast but by the time they start, they stop. Months, however, are long enough to get a bead on how to manage their energies as the forecasting process is condensed.

When obtaining a full picture of the LMT, check the numerical structure of each month for binary and trinary master numbers, endings of hundred month cycles and the beginning of the next LMT century timeline.

For example, at age 8 years and 3 months any person has lived for exactly 99 months. Their 100 month of life begins in the 4th month of their 8th year. At 41 years, 7 months of age a person hits his 499th month of life. His 500th month begins at age 41 years, 8 months. See the advantage? There is a major shift between the 499th and 500th month of life. The LMT 4th Century is ending and the LMT 5th Century is beginning. A LMT Century lasts for 8 years and 4 months. Therefore, the IR Set LIST energy associated with any Century will be Century#/(Expression)/ROPE and last for 100 months. Therefore, changes from one LMT Century to another can be dramatic.

A full Lifetime Monthly Timeline chart from age 1 through age 100 can be found on pages 62 and 63 of *The King's Book of Numerology, Volume 8 – Forecasting, Part 2*. It is an invaluable forecasting tool, listing the number of months of every person's life for a hundred years. For your convenience, the LMT chart is reproduced at the end of this section on the following two pages.

Aside from Century shifts, check for master triads such as 111, 222, 333, etc. Triads are potent because of their energetic saturation. When these triads appear in the LIST position, correlate them with the individual's Basic Matrix and Life Matrix components. Adding the individual's Expression will generate the ROPE for that period of time.

For example, a person with Double Nickel Filters (5 LP & 5 Exp) will experience dramatic changes in the 3rd month of his/her 46th year – a month housing a LIST 555 trimaster. Why? Because of stacking. The 555 LIST energy of change will focus on matters of love, family and domestic issues because the 555 generates a 15-6 energy in reduction. The following 556 month generates a 16-7 LIST. By adding the Expression to the 555 month and 556 month, a ROPE is generated which indicates exactly what will be happening – in general terms, of course. If the 555 appeared in the ROPE position of a person with Double 5 Filters they, indeed, will experience massive changes in their family and love life, changes which will be the most dramatic of their entire life because the 555 only appears once in a person's life as either a LIST or ROPE energy.

An historic example of a LMT month exists in the dramatic presidential defeat of Hillary Clinton in 2016. The election occurred on 8 November 2016 in her 829 month (her age was 69 years and 1 month), generating a 1/(15)/16-7 IR Set which contributed to her fatal decastack of 16-7 energy. A ten part article series on the 2016 U.S. Presidential election is included in KBN8 beginning on page 247. The article highlights the power of numbers in the forecasting process.

Richard Andrew King

LIFETIME MONTHLY TIMELINE (LMT) CHART – AGES 1 TO 100

Age birth	Mo.# 1	Mo.# 2	Mo.# 3	Mo.# 4	Mo.# 5	Mo.# 6	Mo.# 7	Mo.# 8	Mo.# 9	Mo.# 10	Mo.# 11	Mo.# 12
1	13	14	15	16	17	18	19	20	21	**22**	23	24
2	25	26	27	28	29	30	31	32	**33**	34	35	36
3	37	38	39	40	41	42	43	**44**	45	46	47	48
4	49	50	51	52	53	54	**55**	56	57	58	59	60
5	61	62	63	64	65	**66**	67	68	69	70	71	72
6	73	74	75	76	**77**	78	79	80	81	82	83	84
7	85	86	87	**88**	89	90	91	92	93	94	95	96
8	97	98	**99**	**100**	101	102	103	104	105	106	107	108
9	109	110	**111**	112	113	114	115	116	117	118	119	120
10	121	122	123	124	125	126	127	128	129	130	131	132
11	133	134	135	136	137	138	139	140	141	142	143	144
12	145	146	147	148	149	150	151	152	153	154	155	156
13	157	158	159	160	161	162	163	164	165	166	167	168
14	169	170	171	172	173	174	175	176	177	178	179	180
15	181	182	183	184	185	186	187	188	189	190	191	192
16	193	194	195	196	197	198	**199**	**200**	201	202	203	204
17	205	206	207	208	209	210	211	212	213	214	215	216
18	217	218	219	220	221	**222**	223	224	225	226	227	228
19	229	230	231	232	233	234	235	236	237	238	239	240
20	241	242	243	244	245	246	247	248	249	250	251	252
21	253	254	255	256	257	258	259	260	261	262	263	264
22	265	266	267	268	269	270	271	272	273	274	275	276
23	277	278	279	280	281	282	283	284	285	286	287	288
24	289	290	291	292	293	294	295	296	297	298	**299**	**300**
25	301	302	303	304	305	306	307	308	309	310	311	312
26	313	314	315	316	317	318	319	320	321	322	323	324
27	325	326	327	328	329	330	331	332	**333**	334	335	336
28	337	338	339	340	341	342	343	344	345	346	347	348
29	349	350	351	352	353	354	355	356	357	358	359	360
30	361	362	363	364	365	366	367	368	369	370	371	372
31	373	374	375	376	377	378	379	380	381	382	383	384
32	385	386	387	388	389	390	391	392	393	394	395	396
33	397	398	**399**	**400**	401	402	403	404	405	406	407	408
34	409	410	411	412	413	414	415	416	417	418	419	420
35	421	422	423	424	425	426	427	428	429	430	431	432
36	433	434	435	436	437	438	439	440	441	442	443	**444**
37	445	446	447	448	449	450	451	452	453	454	455	456
38	457	458	459	460	461	462	463	464	465	466	467	468
39	469	470	471	472	473	474	475	476	477	478	479	480
40	481	482	483	484	485	486	487	488	489	490	491	492
41	493	494	495	496	497	498	**499**	**500**	501	502	503	504
42	505	506	507	508	509	510	511	512	513	514	515	516
43	517	518	519	520	521	522	523	524	525	526	527	528
44	529	530	531	532	533	534	535	536	537	538	539	540
45	541	542	543	544	545	546	547	548	549	550	551	552
46	553	554	**555**	556	557	558	559	560	561	562	563	564
47	565	566	567	568	569	570	571	572	573	574	575	576
48	577	578	579	580	581	582	583	584	585	586	587	588
49	589	590	591	592	593	594	595	596	597	598	**599**	**600**
50	601	602	603	604	605	606	607	608	609	610	611	612

The King's Book of Numerology, Volume 12 – Advanced Principles

Age	Mo.#	Mo.#	Mo.#	Mo.#	Mo.#	Mo.#	Mo.#	Mo.#	Mo.#	Mo.#	Mo.#	Mo.#
51	613	614	615	616	617	618	619	620	621	622	623	624
52	625	626	627	628	629	630	631	632	633	634	635	636
53	637	638	639	640	641	642	643	644	645	646	647	648
54	649	650	651	652	653	654	655	656	657	658	659	660
55	661	662	663	664	665	**666**	667	668	669	670	671	672
56	673	674	675	676	677	678	679	680	681	682	683	684
57	685	686	687	688	689	690	691	692	693	694	695	696
58	697	698	**699**	**700**	701	702	703	704	705	706	707	708
59	709	710	711	712	713	714	715	716	717	718	719	720
60	721	722	723	724	725	726	727	728	729	730	731	732
61	733	734	735	736	737	738	739	740	741	742	743	744
62	745	746	747	748	749	750	751	752	753	754	755	756
63	757	758	759	760	761	762	763	764	765	766	767	768
64	769	770	771	772	773	774	775	776	**777**	778	779	780
65	781	782	783	784	785	786	787	788	789	790	791	792
66	793	794	795	796	797	798	**799**	**800**	801	802	803	804
67	805	806	807	808	809	810	811	812	813	814	815	816
68	817	818	819	820	821	822	823	824	825	826	827	828
69	829	830	831	832	833	834	835	836	837	838	839	840
70	841	842	843	844	845	846	847	848	849	850	851	852
71	853	854	855	856	857	858	859	860	861	862	863	864
72	865	866	867	868	869	870	871	872	873	874	875	876
73	877	878	879	880	881	882	883	884	885	886	887	**888**
74	889	890	891	892	893	894	895	896	897	898	**899**	**900**
75	901	902	903	904	905	906	907	908	909	910	911	912
76	913	914	915	916	917	918	919	920	921	922	923	924
77	925	926	927	928	929	930	931	932	933	934	935	936
78	937	938	939	940	941	942	943	944	945	946	947	948
79	949	950	951	952	953	954	955	956	957	958	959	960
80	961	962	963	964	965	966	967	968	969	970	971	972
81	973	974	975	976	977	978	979	980	981	982	983	984
82	985	986	987	988	989	990	991	992	993	994	995	996
83	997	998	**999**	**1000**	1001	1002	1003	1004	1005	1006	1007	1008
84	1009	1010	1011	1012	1013	1014	1015	1016	1017	1018	1019	1020
85	1021	1022	1023	1024	1025	1026	1027	1028	1029	1030	1031	1032
86	1033	1034	1035	1036	1037	1038	1039	1040	1041	1042	1043	1044
87	1045	1046	1047	1048	1049	1050	1051	1052	1053	1054	1055	1056
88	1057	1058	1059	1060	1061	1062	1063	1064	1065	1066	1067	1068
89	1069	1070	1071	1072	1073	1074	1075	1076	1077	1078	1079	1080
90	1081	1082	1083	1084	1085	1086	1087	1088	1089	1090	1091	1092
91	1093	1094	1095	1096	1097	1098	**1099**	**1100**	1101	1102	1103	1104
92	1105	1106	1107	1108	1109	1110	**1111**	1112	1113	1114	1115	1116
93	1117	1118	1119	1120	1121	**1122**	1123	1124	1125	1126	1127	1128
94	1129	1130	1131	1132	**1133**	1134	1135	1136	1137	1138	1139	1140
95	1141	1142	1143	**1144**	1145	1146	1147	1148	1149	1150	1151	1152
96	1153	1154	**1155**	1156	1157	1158	1159	1160	1161	1162	1163	1164
97	1165	**1166**	1167	1168	1169	1170	1171	1172	1173	1174	1175	1176
98	**1177**	1178	1179	1180	1181	1182	1183	1184	1185	1186	1187	**1188**
99	1189	1190	1191	1192	1193	1194	1195	1196	1197	1198	**1199**	**1200**
100	1201	1202	1203	1204	1205	1206	1207	1208	1209	1210	1211	1212

Richard Andrew King

Voids

Voids are crucial parts of the destiny puzzle, as every King's Numerology™ student should well know by now. They must be addressed and assessed; never dismissed. Just think of serial killer Ted Bundy's 1 voided Lifepath. It played a major role in his macabre drama. Had it not been voided, he wouldn't have lacked the energy of identity and personal wholeness that he did and, perhaps, would not have attempted to fill up such a void by engaging in his heinous acts.

General George Patton's 3 void, manifesting communication challenges, did cause him problems in his life and nearly cost him his career. Arguably, his saving grace was his immense capability as a military field commander, as detailed in KBN10, Historic Icons – Part 1.

Elvis Presley's 2 and 8 voids; Princess Diana's 2 and 8 voids; Marilyn Monroe's 3-7-8 voids; Muhammad Ali's 2-6-8 voids; Oprah Winfrey's 2 and 4 voids; Sarah Palin's 4 and 7 voids; Albert Einstein's 4-6-7-8 voids and Amelia Earhart's 6 void all played major roles in their lives. Each of these historic individuals is featured in KBN10.

From the Basic Matrix to the Life Matrix to the Name and Letter Matrices, to every person on the planet – voids simply must be accounted for in order to arrive at a true picture of one's destiny. To avoid them would be like refusing to acknowledge an elephant in your kitchen and pretending it wasn't there.

Annual Cycle Patterns (ACPs)

Annual Cycle Patterns are the hub of every yearly forecast. Comprised of the Age Timeline (ATL), Universal Timeline (UTL) and Personal Year Timeline (PTL), they are the major determinants of destiny during every year of a person's life, giving general knowledge for twelve months at a time.

Just as the ACPs are the center of an annual forecast, the Cycle (C) and Universal (U) monthly columns are the core of the ACPs, offering specific month-to-month data in six different components and, thus, pinpointing potential areas of concern via the C & U columns in the ATL, UTL and PTL. Because the ACPs are centered in monthly components, the Lifetime Monthly Timeline (LMT) energy can easily be assessed along with them and is recommended to be so.

From a forecasting perspective, the first thing to look for in the ACP monthly components is stacking. The next thing is voids, followed by associations with the Basic Matrix, Life Matrix, Name and Letter timelines, Cycle of 9s, Decade timelines, etc.

There are three birth months which should especially be noted because of their potential for generating stacking. Those months are January, April and October.

January is the most important birth month from a stacking perspective because the Cycle month (1) and Universal month (1) will be identical for every year of a person's life, creating a potential for massive stacking and its concomitant intensity. For individuals born in January, their first Cycle month will equal the first Universal month (1 & 1); the second Cycle month will equal the second Universal month (2 & 2) and so forth throughout the year. If the person's Expression is a 9, then the LIST and ROPE will be identical, such as in the case of Elvis Presley whose chart revealed a fourteen stack of 5 energy on the day he died (KBN10)! Without a doubt, people born in January potentially have the most intensive destinies of all because of the potential for stacking. For them, when life is good, it's very, very good, but when it is bad, ouch! It is horrendous.

For individuals born in April (their first Cycle month is a 1), of course. January is their tenth Cycle month (also a 1). This creates a three month period where their Cycle and Universal columns will be identical – the months of January, February and March.

People born in October will reflect a similar situation. Their first Cycle month (a 1) resonates with October's tenth Universal month energy (also a 1). Therefore, October, November and December will generate identical Cycle and Universal columns for them.

Split Ciphers

When assessing a chart, Split Ciphers should always be kept in mind. As we've been learning, our lives are energy; numbers are labels for that energy. When we speak, we radiate audio energy. When we say "20 – 18" for the year 2018, we are actually emitting two different energies – that of "20" and "18." When we add 20 and 18, the result is 38, which is really a hidden energy within the year of 2018. Keep this in mind. It has importance in solving the mysteries of destiny.

Richard Andrew King

Number Patterns

Finally, in generating a professional analysis of one's destiny, we're looking for numeric patterns, especially those that are recurring, harmonious, inharmonious, conflictive, supportive and intense via stacking and continuity via linkage.

Our destinies are a puzzle of many parts. Professionally, we must be aware of as many puzzle parts as we can be and assess those parts to generate an accurate picture of the puzzle. One number or two numbers will not, cannot, begin to piece together one's destiny. To be professional takes work. There simply are no short cuts to excellence. Time, continued study, research, application, analysis and an indomitable passion for seeking Truth are the ingredients of a professional numerologist.

CHAPTER 12

THE KING'S BOOK OF NUMEROLOGY™
SERIES SUMMATION
Volumes 1 through 12

The core purpose of The King's Numerology™ in these first twelve volumes has been to validate the reality of a divinity between numbers and life and to move one's understanding of destiny beyond the stage of belief to the knowledge of certainty. Indubitably, inviolably, there is a divine design to all things, especially to our lives and destinies. Pythagoras was right:

Numbers rule the universe. Everything is arranged
according to number and mathematical shape.

Such edified "knowing" will elevate one's consciousness of life and, if thoroughly grasped, will not only change one's perspective of life but revolutionize it. Once we know, we can never not know. Once we've experienced the indisputable connections between numbers and destiny, there is no going back to the delusional fields of uncertainty and unknowing. Numerology plays a major role in our "knowing."

For those who have studied the science of numeric coding there is, irrefutably, a divine design to each of our lives. To say otherwise is akin to saying the world is flat, that germs don't cause disease, and money really does grow on trees. This may be a bold statement to those unfamiliar with numerology, but for those who have devoted their lives to seeking and finding answers to the

Richard Andrew King

puzzle of destiny via numbers, it is an indisputable fact. Light can be described with numbers. Sound can be described with numbers. It is no different with destiny.

There is a belief that numerology is a New Age science. Nothing could be further from the truth. It is just the opposite. Numbers were before man was. Numbers existed when the universe came into being. When man came along and his intelligence grew, he became aware of mathematics and science, which are rooted in numbers. In fact, what is there that cannot be reduced to numbers?

To understand the gifts numerology offers, one has to be a seeker of Truth, of what actually is, not that which fits a political, social, ideological, religious or personal narrative. Truth is truth. It is immutable, timeless. The truth of numerology is that numbers are labels for energy fields describing and defining our lives and destinies. Verily, *Numerology is the numeric manifestation of the architectural design of life and destiny.*

As the great Isaac Newton stated:

God created everything by number, weight and measure.

and

It is the perfection of God's works that they are all done with the greatest simplicity. He is the God of order and not of confusion.

and

In the absence of any other proof, the thumb alone would convince me of God's existence.

And let's not forget Dr. Albert Einstein's revelations:

Everything is determined, the beginning as well as the end, by forces over which we have no control. It is determined for the insect, as well as for the star. Human beings, vegetables or cosmic dust – we all dance to a mysterious tune, intoned in the distance by an invisible piper.

and

Everyone who is seriously involved in the pursuit of science becomes convinced that a spirit is manifest in the laws of the Universe – a a spirit vastly superior to that of man, and one in the face of which we, with our modest powers, must feel humble.

Pythagoras, Sir Isaac Newton and Dr. Albert Einstein were three of the greatest scientific minds in the history of earth. Their quotes above cannot be dismissed. The substance of their findings are correct. The King's Numerology^{tm} corroborates their assessments.

When one studies numerology thoroughly, not just casually, one becomes awed by its foundational intelligence. It is absolutely amazing how precise, accurate and perfect numbers reflect our lives and relationships – frankly, to the nth degree. Indeed, there exists a universal Power so vast it is beyond the comprehension of the human mind. It is that Power we call God. It is this reality which underscores The King's Numerology^{tm} tag line: *Discovering the Divine Design of Your Life.*

Certainly, our lives are divine. When we see how our specific numerology harmonizes and reflects the smallest events in our lives, we cannot help but be amazed and awed at the vastness of the Power that created this universe.

And speaking of God, if people choose to disbelieve in such a Divine Power, even go so far as to deny that such a Power exists, all they have to do is study numerology, truly study it. Ultimately, they will arrive at the conclusion that some Power had to create all this – our lives, destinies, etc.

Without a doubt, numerology is a sacred science. Through it we are able to see into the depths of destiny and to generally know the blueprint of that destiny. Life is not, repeat "not," a random happening. There is an absolute structure to each of our lives, like it or not, agree with it or not, believe it or not. The fact is, our lives are destined and the blueprint of that destiny is contained within our full birth name and birth date. Even common names play a role. This drama we call life is all so perfect, so stunningly perfect. We are never misplaced or out of place. We are exactly

Richard Andrew King

where we are destined to be at any year, month, day, hour or second of our existence. Destiny is that specific.

Here is a major and intensely critical caveat. We must never abuse the sacred knowledge of numerology by using it to negatively affect others. Such knowledge demands a high state of ethics. Because of karma, what we put onto the circle of life circles back to encircle us to either edify and bless us or discipline and punish us.

If we stay on the Light side of this sacred science, we will be rewarded with all that the Light brings. However, if we get sucked into the Dark side, the self-serving side, the how-can-I-manipulate-numbers-to-my-own-personal-advantage side, we'll be moving in the wrong direction and will ultimately suffer the slings and arrows of such ignorant behavior. Therefore, when we keep our intent and actions pure, we're doing the right thing. If our intent and actions are impure, well, good luck sinking into that well of woe. It won't be a positive experience.

The true gift of numerology is to move beyond the mundane to the divine. Numerology, although wonderful, applies only to this level of creation and not to higher levels of existence. Once we grow in our development, we will rise above this very dense dimension of mind and matter.

In this world we don't see things as they are. We see things the way our numbers are. The more proficient we become in understanding the interplay and manifestation of numbers, we see those "numbers" manifesting perfectly in people's lives. People just cannot escape their "numbers." We cannot escape our numbers, and if we cannot escape them, it follows that we are enslaved by them. We are living beings, and the numbers of our lives represent the shackles binding us to this plane of existence. Such knowledge should motivate us to escape our incarceration in this finite world.

Learning to be comfortable with our destiny and not live with delusions of what we cannot be in this incarnation is a true gift of numerology. Hence, we avoid wasting energy, and maybe a lifetime of it, of wishing we had this or that kind of life. The King's Numerology^{tm} point of view is that life is a continuum, not a drama lived between the entrance of birth and the exit of death in this incarnation, but a journey of various stages of eternal existence from lifetime to lifetime. Therefore, it is important to expand our consciousness beyond the apparent boundaries of this life to other lives and plan accordingly for those lives. If we do not achieve or experience what we desire in this life, we may be able to achieve or experience it in future lives.

For example, so many starry-eyed people may seek a celebrity status in this life, or masterful musicianship or commanding an army or being a world-renowned athlete or, or, or, but their destinies may not deliver such dreams, desires or ambitions in *this* life. That does not mean such dreams cannot be realized in another life. Thus, we need to keep working from life to life until those dreams and desires are fulfilled.

The ultimate goal, however, from the King's Numerology[tm] perspective is to see this world for what it actually is, a prison, and get out, escape, return to our True Home in higher vibratory regions, far beyond this world of duality and dense vibratory matter. Sound eccentric? Maybe, but it depends on one's understanding.

As we study numerology, we eventually arrive at the truth – however painful it may be – that we are trapped in this world within the vibratory walls of our destiny. We may choose to believe that we have total free will, but this is simply a massive delusion which has plagued mankind forever.

If we were totally free, we could choose our path in life. Good luck doing that. Our Lifepath was set before we were born. The Life Matrix reveals a specific road map along which we must travel. Our Epochs, Pinnacles and Challenges are set before us. We can't change them.

Our names, too, as well as the letters of those names, establish another layer of the road map of destiny, dictating what we will go through and for how long in specific terms. We cannot escape these energetic shackles of our enslavement in this life.

So where's the unbound freedom and the free will associated with life in this world? Truthfully, total free will doesn't exist. What free will we do have lies in how we react to the events, situations and circumstances of our lives, our destinies. It is the amalgam of these reactions we freely choose to manifest that plant the seed for a future harvest in following incarnations.

Richard Andrew King

The teachings of Saints and Mystics are that this world is not our True Home but a wilderness. As 19th Century Swami Ji Maharaj states:

This world, which is a wilderness, has been mistaken for a residence.

Famed Middle English writer, Geoffrey Chaucer, author of *The Canterbury Tales*, in his poem "Ballade of Good Counsel" states in the third stanza:

What God doth send, receive in gladsomeness;
To wrestle for this world foretells a fall.
Here is no home, here is but wilderness:
Forth, pilgrim, forth; up, beast, and leave thy stall!
Know thy country, look up, thank God for all:
Hold the high way, thy soul the pioneer,
And Truth shall make thee free, there is no fear!

20th Century Saint Charan Singh, remarks:

You do not belong to this world. Just live in the world and get out of it.

and

This world is a bridge. You can walk across it but do not build upon it.

Guru Nanak of the 15th/16th Centuries says:

Wake up! You are a foreigner in this land.

All of this is to underscore the truth of life in this dimension and point the direction in which we should be moving, i.e., in, up and out. Numerology teaches us many things about this life and our destinies within it, but its greatest gift is removing the blindfold from our delusion-stricken vision, allowing us to see the truth of our existence – that we are trapped in a vibratory dungeon of material phenomena, and the only way to ever find true peace and happiness from this dungeon is to escape from it. The only way that can be done is to focus our life's energy on the Spiritual Path of ascent and ultimate freedom.

As a reference point of our journey through these first twelve volumes of *The King's Book of Numerology*^{tm} series, the Table of Contents (TOC) for each volume follows.

Richard Andrew King

THE KING'S BOOK OF NUMEROLOGY™
Volume 1 (1st Edition, 2003)
FOUNDATIONS & FUNDAMENTALS
TABLE OF CONTENTS

Chapters	Title	Page
	Introduction	
Chapter 1	Foundation	1
Chapter 2	The Basic Numbers	8
Chapter 3	Double Numbers	38
Chapter 4	The Purifiers	66
Chapter 5	Master Numbers	74
Chapter 6	The Letters	84
Chapter 7	The Basic Matrix	88
Chapter 8	The Birthpath/Lifepath	94
Chapter 9	The Expression	142
Chapter 10	The Performance/Experience	162
Chapter 11	The Soul	173
Chapter 12	The Nature	185
Chapter 13	Voids	192
Chapter 14	The Inclusion	202
Chapter 15	Name Changes	217
Chapter 16	Planes of Expression	228
Chapter 17	Extended Basic Matrix	234
Chapter 18	Know Thyself	252
	Glossary	258

Richard Andrew King

NUMBERS ARE GOD CODES FOR LIFE AND ALL LIFE CAN BE EXPLAINED WITH THEM AS THEY, THEMSELVES, ARE THE CIPHERS IDENTIFYING THE ENERGY VIBRATIONS AND FIELDS WHICH ARE RESPONSIBLE FOR THE CONSTRUCT OF THIS CREATION. THROUGH NUMEROLOGY, WE CAN SEE HIS HAND WORKING BEAUTIFULLY, PRECISELY, PERFECTLY – TO THE EXCLUSION OF OUR WILL.

~ Richard Andrew King
(Introduction: KBN1)

THE KING'S BOOK OF NUMEROLOGY™
Volume 2
FORECASTING: PART 1
TABLE OF CONTENTS

Chapters	Title	Page
	Author's Forward	9
Chapter One	Into The Looking Glass	13
Chapter Two	Life Cycle Patterns	29
Chapter Three	Pinnacle/Challenge Timeline	89
Chapter Four	Epoch Timeline	123
Chapter Five	Voids	135
Chapter Six	Case Studies	149
Chapter Seven	Name Timeline	163
Chapter Eight	Letter Timeline	185
Chapter Nine	Decade Timeline	201
Chapter Ten	Age Timeline	209
Chapter Eleven	Universal Timeline	237
Chapter Twelve	Personal Year Timeline	255
Chapter Thirteen	Annual Cycle Pattern	265
Chapter Fourteen	The Chart	275

Richard Andrew King

A CAVEAT: ALL ARTS AND SCIENCES NEED CONTINUED STUDY, RESEARCH, ANALYSIS AND REFINEMENT IN ORDER TO REVEAL DEEPER TRUTHS AND REALITIES. IT IS NO DIFFERENT WITH NUMEROLOGY, AND IT IS NO DIFFERENT WITH THE PRINCIPLES OUTLINED IN THIS BOOK. CONTINUED RESEARCH AND DEVELOPMENT ARE ENCOURAGED IN ORDER TO FURTHER ELUCIDATE THE TRUTH REGARDING THE DIVINE BLUEPRINT OF OUR LIVES AND DESTINIES.

~ Richard Andrew King
(Author's Foreword: KBN2)

THE KING'S BOOK OF NUMEROLOGY™

Volume 3

MASTER NUMBERS

TABLE OF CONTENTS

Chapters	Title	Page
	Author's Introduction	9
Chapter One	Numerology – The Divine Science of Numeric Coding	11
Chapter Two	Binary Master Numbers – Power and Profiles	21
Chapter Three	Master Numbers and Voids	47
Chapter Four	Hidden Master Numbers in the Lifepath	59
Chapter Five	Hidden Master Numbers in the Basic Matrix	67
Chapter Six	Hidden Master Numbers in the Name Timeline	73
Chapter Seven	Hidden Master Numbers in the Letter Timeline	81
Chapter Eight	Hidden Master Numbers in the Life Matrix	87
Chapter Nine	Hidden Master Numbers in Influence/Reality Sets	109
Chapter Ten	Voids and Master Numbers in Influence/Reality Sets	127
Chapter Eleven	Master Number Words and Names	145
Chapter Twelve	Famous People and Their Master Numbers	163
Dictionary	The King's Numerology™ – Dictionary	189
Index		227

Richard Andrew King

NUMBER POWER
© Richard Andrew King

NUMBERS TELL THE TIME,
AS WELL, THEY TELL THE TALE;
NUMBERS CALCULATE THE VOYAGE
OF LIFE IN ITS DETAIL

NUMBERS, JUST LIKE COINS,
INCORPORATE TWO SIDES –
POSITIVE AND NEGATIVE,
AS IN THE TURN OF TIDES.

NUMBERS ARE THE CODES OF LIFE;
THEY GAUGE, DESCRIBE, DEFINE
THE FRAMEWORK AND THE STRUCTURE
OF A LIFE THAT IS DIVINE.

NUMBERS ARE LIFE'S BASIS
AND, AS COSMIC LAW AVERS,
THE BLUEPRINT OF OUR DESTINY
HAS ITS DESIGN IN NUMBERS!

~ Richard Andrew King
(Chapter One: KBN3)

THE KING'S BOOK OF NUMEROLOGY™
Volume 4
INTERMEDIATE PRINCIPLES
TABLE OF CONTENTS

Chapters	Title	Page
	Author's Introduction	9
Chapter One	Influence/Reality Set Formats	11
Chapter Two	Your Specific Expression – Know This Number	21
Chapter Three	Dual Basic Matrix Components	35
Chapter Four	Linkage	55
Chapter Five	Stacking	75
Chapter Six	Binary Capsets	83
Chapter Seven	Trinary & Quaternary Capsets	111
Chapter Eight	Subcap Challenges	119
Chapter Nine	Name Suffixes	127
Chapter Ten	Common Names	137
Chapter Eleven	Fun Number Facts	147
Chapter Twelve	Numerological Potpourri	157
Dictionary		183
Index		227

Richard Andrew King

ONE OF THE MOST POTENT BENEFITS OF THE SCIENCE OF NUMERIC CODING IS THAT IT DESTROYS THE DELUSIONS AND ILLUSIONS KEEPING US CHAINED TO A MATERIAL, MUNDANE, MYOPIC, LIMITED MINDSET AND CONSCIOUSNESS. ONCE WE UNDERSTAND THE TRUTHS OF NUMEROLOGY WE'LL NEVER BE THE SAME AGAIN, CAN NEVER BE THE SAME AGAIN, ANY MORE THAN A CHILD CAN RETURN TO THE WOMB OR A SNAKE CAN RETURN TO ITS OLD SKIN. IN EFFECT, WE TRANSCEND WHAT HAS BEEN, MOVING EVER CLOSER TO THE REALITY OF WHAT IS.

~ Richard Andrew King
(Author's Introduction: KBN4)

THE KING'S BOOK OF NUMEROLOGY™

Volume 5

IR SETS – LEVEL 1

TABLE OF CONTENTS

Chapters	Title	Page
	Author's Introduction	9
Pre-notes: IR Sets – Level 1		11
The #1 IR Set Patterns		19
The #2 IR Set Patterns		53
The #3 IR Set Patterns		75
The #4 IR Set Patterns		115
The #5 IR Set Patterns		137
The #6 IR Set Patterns		165
The #7 IR Set Patterns		191
The #8 IR Set Patterns		229
The #9 IR Set Patterns		271
Keywords		307
Index		313
Richard Andrew King - Books		317

Richard Andrew King

IT TAKES COURAGE TO SEE THE BLUEPRINT OF ONE'S LIFE, BUT WHAT'S THE ALTERNATIVE? TRAVELING BLIND AND UNPROTECTED ON A JOURNEY WHERE WE HAVE NO IDEA WHAT TO EXPECT? OUR DESTINIES ARE NOT UNKNOWN. WE CAN KNOW THEM IF WE CHOOSE AND BE GRATEFUL RECIPIENTS OF SUCH KNOWLEDGE. WE CAN KNOW LIFE ON LEVELS WE NEVER KNEW EXISTED, LEVELS WHICH WILL LIFT US INTO HIGHER REALMS OF CONSCIOUSNESS AND REALITY, FOR WITH EVERY STEP WE TAKE UP THE MOUNTAIN REALITY CHANGES.

~ Richard Andrew King
(Author's Foreword: KBN5)

THE KING'S BOOK OF NUMEROLOGY™

Volume 6

LOVE RELATIONSHIPS

TABLE OF CONTENTS

PART 1

Originally published as *The 5 Minute Lover* and
Your Love Numbers – Discovering the Secrets of Your Life, Loves & Relationships

Chapters	Title	Page
	Author's Introduction	11
1	Love and Light	17
2	The Lifepath [LP-Birth Date]	27
3	The Expression [Exp - Birth Name]	61
4	The Performance [PE - Role in Life]	91
5	The Soul [Desires/Needs/Wants]	121
6	The Nature [Personality]	139
7	The Loveline	159
8	The Love Match	175
9	The Love Mix	189
10	Love Bumps	197
11	Love Voids	207
12	Love Notes	225
	Expanded Keywords/Key Phrase Chart	229

Richard Andrew King

THE THREE MOST IMPORTANT FACTORS IN ALL GREAT RELATIONSHIPS ARE:

1. SOUL LAYER RELEASE

2. EXPRESSION TO PE

3. A SUFFICIENT AMOUNT OF "MER" – MUTUAL ENERGETIC RESONANCE BETWEEN THE PARTIES INVOLVED.

~ Richard Andrew King
(KBN6)

THE KING'S BOOK OF NUMEROLOGY™

Volume 6

PART 2

LOVE RELATIONSHIPS: CASE STUDIES

Love Relationships: Part 2 – Case Studies		235
Love Relationships: Part 2 – Case Studies Table of Contents		237
Preface to Part 2: Case Studies		239
Case Studies: Common Marriages Rated As Excellent		241
# 01	Roberta & Carl	243
# 02	Elizabeth & Daniel	247
# 03	Joan & John	251
# 04	Joan & Barrymore	255
# 05	Catherine & Harold	259
# 06	Elizabeth & Frederick	263
# 07	Elizabeth & Stephen	267
# 08	Margarita & Carlos	271
# 09	Shari & Christopher	275
# 10	Barbara & Fred	279
Case Studies: Celebrity Marriages & Divorces		283
# 11	Tiger Woods & Elin Nordegren	285
# 12	Princess Diana & Prince Charles	289
# 13	Paul McCartney & Heather Mills	293
# 14	Jennifer Garner & Ben Affleck	297
# 15	Bruce Jenner & Kris Kardashian	301
Case Studies: Hollywood's Enduring Marriages		305
# 16	Ron Howard & Cheryl Alley	307
# 17	Tom Hanks & Rita Wilson	311
# 18	Suzanne Somers & Alan Hamel	315
# 19	Alan Alda & Arlene Weiss	319
# 20	Paul Newman & Joanne Woodward	323
Summation: Case Studies		327
Index		329

Richard Andrew King

LOVE AND LIGHT. WHAT DO THEY HAVE IN COMMON? THEY ARE THE BASIS OF LIFE. WITHOUT LIGHT, LIFE AS WE KNOW IT COULD NOT EXIST. WITHOUT LOVE, LIFE AS WE KNOW IT WOULD BE INTOLERABLE. WE ALL NEED LIGHT TO SURVIVE AND WE ALL NEED LOVE TO SURVIVE. A LOVELESS LIGHTLESS LIFE IS NO LIFE AT ALL.

~ Richard Andrew King
(Chapter One: KBN6)

THE KING'S BOOK OF NUMEROLOGY™

Volume 7

PARENTING WISDOM - NUMEROLOGY & LIFE TRUTHS

TABLE OF CONTENTS

PART 1: NUMEROLOGY

Chapter	Title	Page
	Author's Introduction	13
	Foreword – Dr. Victoria Ford, J.D.	15
1	For the Love of Children	17
2	The King's Numerology™ – Basic Matrix	25
3	The Numbers	29
4	The Lifepath (LP)	45
5	The Expression (EXP)	83
6	The Performance/Experience (PE)	117
7	Soul (Desire) Layers	129
8	Nature (Personality) Layers	151
9	Voids	171
10	Names & Letters	191
11	The 1st E-P-C Triad	199
12	The Teen Years	219
13	Parenting Wisdom & Beyond	225
	Appendix – Keywords	231

Richard Andrew King

PARENTING IS THE MOST IMPORTANT AND CRITICAL JOB IN LIFE BECAUSE IT ENCOMPASSES THE CULTIVATING AND SCULPTING OF LIFE ITSELF AS REFLECTED IN OUR CHILDREN – THE SANCTITY OF LIFE IN MANIFEST FORM.

~ Richard Andrew King
(Back Cover Text: KBN7)

THE KING'S BOOK OF NUMEROLOGY™

Volume 7

Parenting Wisdom – Numerology & Life Truths

PART 2: LIFE TRUTHS

Segment	Page
Parenting Wisdom – Part 2: Numerology & Life Truths	235
Author's Introduction	239
A Divine Reality	241
A Man's Worth Is Only Worth What His Word's Worth	245
Balance Is Primary	249
Be A Living Example	253
Better To Have A Gold Character Than A Gold Medal	255
Boundaries, Rules, And Regs	259
Competence Creates Confidence	265
Do The Right Thing Because It's The Right Thing To Do	269
Don't Dummy Down	273
Don't Rush In	277
First Comes Ticker	281
Give 'Em A Spine	285
Grown Ups, Own Up	289
High Bar, High Life; Low Bar, Low Life	291
How To Spoil A Child	297
It's Not All About Them	299
Living With Grace	303

Richard Andrew King

FOR THE LOVE OF CHILDREN

© Richard Andrew King

WHEN I LOOK AT THE SMILE ON A CHILD'S FACE
I SEE HAPPINESS I PRAY WILL NEVER DIE;
I SEE INNOCENCE ALIVE AND WELL
AND . . . PURITY.

THERE IS JOY IN THAT SMILE -
UNADULTERATED AND REAL.
NONETHELESS, I FEEL THE PAIN
OF KNOWING IT MAY NOT LAST
AND I AM LOST FOR WORDS.
SECRET TEARS FALL QUIETLY
BEHIND THE VEIL OF MY GAZE.

HOW HAPPY WOULD THE WORLD BE
IF THAT SMILE COULD EXIST ETERNALLY?
HOW LOVING WOULD ALL LIFE BE
IF THAT PURITY COULD ENDURE?
WHY NOT, I ASK?
WHY NOT?
WHY?

~ Richard Andrew King
(Page 23: KBN7)

THE KING'S BOOK OF NUMEROLOGY™

Volume 7

Parenting Wisdom – Numerology & Life Truths

PART 2: LIFE TRUTHS, CONT'D

Make It A Game	305
Make It A Game	305
Managing Opposition	313
No Second Chance Guarantee	315
No Whining	319
Parental Sovereignty Of Children	321
Pity Pot Poison	323
Sticks And Stones	325
Tender Love Versus Tough Love	327
The Five Needs Of Children	331
The Four Cornerstones Of A Substantive Life	335
The Process Is The Product	339
The Temptations Of S.A.D.	343
The Two Sides Of Life	349
Where Have All The Manners Gone?	353
Your Life, Your Responsibility	357
You're On Your Own – Y.O.Y.O.	361
Glossary	365
Index	377

Richard Andrew King

THERE IS AN UNDERLYING ORDER TO ALL THINGS, INCLUDING OUR DESTINIES. WHEN WE KNOW THAT ORDER, WE CAN APPLY IT TO THE BENEFIT AND WELL BEING OF OUR MOST PRECIOUS TREASURE, OUR CHILDREN. WE CAN RAISE THEM TO BE AWARE, BALANCED, WHOLE, ENLIGHTENED, EVOLVED. THE PRIMARY PURPOSE OF THIS WORK IS TO HELP PARENTS RAISE THEIR CHILDREN SO THEY, THE CHILDREN, CAN ACHIEVE THEIR HIGHEST POTENTIAL AND LIVE A LIFE OF VALUE, FULFILLMENT, SUBSTANCE AND MEANING.

~ Richard Andrew King
(Author's Introduction: KBN7)

THE KING'S BOOK OF NUMEROLOGY™
Volume 8
FORECASTING, PART 2
TABLE OF CONTENTS

Chapters	Title	Page
	PART 1	
	Author's Introduction	9
1	The X-Y Paradigm	11
2	Cycle of Nines	21
3	Timeline Transitions	41
4	Lifetime Monthly Timeline (LMT)	57
5	Annual Cycle Patterns – Monthly Cycles	71
6	Monthly Cycle Patterns (MCPs)	97
7	Life Changes & the Number 5	139
8	Master Filters	149
9	Master Amalgams	159
10	Crown Roots/Pillars	179
11	Addresses – Homes and Businesses	215
12	Numerology Forecasting – Step-by-Step Analysis	223
	PART 2	
	2016 Presidential Election – Articles: 1 to 10	245-317
	Expanded Keywords Chart	325
	Index	331

Richard Andrew King

LIFE IS DESTINED, AND THE BLUEPRINT OF DESTINY IS, INDISPUTABLY, SECRETLY HIDDEN IN OUR BIRTH NAMES AND BIRTH DATES. INDEED, GOD DID NOT DROP US HERE WITHOUT A PLAN OR A WAY OF KNOWING THAT PLAN IF WE SO CHOOSE.

~ Richard Andrew King
(Author's Introduction: KBN8)

THE KING'S BOOK OF NUMEROLOGY™

Volume 8

PART 2

2016 PRESIDENTIAL ELECTION

ARTICLE SERIES: PARTS 1-10

Part	Page	Title	Pub Date
Part 1	249	Turbulent 2 Landscape	4 March 2016, Friday
Part 2	253	Clinton/Trump – Contrast of the 99ers	22 April 2016, Friday
Part 3	263	Feelin' the Bern?	20 May 2016, Friday
Part 4	269	Hillary Clinton and Her Coming Tsunami of Darkness	4 August 2016, Thursday
Part 5	281	Donald Trump – Megaquake of Change	17 August 2016, Wednesday
Part 6	289	1st Presidential Debate – Dueling Octostacks	9 September 2016, Friday
Part 7	293	Hillary's 16-7 August Quintstack Review – A Titanic Headache	28 September 2016, Wednesday
Part 8	301	Donald Trump & the #88 – A United States President?	21 October 2016, Friday
Part 9	309	Hillary's Tsunami of Darkness Makes Landfall Right on Schedule	4 November 2016, Friday
Part 10	317	Final Numeric Notes in a Nutshell	15 November 2016, Tuesday

Richard Andrew King

NUMBERS, LIKE COINS, HAVE TWO SIDES – ONE POSITIVE, ONE NEGATIVE; ONE LIGHT, ONE DARK. UNFORTUNATELY, THE EARTH NOW EXISTS IN A BIPOLAR ENERGY FIELD RULED BY THE NUMBER 2. THIS ENERGY FIELD IS FURTHER ENCLOSED WITHIN THE MORE EXPANSIVE CLOAK OF A BIPOLAR UNIVERSE. BIPOLAR WITHIN BIPOLAR – AN EXTREMELY DIFFICULT CONSTRUCT.

~ Richard Andrew King
(Page 249: KBN8)

THE KING'S BOOK OF NUMEROLOGY™
Volume 9
NUMERIC BIOGRAPHY – PRINCESS DIANA
TABLE OF CONTENTS

Chapters	Title	Page
	Author's Introduction	9
1	Beyond the Veil	11
2	Cosmic Numbers	25
3	Millennia Bridge	49
4	Blueprint of a Princess	63
5	A Path of Tears	85
6	Queen of Hearts/Princess of Love	105
7	Troubled Princess	127
8	Blueprint of a Prince	141
9	Marital Madness	161
10	Letters of Destiny	193
11	A Time to Die	217
12	Reflections	233
	Bibliography	253
	Keywords & Phrases	261
	Index	271
	Richard Andrew King – Books & CDs	275

Richard Andrew King

SHE WAS ENGLAND'S BRIGHTEST STAR, A STAR-CROSSED, REGAL, ROYAL ROSE WHOSE LOVE AND KINDNESS SPRINKLED STARDUST ON THE FURROWED BROW OF THE BRITISH EMPIRE, PLANTING SEEDS OF COMPASSION IN THE HEARTS OF KINGS AND BUILDING A BRIDGE TO USHER HER COUNTRY AND HER PEOPLE INTO THE UNCHARTED DOMAIN OF A NEW MILLENNIUM AND . . . A NEW CONSCIOUSNESS.

~ Richard Andrew King
(Chapter One: KBN9)

THE KING'S BOOK OF NUMEROLOGY™
Volume 10
HISTORIC ICONS – PART 1
TABLE OF CONTENTS

Chapters	Title	Page
	Author's Introduction	9
Preface A	Foundations of Fame	11
Preface B	The Keys of Fame	17
Historic Icon #1	Albert Einstein	29
Historic Icon #2	Amelia Earhart	39
Historic Icon #3	Elvis Presley	53
Historic Icon #4	General George Patton	71
Historic Icon #5	Howard Hughes	89
Historic Icon #6	John F. Kennedy	101
Historic Icon #7	Marilyn Monroe	121
Historic Icon #8	Michael Jackson	141
Historic Icon #9	Muhammad Ali	159
Historic Icon #10	Oprah Winfrey	175
Historic Icon #11	Princess Diana	191
Historic Icon #12	Sarah Palin	211
	Power, Fame & Kings	223
	Appendix – Keywords	231
	Glossary	237
	Index	245

Richard Andrew King

ONCE WE SEE THE RELATIONSHIP BETWEEN THE LIVES OF THESE FEATURED ICONS AND THEIR FULL NAMES AND BIRTH DATES, IT WILL REVOLUTIONIZE OUR LIVES. HOW COULD IT NOT? LIFE IS NOT HAPPENSTANCE. THERE IS A POWER AT WORK FORMULATING OUR DESTINIES THAT TRANSCENDS HUMAN COMPREHENSION, A POWER SO VAST AND INTELLIGENT THAT WE CANNOT BUT BE HUMBLED BY ITS REALITY.

~ Richard Andrew King
(Author's Introduction: KBN10)

THE KING'S BOOK OF NUMEROLOGY™

Volume 11

THE AGE OF THE FEMALE – PART 1

A Thousand Years of Yin

TABLE OF CONTENTS

Chapter	Title	Page
	Author's Introduction	11
1	A Thousand Years of Yin	15
2	Millennia Shift	25
3	Yin Power	41
4	Number Power	55
5	Approaching Signs I	69
6	Approaching Signs II	89
7	Current Signs	123
8	Concerns & Dangers	143
9	Positives & Pluses	163
	Works Cited	181

Richard Andrew King

A THOUSAND YEARS OF YANG, GONE.

A THOUSAND YEARS OF HIM BEEN.

NOW, A THOUSAND YEARS OF YIN BEGIN

AS THE COSMIC CLOCK ASSURES

AND THE TIDES OF TIME SECURE –

THE NEXT ONE THOUSAND YEARS

BELONG TO HER.

~ Richard Andrew King
(Chapter One: KBN11)

THE KING'S BOOK OF NUMEROLOGY™

Volume 11

THE AGE OF THE FEMALE – PART 2

Heroines of the Shift

TABLE OF CONTENTS

Chapter	Title	Page
	Author's Introduction	189
1	Yin Rise	191
2	Nobel Yin	205
3	Athletic Yin	245
4	Notable Yin	279
5	Yin Speak	325
	Appendix – Keywords	359
	Index	365
	King – Books/CDs	371
	Works Cited – Part 2	383
	Contact Information	393

Richard Andrew King

YIN RISE

SUN RISE, MOON RISE, YIN RISE

EYES TURN HEAVENWARD TO SKIES AGLOW

WITH THE CRESTING WAVE

OF THE COSMIC WIND

CATAPULTING YIN INTO ASCENDANCE.

NO MORE CONCEALED, HER POWER REVEALED,

SOARING WINGS AND SPREADING SAILS

LIFT HER HIGH WHERE NONE DENY

THE PRESENCE OF HER PRESENCE.

IN EVERY FIELD SHE WIELDS HER FORCE,

IN EVERY FIELD HER SEED IS SEWN.

SCEPTER, KINGDOM, CROWN AND THRONE

FOR A THOUSAND YEARS ARE HERS TO OWN.

~ Richard Andrew King
(Part 2, Chapter One: KBN11)

THE KING'S BOOK OF NUMEROLOGY™
Volume 12
ADVANCED PRINCIPLES
TABLE OF CONTENTS

Chapters	Title	Page
	Author's Introduction	
Chapter 1	The Numerology of Dislike	11
Chapter 2	The Numerology of Betrayal	25
Chapter 3	Nemesis Numbers	57
Chapter 4	Common Name Dynamics	83
Chapter 5	Single Name Analysis Profile - SNAP	91
Chapter 6	Numerology and Past Lives	103
Chapter 7	Family Ties	115
Chapter 8	Life Journey Shifts & Changes	129
Chapter 9	Voids, Vacuums & Karmic Scales	183
Chapter 10	The Life Matrix Diamond	197
Chapter 11	Professional Chart Analysis	217
Chapter 12	KBN Series Summation: Volumes 1 - 12	243

Richard Andrew King

INDUBITABLY, INVIOLABLY, THERE

IS A DIVINE DESIGN TO ALL THINGS,

ESPECIALLY OUR LIVES AND DESTINIES.

~ Richard Andrew King
(Chapter 12: KBN12)

APPENDIX – KEYWORDS

EXPANDED KEYWORDS/KEY PHRASE CHART

Note 1: every number maintains a positive and negative side (polarity), just as every coin has two sides. Furthermore, we cannot hold a coin without holding both sides simultaneously. The same is true for numbers and our lives reflect both the positive and negative aspects of each vibration to some degree. In other words, no number is perfect, no chart is perfect, no human being is perfect. We all have assets and liabilities, good karmas and bad karmas.

Note 2: every single number has ten binary or two-digit numbers attached to it and which, when added together reduce to form that specific single number.

Note 3: it would be impossible to list every word in the English language which is attached to each of the nine basic numbers. After all, there are only nine basic numbers and hundreds of thousands of words. Therefore, a complete keyword list would be impossible to generate. Below, however, are more words and phrases than simply those used in the basic keyword chart.

Note 4: if voided in a chart, especially if a voided challenge occurs, the influences can be quite negative, reflecting the dark side of a number.

ONE - 1
(Fire) (Symbols: Sun, Staff)

10	19	28	37	46	55	64	73	82	91

The Primal Force, first cause, yang, fire, vitality, action, man, male, masculine, father, self, identity, creativity, ego, skill, individual, self-confidence, boss, leader, director, doer, initiator, creator, authority figure, pioneer, star, center of attention, willpower, self-control, independence, self-sufficiency, determination, activates, initiates, creates, dominates, leads, attains, driving, strong, courageous, powerful, dynamic, decisive, unbending, steadfast, dominant, linear, single-minded, unique, original, starts, new beginnings, creation, genesis, assertive, aggressive, overbearing, self-indulgent, ego-maniacal, selfish, self-obsessed, tom-boy, rational, reasonable, logical, unemotional, radiating, initiating, purpose, direction. TIME FRAME: a time of initiation, initiating, action, seed planting, new beginnings, starts; a period of the self and its attainments; being accountable and responsible; being the leader or bread-winner; issues of identity, self-worth, males and all things Yang; moving ahead; getting new direction; planting flags; solo excursions; tests of courage and standing alone against all people and all odds. Ones make things happen.

TWO - 2
(Water) (Symbols: Moon, Scales, Twin Towers)

11	20	29	38	47	56	65	74	83	92

Yin, water, woman, female, feminine, mother, others, relationships, especially those that are close, personal and intimate; 2s take sides, support, separate, helper, assistant, adversary, adversity, adversarial, assistance, follower, dependent, diplomatic, cooperative, cooperation, collaboration, consideration, teamwork, passive, patient, non-obtrusive, intuitive, receptive, responsive, agreeable, amenable, affable, kind, warm, devoted, sweet, gentle-hearted, peacemaking, harmonizing, equalizing, submissive, rhythmic, equalizing, equilibrium, competition, rivalry, contention, confliction, duality, duplicity, deceit, indecisive, division, the great divide, 'us vs. them,' intuitive, behind the scenes, bending, yielding, non-assertive, together, taking sides, opposition, vacillation, irrational, illogical, unreasonable, emotional, reflecting (as in the Moon reflecting light, water reflecting an image) and absorbing (vs. radiating of the 1), acquiescing. TIME FRAME: a period of others, serving them, being helpful and supportive; being the helper, partner, team player, opponent, adversary, inhibitor, diplomat, judge, arbitrator, go-between; lessons of tolerance and intolerance; a time of all things Yin; period of competition, stress, adversarial conditions, tensions, tug-o-wars; learning to get along; being balanced; finding the middle path; being deceptive or dealing with deception and/or the interference or inhibition of others and either their helpfulness or hindering; a time of high energy and friction.

THREE - 3
(Air) (Symbols: Triangle, Trident)

12	21	30	39	48	57	66	75	84	93

Trinity, triads, air, the triangle (Ancient symbol of Perfection), The Golden Mean of Aristotle, Yin and Yang in perfect balance (the symbol of the Tao), art, artistry, artistic, image (moving or still), fashion, words, communication, expression, personal integration, fulfillment, complete approach to health, happiness, wholeness, holiness, holistic, well-being, marriage, joy, enjoyment, pleasure, parties, friends, good times, talkative, verbal, gregarious, approachable, gossip, social, outgoing, fun-loving, entertaining, light-hearted, vibrant, alive, creative, imaginative, happy, optimistic, cheerful, charming, health, beauty, vanity, writing, acting, performing, glamorous, ease, disease, dis-ease, hostility, poisonous words, harsh, critical, stern, harsh, vain, egotistical; often found in charts of politicians. TIME FRAME: a time of self-expression and fulfillment, being creative, using words, being involved with health, beauty, disease, dis-ease, acting, writing, painting, modeling, sculpting; a time of children and seeking perfection and balance; a time of happiness (if positively aspected) and unhappiness and harshness (if negatively aspected); can give a sense of entitlement or ease of life coming toward the self; issues of purity, holiness, unholiness, pure pleasure or debauchery, harshness and communication which is either uplifting or destructive. It is a time of integration and self-realization, a time where the goodness or meanness of life will reveal itself; a time of happiness and/or sadness; pleasure and/or pain.

FOUR - 4
(Earth) (Symbols: Square, Roots, Anchors, Chains)

13	22	31	40	49	58	67	76	85	94

Earth, order, structure, framework, form, foundation, boundaries, rules, regulations, guidelines, routine, status quo, concrete, confines, confinements, proprieties, mechanics, work, service, servant, matter, materialism, transformation, transmutation, security, stability, effort, hard, stubborn, recalcitrant, <u>resistance</u>, <u>resistant</u>, confinement, toil, physical strength, solid power, steadfast, sturdy, the rock, anchor, roots, chains, obstacles, tradition, convention, duty, loyalty, dependability, discipline, control, commitment, construction, prudent, clerical, industrious, down to earth, frugal, practical, organizing, house, beams, foundations, constancy, regimentation, classification, organization, organized, systemize, non-adventurous, predictable, obstinate, boring, routine, patterns, status quo, plodding along, unchanging, the order of things, events, situations, circumstances and relationships; if voided or challenged can be unstable, unfaithful, dishonest, weak, insecure, faithless. TIME FRAME: a time of work, effort, restriction (especially in conjunction with 5 energy), limitation, grinding it out, being consistent, not changing, conforming, nuts & bolts; a time when the focus is on the structures of life - financial, moral, ethical, routines, regimes, order, discipline; it is a time of learning about boundaries and borders, rules and regulations, service and work, faithfulness and devotion, sacrifice and surrender.

FIVE - 5
(Fire) (Symbols: Wings, Wheels, Needles, Broken Chains)

14	23	32	41	50	59	68	77	86	95

Free, freedom, fire, change, movement, detachment, detaching, shifting, wild, wayward, careless, adventure, adventurous, roam, roaming, liberation, liberate, unrestrained, undisciplined, unsettled, non-restriction, nonrestrictive, shifts, slavery mercurial, spontaneous, excitement, experience, experiential, variety, talent, versatility, people, senses, sexuality, sensations, stimulation, motion, energy, mercurial, multi-faceted, many sided, assortment, exuberant, enthusiastic, exciting, spontaneous, foot-loose, flamboyant, dashing, energetic, exploring, exposure, exhibitionist, adventurous, travel, unpredictable, unconventional, uncertain, unstable, instability, the crowd, diverse, diversity, letting go, free-spirited, rebellious, liberation, liberating, stimulating, stimulants, non-complacent, temptation, temperance, restraint, indulgence, animated, exuberant, flamboyant, volatile. TIME FRAME: a time of freedom, change, shifting, movement, uncertainty, detachment, letting go, releasing, wiping out the old, exploring, investigating, experimenting, sexuality, sensual gratification; temperance and fidelity challenged; not a time to cling, but a time to let go, detach, release and move on; also a time testing our true understanding of freedom which is not action devoid of consequence but action taken in consideration of consequence, action taken in pursuit of sensual pleasures, sense gratification and wild sorties into the realms of indulgence create slavery and bondage and all the suffering, woes and wailings associated with such incarceration, action of freedom taken in consideration of consequence by following the inner voice of conscience, temperance and restraint, the end result will be true freedom and liberation from sensual enslavement. The key note during a Five period is to be wise; look ahead to the results of your actions; exercise moderation and fidelity and do not step into the regions of material indulgence.

Richard Andrew King

SIX - 6
(Water) (Symbol: Heart)

15	24	33	42	51	60	69	78	87	96

Love, hate, home, water, hearth, matters of the heart, romance, domesticity, adjustability, responsibility, accountability, personal love, art, artistic, beauty, community, harmonious, caring, warm, nurturing, understanding, soft, comfortable, dependable, conscientious, kind, responsive, protective, protecting, music, sex, singing, harmonizing, hatred, cruelty, family discord, family issues and concerns, addiction, jealousy, envy, resentment. TIME FRAME: a time of matters of the heart, love issues, domestic (individual, personal, community, national, global) energies, concerns, responsibilities, possible addictions, romance, lust, sexuality.

SEVEN - 7
(Air) (Symbols: Hurricane, Thinker, Cross)

16	25	34	43	52	61	70	79	88	97

Spirit, spiritual, mystical, meticulous, air, bliss, chaos, thought, the thinker, introspection, perception, investigation, inquisition, intuition, reflection, examination, judgment, recession, repose, receding, distancing, counseling, alienation, study, testing, reflecting, evaluating, reviewing, learning, processing, isolation, isolated, solitary, solitude, separate, separation, seclusion, secrecy, privacy, analysis, religion, rest, quiet, calm, peace, tranquility, inwardness, the 'within', perfection, poise, wisdom, saints/sinners, light/dark, curious, distant, cool, cold, removed, withdrawn, shy, reclusive, alone, lonely, loneliness, refined, non-social, purification, stressed, distressed, troubled, turmoil, torment, tumult, trauma, unworldly, considerate, inconsiderate, cold, cruel, calculating, harsh, ruthless, brutal thoughtful, thoughtless, private, secret, secretive, stealthy, hide, hidden, investigative, trouble, problems, worry, concern, anxiety, anxious, scandal, scandalous, misery, miserable, grief, deep, despair, anguish, chaos, chaotic, distressful, soul-searching, cynical, cynicism. TIME FRAME: a time for the building of inner strength and developing the inner self and all things spiritual; a time of being alone; a time of testing; a time of reflecting, analyzing, studying, teaching, pondering, going within and searching, asking questions and seeking answers, becoming mature through the fires of the heart and emotions, being brought to our knees in humble supplication of the power of God, Source, Spirit, the Lord; the time of the hurricane; choices of fidelity or adultery; peace or chaos; a time of purification by fire; a time to float across to the other side on a river of your own tears; the time to find and cling to God.

EIGHT - 8
(Earth) (Symbol: Lemniscate)

17	26	35	44	53	62	71	80	89	98

Earth sign, interaction, involvement, connection, disconnection, orchestration, coordination, manipulation, administration, circulation, association, associating, continuation, continuity, opportunity, responsive, (non-responsive if void), mixing, karmic conduit, circuits, circulate, systems, worldly success-power-wealth, opportunist, materialism, material comfort, management, marketing, promotion, commerce, business, flow, efficiency of motion-movement-management, being in the loop, administrator, executive, coordinating, socialization, socializing, external power, leadership, organization, involve, engage, usury, social importance and power, externalization, the 'without,' can also reference a lack of understanding of 'give and take' and 'cause and consequence.' TIME FRAME: a time of connection/disconnection, interaction, management, procrastination (if negatively afflicted), marketing, making business contacts, socializing, organizing and administrating, executing as one who is an executive; a time of association, administration, manipulation, orchestration, circulation, coordination; a time of bringing things together and making it happen; a time to be careful of using others to our advantage; a time of success or failure where all things work together harmoniously (for success) or fall apart to create failure.

NINE - 9
(Grand Elemental - All Elements) (Symbol: Crown)

18	27	36	45	54	63	72	81	90	99

Universality, timeless, macrocosm, endings, conclusions, completions, climaxes, chameleon, volunteer, inclusions, humanitarian, humanitarianism, teacher, impersonal love, broadcast, broadcaster, broadcasting, public exposure, pushy, magnanimous, regal, royal, philanthropic, philosophical, all encompassing, understanding, generous, tolerant, broad-minded, global, worldly, strong, dominant, domineering, controlling, artistic, intense emotion, acting, theatrical, charismatic, travel, the 'many,' healer, healing, the universal giver, expansion, the world, represents the universal languages of music, art, love. TIME FRAME: a time of conclusions, endings, resolutions, terminations, finalizations, volunteering, being public and being in the public eye and spotlight; moving within the macrocosm and life stage, moving among the masses, being famous or infamous; a time of travel - mentally or physically; a time of higher education and the advancement of thought and philosophy; a time to be universal and far-reaching; a time to be the great communicator, the powerful ruler, the icon of a culture; a time to serve humanity and expand one's thought beyond the finite boundaries of the self; a time to act, expand and be known. It is life stage for theater, medicine, sport and war; strong, even dominant personality and persona, possibly including or bordering on being over-bearing, domineering, imperious.

KBN-12 INDEX

Topic	Pages
Abraham Lincoln	186-187
Albert Einstein	183-184, 240, 244, 245, 277
Amelia Earhart	81, 190, 240, 277
Ballade of Good Counsel	248
Bernie Madoff	37, 51
Bishop Mandell Creighton	45
Britain's Got Talent	168, 170
Callista Bisek	35
Charles Darwin	185-186
Charles Kuhl	188, 190
Common Name Dynamics	83-90 (Chapter 4)
Confucius	58
Crown Diamond	204
Cycle of 9s	60, 64-65, 71, 126, 186, 234, 241
Decade Timeline	60, 63-64, 71, 77, 119, 126, 186, 194, 220, 226, 233-235, 241, 253
Dina Parr	46
Dirty Dancing	17, 19
Disunited Triad	192
Donald Trump	22-23, 273
Dr. Samuel Johnson	42, 48
E Online	46
Elin Nordegren	37, 40, 54, 263
Elvis Presley	66, 67-68, 81, 190, 219, 230, 240-241, 277
External Dynamics	86
Family Ties	115-128 (Chapter 7)
Garth Brooks	219
General Dwight D. Eisenhower	211, 215
General George Patton	81, 135, 188, 211, 240, 277
Geoffrey Chaucer	248
Grand 9 Cycle	234
Grand Amplifier	18, 65-66, 99, 148
Grand Elemental	18, 43-44, 66, 96, 99, 148, 166, 168, 221
Grand Ruler	18, 65-66, 99, 148, 168
Great Purifier	17, 26, 34, 57-58-61, 64, 70-73, 81-82, 142, 202, 225, 233
Guru Nanak	55, 248
Helen Keller	58
Henry Wadsworth Longfellow	36
Hillary Clinton	81, 237, 273
House of Windsor	279
Howard Hughes, Jr.	81, 230, 277
I Dreamed a Dream	168, 170
Internal Dynamics	86-87
Jackie Battley	35
Jennifer Grey	17-18
John Edwards	34
John F. Kennedy	81, 84, 230, 277
John Lewis	22-23
Kahlil Gibran	59
Karate Institute of America	58
Karmic Scales of Justice	195
KBN Series Summation	243-290 (Chapter 12)
Kobe Bryant	37
Lance Armstrong	67-68, 83, 87, 89

Richard Andrew King

Les Misérables	168
Life Journey Shifts & Changes	129-182 (Chapter 8)
Life Matrix Diamond	197-216 (Chapter 10)
Life Matrix Master Diamond	211, 213, 215
Lifetime Monthly Timeline	31, 33, 60, 63-64, 71, 226, 236-238, 240, 271
Lord Acton	42, 45
Loveline Match & Mix	116, 313
Marianne Ginther	35
Marilyn Monroe	20-21, 69-70, 81, 141-142, 240, 277
Michael Jackson	37, 81, 146, 149-162, 198, 204, 230, 277
Mix Dynamic Energy	84-86
Muhammad Ali	240, 277
Mutual Energetic Resonance (MER)	11, 262
Nemesis Numbers	7, 57-82 (Chapter 3) 283
Newt Gingrich	35
Nikola Tesla	183-184
Number of Man	15, 210
Numerology of Betrayal	25-56 (Chapter 2)
Numerology of Dislike	11-24 (Chapter 1)
Numerology of Past Live	103-114 (Chapter 6)
O.J. Simpson	37
Oprah Winfrey	81, 180, 191, 205, 230, 240, 277
Patrick Swayze	17
Prince Charles	17, 263
Princess Diana	17, 68-69, 230, 240, 263, 275, 277
Professional Chart Analysis	217-242 (Chapter 11)
Pythagoras	190, 243, 245
Pythagorean maxim	15
Queen Elizabeth II	219
Rachel Uchitel	38, 40
Rielle Hunter	34
Royal Family	69
Saint Charan Singh	37, 120, 248
Saint Dadu	25, 104, 106, 109
Saint Jagat Singh	47, 104
Sarah Palin	240, 277
Single Name Analysis Profile (SNAP)	91-102 (Chapter 5)
Sir Isaac Newton	105, 245
Sir Walter Scott	233
Soul/Nature Overview (SNO)	94
Split Linkage	236
Superior Man	58
Susan Boyle	168-170
Suzanne Necker	42-43
Swami Ji Maharaj	248
Ted Bundy	224, 230, 240
The Canterbury Tales	248
Tiger Woods	36-54, 64-65, 94, 171, 174-175
Tony Curtis	20-21
Voids, Vacuums & Karmic Scales	183-196 (Chapter 9)

RICHARD ANDREW KING
~ BOOKS ~
RichardKing.net and Major Online Retailers

(NOTE: Consider using KBN11 Index Format)

The King's Book of Numerology (KBN1)
Volume 1-Foundations & Fundamentals

The King's Book of Numerology, Volume 1-Foundations & Fundamentals provides complete descriptions of Basic Numbers, Double Numbers, Purifier Numbers, Master Numbers, the Letters in Simple and Specific form as well as the Basic Matrix, the numerological blueprint of our lives.

"*The King's Book of Numerology* series contains new information that informs and predicts more completely and accurately than any previously published numerological work. It brings back the empowered sciences of long ago, information long since lost upon this plane."
~ G. Shaver

"The best numerology book I've ever read." ~ M.W.

"I've learned as much about numerology from *The King's Book of Numerology* the last few days than I have in my past five years of study." ~ Frank M.

The King's Book of Numerology II (KBN2)
Forecasting – Part 1

The King's Book of Numerology II: Forecasting – Part 1 is dedicated to opening the door to the divine blueprint of our lives. That plan, that divine blueprint of destiny, is exact, precise, unchangeable, unalterable and . . . knowable, at least in general terms.

Once this awareness of a predetermined fate becomes established through application of numbers and their truths, our understanding and consciousness of life will, no doubt, change. We will begin to see ourselves as part of an immense spiritual super-structure far beyond our current ability to comprehend, understand or perceive. Life will take on new meaning and, perhaps, we will even begin to awaken to greater spiritual truths. Subjects covered: Life Cycle Patterns, The Pinnacle/Challenge Matrix, Epoch Timeline, Voids, Case Studies and much more.

The King's Book of Numerology 3 (KBN3)
Master Numbers

The King's Book of Numerology 3 – Master Numbers delves deeply into the subject of master numbers – multiple digit numbers of the same cipher, focusing especially on binary master numbers: 11-22-33-44-55-66-77-88-99.

Master numbers are the nuclear component of the numeric spectrum and play powerful roles in the destinies of individuals. They cannot be ignored.

KBN3 reveals the process of discovering hidden master numbers in all facets of a King's Numerology™ chart, how voids effect the life and much more.

The King's Book of Numerology 4 (KBN4)
Intermediate Principles

The King's Book of Numerology 4 – Intermediate Principles will expand your consciousness of the mysteries of life and destiny by taking you deeper into the secret world of numbers and their meaning.

Life is energy. People are energy. Numbers are arithmetic codes describing and defining the energies that comprise our lives and destinies. Like priceless treasures discovered during an archaeological dig, numbers and number patterns buried beneath the surface of single numbers contain a treasure trove of untold wealth and secret riches of knowledge and wisdom.

Intermediate Principles chapters include Common Names, Linkage, Stacking, Name Suffixes, Binary Capsets, Influence/Reality Set Formats, Dual Basic Matrix Components, Subcap Challenges, and much more.

The King's Book of Numerology 5 (KBN5)
I/R Sets – Level 1

IR SETS are the crux, core and substance of numerology forecasting, indispensable to the King's Numerology^{tm} system and to anyone choosing to know where they've been, where they are now and where they're headed. They are obligatory for any serious and professional numerologist.

The King's Book of Numerology 5: I/R Sets – Level 1 offers a general explanation of each of the 81 IR Sets in order to create a foundation on which to build a greater understanding of how life's events affect us. KBN5 is a starting point from which to grow greater knowledge of one's self and destiny.

IR SETS are a gift for those willing to receive them, study them and apply their vast level of knowledge to make our lives more understandable, manageable, easier, better, whole.

The King's Book of Numerology 6 (KBN6)
Love Relationships

Note: This is a "stand alone" book. Its knowledge is not dependent on prior KBN publications.

The *King's Book of Numerology, Volume 6 – Love Relationships* (KBN6) guides you through this revolutionary method of understanding the Secrets of Love and Happiness via the mystical science of numbers. If you can add 1 + 1, you can quickly learn how to utilize and benefit from the great truths shared within this book.

The fundamental Secret of all great relationships, marriages and partnerships revolves around the quality and quantity of *Mutual Energetic Resonance* between the partners. This resonance (MER) is easily identified from the natal data of the individuals involved – their full birth names and birth dates. In fact, this birth data is where the mysteries of everything, including love relationships and destiny, all begins.

KBN6 is divided into two parts: Part 1 is the original book *Your Love Numbers*; Part 2 puts the King's Numerology^{tm} number science to the test with twenty marital case studies broken into three segments: Section I. Marriages rated as excellent; Section II. Celebrity marriages ending in divorce; and Section III. Hollywood marriages that have endured. These case studies are powerfully insightful because they reveal, without question, the dramatic and irrefutable correlation between love and numbers.

Richard Andrew King

The King's Book of Numerology 7 (KBN7)

Parenting Wisdom

The King's Book of Numerology, Volume 7: Parenting Wisdom – Numerology & Life Truths (KBN7) is a compilation of two books in one. The reason for this is twofold: 1. To place the *Parenting Wisdom* series in one convenient resource; 2. As a continuing effort to place all King's Numerology™ books under one banner. KBN7 is also a "stand alone" book. Its knowledge is not dependent on having read prior KBN publications.

KBN7-Part 1: *Parenting Wisdom for the 21st Century – Raising Your Children by Their Numbers to Achieve Their Highest Potential* reveals the secrets to understanding a child's Basic Matrix and destiny through the most ancient of all sciences, numbers. Using numerology to help raise children is a revolutionary idea, reaping great rewards for children in helping them understand themselves, their life's journey and destiny.

KBN7-Part 2: *Parenting Wisdom – What to Teach the Children* offers thirty-three time-tested universal principles of life which parents can use to create a strong foundation for their children, allowing them to develop into whole, fulfilled and substantive adults. These thirty-three fundamental concepts offer parents a road map and paradigm of what to teach the children.

The King's Book of Numerology 8 (KBN8)

Forecasting, Part 2

The King's Book of Numerology, Volume 8 – Forecasting, Part 2 (KBN8) broadens and expands the knowledge of numerology forecasting into areas of greater depth and specificity, giving students and practitioners of this divine numeric science tools unknown heretofore, allowing them to rise to the zenith of understanding in decoding life and destiny, and once again proving that life is destined and that the blueprint of destiny is, indisputably, secretly hidden in our birth names and birth dates. Indeed, God did not drop us here without a plan or a way of knowing that plan if we so choose.

The King's Book of Numerology, Volume 8 – Forecasting, Part 2

Contents

The X-Y Paradigm, Cycle of Nines, Timeline Transitions, Lifetime Monthly Timeline (LMT), Annual Cycle Patterns – Monthly Timelines, Monthly Cycle Patterns (MCPs), Life Changes and the Number 5, Master Filters, Master Amalgams, Crown Roots/Pillars, Addresses – Homes and Businesses, Numerology Forecasting – Step-by-Step Analysis, and the 2016 Presidential Election Series – Articles: 1 to 10

The King's Book of Numerology, Volume 12 – Advanced Principles

The King's Book of Numerology 9 (KBN9)
Numeric Biography – Princess Diana

The King's Book of Numerology, Volume 9 – Numeric Biography, Princess Diana was originally published as *Blueprint of a Princess – Diana Frances Spencer, Queen of Hearts*, in 1998 and reprised in 2017 – the 20th Anniversary of Diana's death – to be included in *The King's Book of Numerology Series*.

KBN9 thoroughly explains the life, destiny and heartbreak of Princess Diana based on the King's Numerology^{tm} and its system of numeric coding.

For a more thorough explanation, see the following *Blueprint of a Princess* description.

The King's Book of Numerology 10 (KBN10)
Historic Icons – Part 1

The King's Book of Numerology, Volume 10 – Historic Icons, Part 1 (KBN10) was initially published as *Destinies of the Rich & Famous – The Secret Numbers of Extraordinary Lives* and has been added to The King's Book of Numerology^{tm} series to expand its platform.

WHY do individuals become historic icons? What is it in their numbers allowing them to be rich or successful or famous or universally known globally and historically? Is it luck? Hard work? Advantage by family name? No. It is destiny, purely and simply, and the blueprint of that destiny is contained within the full birth name and birth date of each of these featured icons.

KBN10 highlights the following twelve famous historic individuals and offers explanations via The King's Numerology^{tm} as to why they have become globally historic figures – Dr. Albert Einstein, Amelia Earhart, Elvis Presley, General George Patton, Howard Hughes, John F. Kennedy, Marilyn Monroe, Michael Jackson, Muhammad Ali, Oprah Winfrey, Princess Diana and Sarah Palin.

Richard Andrew King

The King's Book of Numerology 11 (KBN11)
The Age of the Female – Volumes 1 & 2

Blueprint of a Princess
Diana Frances Spencer - Queen of Hearts

The tragic death of Princess Diana of Wales - the most famous, the most photographed, the most written about woman of the modern world and possibly of all time - was one of the most shocking and saddening events of the late Twentieth Century. Not since the assassination of American President John Fitzgerald Kennedy in 1963, has such an event captured the attention of the world. On that ill-fated Sunday of 31 August 1997, and the following week until her funeral, there was much discussion and reflection of the Queen of Hearts, the People's Princess, England's Rose. But in all of the media news coverage, there was no discussion given to the cosmic aspects of her life and death.

Blueprint of a Princess is dedicated to addressing those issues through The King's Numerology^{tm}. Its purpose and hope is to offer some consolation and explanation as to that one question so poignantly written on a card of condolence left with the multitude of flowers before the gates of Buckingham Palace. . . "Why?"

After learning from King's numerological teaching, it is impossible to conceive of going back to that 'twilight naive and foggy' state of being where one can only guess or hint at the truths, motivations and directions of one's life that are Pre-King. Not only do I recommend this book, but I suggest it and his other numerology books as absolutely necessary for the library of anyone even remotely interested in the science of numerology.

~ Hunter Stowers

The King's Book of Numerology 12 (KBN12)
Advanced Principles

Numerology is the numeric manifestation of the architectural design of life and destiny.

The King's Book of Numerology, Volume 12 – Advanced Principles (KBN`12) offers seasoned King's Numerology^{tm} followers further insights, knowledge and understanding into the divine science of numeric coding, allowing for the expansion of human consciousness beyond the mundane world of phenomena to the mystical world of Divine Reality.

Chapters in KBN12 are:

1. The Numerology of Dislike
2. The Numerology of Betrayal
3. Nemesis Numbers
4. Common Name Dynamics
5. Single Name Analysis Profile – SNAP
6. Numerology of Past Lives
7. Family Ties
8. Life Journey Shifts and Changes
9. Voids, Vacuums and Karmic Scales
10. The Life Matrix Diamond
11. Professional Chart Analysis
12. The King's Book of Numerology^{tm} Series Summation
    Volumes 1 through 12

Richard Andrew King

99 Poems of the Spirit

99 Poems of the Spirit draws from the writings of Perfect Saints, Masters, Mystics and Sacred Scriptures. Designed to lift the consciousness, mind and heart, all of the poems are original works by Richard Andrew King. Their purpose is to help connect the reader with the mystic side of life in order to enhance the process of self-realization while advancing on the spiritual path and climbing the ladder leading to the ultimate attainment of God Realization. It is a treasure chest of poetic spiritual gems offered to excite, educate and stimulate the mind and soul in the glorious journey of spiritual ascent.

Messages from the Masters
Timeless Truths for Spiritual Seekers

In a time where there is more need for enlightenment than ever before, *Messages from the Masters: Timeless Truths for Spiritual Seekers* offers timeless truths for genuine seekers thirsty for spiritual nectar.

Masters are the PhDs of the universe, the Light Bearers of the Divine Flame. Their knowledge and wisdom are supreme. They have no equal. Although appearing human, they are not. Masters are the exalted Sons of God. Their chief duty is to rescue souls, liberating them from the maniacal maelstrom and madness of the material world and returning them to their eternal Home with the Lord.

Messages from the Masters is a rich source of hundreds of quotes from a cavalcade of nine Perfect Saints throughout the last six hundred years: Guru Ravidas, Kabir, Guru Nanak, Tulsi Sahib, Swami Ji Maharaj, Baba Jaimal Singh, Sawan Singh, Jagat Singh and Charan Singh. The messages in this book focus on the importance of the Divine Diet, the priceless Human Form, Reincarnation, the World, the Negative Power and Soul Food.

Warning! *Messages from the Masters* is not for the faint of heart or the worldly-minded. Masters come into the world to sever our attachment to it, not make it a paradise. Although the epitome of love and wisdom, they shoot straight from the hip, pull no punches, favor no religion. Their universal message of soul liberation is reflected in the statement of Saint Maharaj Charan Singh: *Just live in the creation and get out of it*!

The Age of the Female
A Thousand Years of Yin

The Age of the Female: A Thousand Years of Yin highlights the profound and extraordinary ascent of the female in the modern world, placing her center stage in the global spotlight as presidents and leaders of nations, titans of industry, corporate executives, military generals, media magnets, doctors, lawyers and a whole host of other prestigious titles normally associated with the male. Why has her rise to prominence been so rapid, especially in consideration of historic time? Why also has there been an increased interest in other people's lives in our society, in competitive athletics, personal data collection and the exploration of space and other worlds? *The Age of the Female: A Thousand Years of Yin* answers these questions. It is an insightful and exciting read into these mysteries, offering compelling and irrefutable evidence through the ancient science and art of numerology that, indeed, the age of the female has arrived and the next thousand years belong, not to him, but to her.

The Age of the Female II
Heroines of the Shift

The Age of the Female II: Heroines of the Shift continues the remarkable journey of the female's ascent in the modern world of the 2nd Millennium. This installment is a general read in five chapters honoring the accomplishments of women in categories of female firsts, female Nobel laureates, female athletes, female icons and female quotations.

The achievements of the women featured in *The Age of the Female II: Heroines of the Shift* are deserving of respect and admiration. Their lives, challenges and successes are motivational catalysts for every individual to be the best he or she can be and to honor the very essence of what it is to be human. *The Age of the Female II: Heroines of the Shift* is intended to be an inspiring and educational read for everyone, not just women but men, too, offering knowledge and insight of the depth, power and daring-do of women as their Yin energy rises upon the global stage in this millennium which destiny has irrefutably marked as the Age of the Female.

Richard Andrew King

Your Love Numbers
Discovering the Secrets of Your Life, Loves and Relationships

Your Love Numbers reveals the secret formula defining all great relationships and how to assess the love potential of any relationship in a matter of minutes.

Your Love Numbers teaches you how to assess a relationship or potential relationship in minutes, saving you endless time, energy, effort and possible heartache in the end. By knowing ourselves and the people we love, our relationships will be potentially more rewarding, satisfying, productive, peaceful, lasting and loving . . . for everyone - our family, spouses, partners, children, friends.

Your Love Numbers explains the mystery of love through the most ancient of all sciences . . . numbers, your numbers, calculated using only your full name and date of birth and those of the people you love! "Numbers rule the universe; everything is arranged according to number and mathematical shape," said Pythagoras. Everything - including light, sound and love can be measured in numbers! *Your Love Numbers* is based on thirty years of relationship research by master numerologist, Richard Andrew King. Applying his unique and revolutionary new theories, love and attraction between people can be determined using very easy to learn concepts. With a little study and practice, all this can be done in a minutes.

YourLoveNumbers.com

The Galactic Transcripts

The Galactic Transcripts will take you on a journey that is as provocative as it is mysterious. Its thirty-seven transmissions are channeled from a non-earth, alien group who identify themselves as members of the Space Brotherhood.

The Galactic Transcripts offer us descriptions of other worlds, their inhabitants, morals, ethics, and histories. They even forewarn of the coming cleansing of earth and the cataclysms preceding it. Other messages shed light on the original colonization of earth, telepathic communication, the power of love, the program of the Radiant One, and much more.

Those who have read *The Galactic Transcripts* have found them to be life-altering, profound, inspirational, transformative. Will they have that effect on you? Open your mind and allow the transcripts to take you beyond the limitations of our world and into new, undiscovered worlds far beyond our galaxy.

RichardKing.net
TheGalacticTranscripts.com

The Black Belt Book of Life
Secrets of a Martial Arts Master

The mystery and mystique of the martial arts is not only ages old, it's legend. Revered throughout the world, martial arts is a treasure chest of life secrets that transcend the boundaries of combat to include the expanse of life and living. Arguably, it is the greatest developmental system on earth for teaching the integration of body, mind and spirit

The Black Belt Book of Life: Secrets of a Martial Arts Master is not about physical fighting strategies and tactics. It is about concepts and principles we learn though martial arts training that can help us in the struggle of life, in the journey to conquer ourselves and gain the golden ring of our own completeness because in the end a true Black Belt should be a realized soul who, having engaged the enemy - himself - finds himself at the end of the journey, triumphant.

The Black Belt Book of Life: Secrets of a Martial Arts Master reveals many secrets of martial arts training, sharing these truths in quick and easy to read vignettes to benefit martial artists and the general public as well. It is a book for all readers, not just martial artists, both males and females, especially the youth of today who are in search of a foundation to guide their lives.

The Karate Consciousness
From Worldly Warrior to Mystic Master

The Karate Consciousness – From Worldly Warrior to Mystic Master is dedicated to the philosophy that karate is both an excellent system for the integration of body, mind and spirit as well as an excellent vehicle for the evolution of one's consciousness of life from a mundane perspective to a more elevated and edified reality.

Just as many martial arts systems are comprised of an ascending ladder of colored belts to designate accomplishment, so life is also comprised of an ascending ladder of levels of consciousness from worldly to divine.

The Karate Consciousness – From Worldly Warrior to Mystic Master shares concepts and perspectives which may help the karate practitioner in climbing the "Ladder of Consciousness." Among such concepts are the Power in the Flock Syndrome, the Continuum, the D.C. Factor, the Great Law of Karma and much more.

Richard Andrew King

Destinies of the Rich & Famous
The Secret Numbers of Extraordinary Lives

Why are rich and famous people rich and famous? Is it luck? Hard work? Advantage by family name? What makes them special? What secrets are the basis of their success?

Destinies of the Rich & Famous explores the secret numbers of the following famous global icons and explains through The King's Numerology™ why they are both rich and famous - Dr. Albert Einstein, Amelia Earhart, Elvis Presley, General George Patton, Howard Hughes, John F. Kennedy, Marilyn Monroe, Michael Jackson, Muhammad Ali, Oprah Winfrey, Princess Diana and Sarah Palin

Destinies of the Rich & Famous answers these questions and much more. Too, it reveals the clear correlation between a person's life and his or her natal data - the date of birth and full name of birth, illustrating the reality that fame and fortune and destined!

DestiniesOfTheRichAndFamous.com

Parenting Wisdom
Raising Your Children By Their Numbers
To Achieve Their Highest Potential
ParentingWisdom.net

This book is a must for any parent and all parents to be. It is vital to read this book now before you name your children. If you already have children, then it is just as important to understand them.

Richard Andrew King should be called Dr. King. His books are of the magnitude that will be read with reverence for generations to come. ~ Dr. Victoria Ford, J.D.

Parenting Wisdom for the 21st Century - Raising Your Children by Their Numbers to Achieve Their Highest Potential is a revolutionary addition to the process of arguably the most important job in the world, parenting.

The powerful information contained within this work will reveal the hidden desires driving your children, the paths they will follow in life, the roles they will give on the great life stage and much more – all designed to augment your parenting wisdom and support life's paramount parental purpose . . . to love the children and help them achieve their highest potential.

Parenting Wisdom 2
What To Teach The Children

This work is a companion book to *Parenting Wisdom For The 21st Century – Raising Your Children By Their Numbers To Achieve Their Highest Potential.*

Parenting is the most important and critical job in life because it encompasses the cultivating and sculpting of life itself as reflected in our children – the sanctity of life in manifest form.

In the process of parenting one of the most germane questions is, "What do we teach the children?" Parenting Wisdom offers thirty-three time-tested, universal principles which parents can use to create a strong foundation allowing children to develop into whole, fulfilled, and substantive adults.

The thirty-three principles include: The Five Needs of Children, Boundaries, Rules, And Regs, Your Life, Your Responsibility, Tender Love Versus Tough Love, The Four Cornerstones of a Substantive Life, The Temptations of S.A.D. (Sex, Alcohol, Drugs) and much more . . .

ParentingWisdom.net

FOR ALL OF

RICHARD ANDREW KING'S BOOKS,

VISIT RICHARDKING.NET/BOOKS

AND ONLINE RETAILERS.

REQUEST THEM AT YOUR LIBRARY

AND LOCAL BOOK STORES.

Richard Andrew King

RICHARD ANDREW KING
~ CDs ~

RichardKing.net, CDBaby.com, and Online Retailers

Priceless Poetry & Prose 1
Dramatizations of Famous Literary Works

Wonderfully entertaining and educational artistic dramatizations of famous literary works for adults, children, teachers and students alike. Enjoy the timeless words of Shakespeare, Lincoln, Tennyson, Longfellow, Patrick Henry, Emily Dickinson, Chaucer and more.

Priceless Poetry & Prose 2
Selected Works of Edgar Allan Poe

Be enveloped in the mysterious and haunted world of one of America's most loved poets, Edgar Allan Poe. Highly entertaining and educational, enjoy classic poems such as, The Raven, Annabel Lee, Ulalume, Alone, Lenore and more.

Poems of the Spirit
Selected Original Poems of Richard Andrew King

A collection of original spiritual poems designed to edify the mind and uplift the spirit. Not for the faint of heart or worldly-minded, these works reflect timeless truths from scriptures, saints and mystics throughout the ages - messages enabling the individual to break the shackles of worldly ties in quest for spiritual realization.

Echoes from the Heart
Selected Original Songs of Richard Andrew King

An original collection of twelve of Richard's tug-at-your-heart ballads, cowboy songs, patriotic tributes and spiritual tunes for your soul. A few titles are *Waiting for You*, *Don't Forget the Heroes*, *One More Broken Heart*, *The Promise*, *Rodeo Cowboy*, *You Can't Push the River*, *No Itty Bitty Cowboy* and *Catch Me When I Fall*.

Richard Andrew King

ORDER INFORMATION

To order Books and CDs, go to
RichardKing.Net
or major online retailers

CONTACT

Richard Andrew King
PO Box 3621
Laguna Hills, CA 92654
RichardKing.Net
Rich @ RichardKing.net

NOTES

MATCH & MIX CHARTS

Full Natal Name and Date of Birth Person #1: _____ / Day/Month/Year

Full Natal Name and Date of Birth Person #2: _____ / Day/Month/Year

Basic Matrix	LP	Exp	PE	Soul	MS	Nature	MN	Voids
Name #1								
Name #2								
Mix								

LOVELINE MATCH – BASIC MATRICES

	Name #1	#1	#2	Name #2	
External	Life Path (Life Script)			Life Path (Life script)	**External**
	Expression (Actor)			Expression (Actor)	
	P/E (Role in life)			P/E (Role in life)	
Internal	Soul (Needs & Wants)			Soul (Needs & Wants)	**Internal**
	Material Soul			Material Soul	
	Nature (Personality)			Nature (Personality)	
	Material Nature			Material Nature	
	First Name #1			First Name #2	
	Numeric Day of Birth			Numeric Day of Birth	
	Voids			Voids	

LOVELINE MATCH & MIX

	Name #1	#1	MIX	#2	Name #2	
External	Life Path				Life Path	**External**
	Expression				Expression	
	P/E				P/E	
Internal	Soul				Soul	**Internal**
	Material Soul				Material Soul	
	Nature				Nature	
	Material Nature				Material Nature	
	Name #1				Name #2	
	Numeric Day of Birth				Numeric Day of Birth	
	Voids				Voids	
	Total Connections				**Total Connections**	

Richard Andrew King

NOTES

NOTES

NOTES

Richard Andrew King

NOTES

NOTES

Richard Andrew King

NOTES

NOTES

www.ingramcontent.com/pod-product-compliance
Lightning Source LLC
Chambersburg PA
CBHW080543230426
43663CB00015B/2687